# Assessment of Cataloging and Metadata Services

Written by experienced practitioners and researchers, *Assessment of Cataloging and Metadata Services* provides the reader with many examples of how assessment practices can be applied to the work of cataloging and metadata services departments. Containing both research and case studies, it explores a variety of assessment methods as they are applied to the evaluation of cataloging productivity, workflows, metadata quality, vendor services, training needs, documentation, and more. Assessment methods addressed in these chapters include surveys, focus groups, interviews, observational analyses, workflow analyses, and methodologies borrowed from the field of business. *Assessment of Cataloging and Metadata Services* will help managers and administrators as they attempt to evaluate and communicate the value of what they do to their broader communities, whether they are higher education institutions, another organization, or the public. This book will help professionals with decision-making and give them the tools they need to identify and implement improvements.

The chapters in this book were originally published in a special issue of *Cataloging & Classification Quarterly*.

**Rebecca L. Mugridge** is Dean of University Libraries at the University at Albany – State University of New York, USA. Prior to this she was Associate Director for Technical Services and Library Systems. She has worked at Pennsylvania State University (Penn State), State College, USA; Yale University, New Haven, USA; Robert Morris University, Moon, USA; and the University of Pittsburgh, USA. Ms. Mugridge has a BA in history from Penn State, an MLS from the University of Pittsburgh, and an MBA from Robert Morris University.

# Assessment of Cataloging and Metadata Services

*Edited by*
Rebecca L. Mugridge

Routledge
Taylor & Francis Group

LONDON AND NEW YORK

First published 2019
by Routledge
2 Park Square, Milton Park, Abingdon, Oxon, OX14 4RN, UK

and by Routledge
52 Vanderbilt Avenue, New York, NY 10017

First issued in paperback 2020

*Routledge is an imprint of the Taylor & Francis Group, an informa business*

*British Library Cataloguing-in-Publication Data*
A catalogue record for this book is available from the British Library

ISBN 13: 978-0-367-66533-3 (pbk)
ISBN 13: 978-1-138-32665-1 (hbk)

Typeset in Minion Pro
by codeMantra

**Publisher's Note**
The publisher accepts responsibility for any inconsistencies that may have arisen during
the conversion of this book from journal articles to book chapters, namely the possible
inclusion of journal terminology.

**Disclaimer**
Every effort has been made to contact copyright holders for their permission to reprint
material in this book. The publishers would be grateful to hear from any copyright
holder who is not here acknowledged and will undertake to rectify any errors or
omissions in future editions of this book.

# Contents

## Research Studies

## Case Studies in Metadata Quality and Workflow Assessment

CONTENTS

# Citation Information

The chapters in this book were originally published in the journal *Cataloging & Classification Quarterly*, volume 55, issues 7–8 (October 2017). When citing this material, please use the original page numbering for each article, as follows:

**Introduction**

*Assessment of Cataloging and Metadata Services: Introduction*
Rebecca L. Mugridge
*Cataloging & Classification Quarterly*, volume 55, issues 7–8 (October 2017) pp. 435–437

**Chapter 1**

*Defining, Assessing, and Rethinking Quality Cataloging*
Karen Snow
*Cataloging & Classification Quarterly*, volume 55, issues 7–8 (October 2017) pp. 438–455

**Chapter 2**

*A Librarian-Centered Study of Perceptions of Subject Terms and Controlled Vocabulary*
William N. Schultz Jr. and Lindsay Braddy
*Cataloging & Classification Quarterly*, volume 55, issues 7–8 (October 2017) pp. 456–466

**Chapter 3**

*Initiating Cultural Shifts in Perceptions of Cataloging Units through Interaction Assessment*
Andrea Payant, Becky Skeen, and Liz Woolcott
*Cataloging & Classification Quarterly*, volume 55, issues 7–8 (October 2017) pp. 467–492

**Chapter 4**

*Failure Modes and Effects Analysis (FMEA) for Cataloging: An Application and Evaluation*
Jennifer Meekhof and Amy B. Bailey
*Cataloging & Classification Quarterly*, volume 55, issues 7–8 (October 2017) pp. 493–505

**Chapter 5**

*An Investigation of Title Ambiguity in the Health Sciences Literature*
Dick R. Miller, Joanne Banko, Thea S. Allen, Ariel Vanderpool, and Ryan Max Steinberg
*Cataloging & Classification Quarterly*, volume 55, issues 7–8 (October 2017) pp. 506–521

For any permission-related enquiries please visit:
http://www.tandfonline.com/page/help/permissions

# Notes on Contributors

**Emily Alinder Flynn** is the Metadata & ETD Coordinator at the Ohio Library and Information Network (OhioLINK), Columbus, USA.

**Thea S. Allen** is a Metadata Librarian at Lane Medical Library at Stanford University School of Medicine, USA.

**Kelly J. Applegate** is a Metadata Specialist at The MediaPreserve – Preservation Technologies, Cranberry Township, USA.

**Janet Ashton** is the West European Languages Cataloguing Team Manager at The British Library, Wetherby, UK.

**Amy B. Bailey** is the Head Cataloging Assistant Librarian for Cataloging at Indiana University Libraries, Bloomington, USA.

**Joanne Banko** is a retired Librarian at Lane Medical Library at Stanford University School of Medicine, USA.

**Leigh Billings** is a Slavic Cataloger at the University of Michigan Library, Ann Arbor, USA.

**Lindsay Braddy** is the Assistant Manager of Access Services at Skokie Public Library, USA.

**Karl Debus-López** is the Chief of the U.S. Programs, Law, and Literature Division at the Library of Congress, Washington, DC, USA.

**Robert B. Freeborn** is a Music and AV Cataloging Librarian in the Department of Cataloging and Metadata Services at the University Libraries at Pennsylvania State University, University Park, USA.

**Caroline Kent** is the Metadata Creation Manager at The British Library, Wetherby, UK.

**Erin Kilkenny** is a Cataloging Assistant at OhioLINK, Columbus, USA.

**Gerald Langford** works in the Cataloging and Discovery Services Department at the University of Florida, Gainesville, USA.

**Nerea A. Llamas** is the (interim) Associate University Librarian for Research, and Head of International Studies, at the University of Michigan Library, Ann Arbor, USA.

**Jimmie Lundgren** is the Head of the Contributed Cataloging Unit in the Cataloging Services Department at the University of Florida, Gainesville, USA.

**Marilyn McCroskey** is the Head of Cataloging at Meyer Library at Missouri State University, Springfield, USA.

NOTES ON CONTRIBUTORS

**Jennifer Meekhof** is the Resource Description Manager at the University of Michigan, Ann Arbor, USA.

**Dick R. Miller** is the Associate Director of Resource Management at Lane Medical Library at Stanford University School of Medicine, USA.

**Rebecca L. Mugridge** is the Dean of University Libraries at the University at Albany – State University of New York, USA.

**Hikaru Nakano** is an Associate Librarian at the University of Florida, Gainesville, USA.

**Allison Jai O'Dell** is a Database and Information Developer at Mercy for Animals, Los Angeles, USA.

**Clément Oury** is the Head of Data, Network and Standards in the Data, Network and Standards Department at the ISSN International Centre, Paris, France.

**Andrea Payant** is a Cataloging Assistant at Merrill-Cazier Library at Utah State University, Logan, USA.

**Seth Robbins** is the Manager of Scholarly Communications and Repository at the Main Library at the University of Illinois at Urbana-Champaign, USA.

**Regina Romano Reynolds** is the ISSN Coordinator at the Library of Congress, Washington, DC, USA.

**Caroline Saccucci** is the CIP and Dewey Program Manager and Section Head at the Library of Congress, Washington, DC, USA.

**William N. Schultz Jr.** is a Cataloging Librarian at Booth Library at Eastern Illinois University, Charleston, USA.

**Trey Shelton** is an E-Resources Librarian at the University of Florida, Gainesville, USA.

**Becky Skeen** is the Special Collections Cataloging Librarian at Merrill-Cazier Library at Utah State University, Logan, USA.

**Karen Snow** is an Associate Professor, and Director of the Doctoral Program – SOIS, at the School of Information Studies, Dominican University, River Forest, USA.

**Beth E. Snyder** is the Technical Services Coordinator for Slavic, East European, and Eurasian Studies and Near Eastern Studies at the University of Michigan Library, Ann Arbor, USA.

**Ayla Stein** is a Metadata Librarian, Assistant Professor, and Interim Coordinator of Repository Services at the Main Library at the University of Illinois at Urbana-Champaign, USA.

**Ryan Max Steinberg** is a Software Developer at Lane Medical Library at the Stanford University School of Medicine, USA.

**Yunah Sung** is the Korean Studies Librarian & Coordinator for Asia Library Technical Services at the University of Michigan Library, Ann Arbor, USA.

**Ariel Vanderpool** is a Resource Acquisition Specialist at Lane Medical Library at Stanford University School of Medicine, USA.

**David Van Kleeck** is an Authorities, Identities, Metadata, and Cataloging Librarian at the University of Florida, Gainesville, USA.

**Camilla Williams** is a CIP Program Specialist at the Library of Congress, Washington, DC, USA.

**Liz Woolcott** is Head of Cataloging at Merrill-Cazier Library at Utah State University, Logan, USA.

**Michele Zwierski** is Head of Database Management at Nassau Library System, Uniondale, USA.

# Assessment of Cataloging and Metadata Services: Introduction

Rebecca L. Mugridge

Assessment is a topic of great interest to the cataloging and metadata community. In the last decade it has gotten significantly more attention, partly as a response to movements in the academic library community and its focus on the value of libraries and what we do. I have long felt that cataloging and metadata departments regularly conduct a variety of forms of assessment, but that we are not good at sharing those assessment activities or communicating the results of our efforts. We carry out assessments of productivity, workflows, cataloging and metadata quality, vendor services, training needs, documentation, and more. Methods of conducting assessment can include focus groups, surveys, benchmarking, observational analyses, interviews, and methodologies that we borrow from other disciplines such as business. Interest in assessment continues to grow as evidenced by the number of conference programs, webinars, and other continuing education offerings that attract many attendees. There is clearly a need for practical ideas on how to conduct assessment and communicate the results of that assessment to administrators and other stakeholders.

With this special issue, I hoped to satisfy that need by gathering a variety of articles that address many aspects of assessment of cataloging and metadata services. In addition to articles and studies that discuss the assessment of cataloging and metadata quality, workflows, and productivity, I was looking for articles that address the impact of cataloging and metadata on the larger organization and society, assessment of vendor services, international assessment efforts, and various methods of assessment. I am pleased to be able to present all of those and more in this special issue. The papers are organized into two broad sections: (1) Research Studies; and (2) Case Studies in Metadata Quality and Workflow Assessment.

The five research studies in this special issue address a variety of topics that shed light on many aspects of managing cataloging and metadata services and providing quality metadata to support research and learning. "Defining, Assessing, and Rethinking Quality Cataloging" by Karen Snow is a thoughtful discussion about how we define and think about quality in our cataloging activities. William Schultz and Lindsay Braddy share the results of their study of librarians' perceptions of the value of subject terminology and controlled vocabularies in "A Librarian-Centered Study of Perceptions of Subject Terms and Conrolled Vocabulary." Andrea Payant, Becky Skeen, and Liz Woolcott conducted a study about how cataloging staff interact with others throughout the library and present their results in "Initiating Cultural Shifts in Perceptions of Cataloging Units through Interaction Assessment." A method for assessing quality that comes from the business world, Failure Modes and Effects Analysis, is used to evaluate cataloging quality at ProQuest, in a study by Jennifer Meekhof and Amy Bailey, "Failure Modes and Effects Analysis (FMEA) for Cataloging: An Application and Evaluation." Finally, Dick Miller, Joanne Banko, Thea Allen, Ariel Vanderpool, and Ryan Steinberg look at the quality of title metadata in "An Investigation of Title Ambiguity in the Health Sciences Literature."

Case studies included in this collection encompass both the assessment of various metadata elements as well as the assessment of cataloging and metadata workflows. In the first of several articles that address metadata quality, Karl Debus-López, Marilyn McCroskey, Regina Reynolds, Caroline Saccucci, Camilla Williams, and Michele Zwierski share the results of a two-year-long project to assess and re-design the Cataloging-in-Publication information and data block in "Transforming the CIP Data Block: Assessing User Needs to Re-envision a Venerable Library Icon." This is a significant development in a service that the Library of Congress has been offering for nearly 50 years and I am proud to document the process of assessment and outreach in this special issue. Janet Ashton and Caroline Kent tackle "New Approaches to Subject Indexing at the British Library" in an assessment of the use of faceted subject terminology (FAST) in their cataloging. David Van Kleeck, Hikaru Nakano, Gerald Langford, Trey Shelton, Jimmie Lundgren, and Allison Jai O'Dell present the results of their study that compared the quality of vendor records with that of records available through the WorldShare Management Services platform in "Managing Bibliographic Data Quality for Electronic Resources." Robert Freeborn discusses a project to reclassify a collection of sound recordings from a home grown classification to Library of Congress Classification and how they assessed the usage of the collection after the reclassification in "Planning, Implementing, and Assessing a CD Reclassification Project."

With "Assessing the ISSN Register: Defining, Evaluating and Improving the Quality of a Shared International Bibliographic Database," Clément Oury addresses not only metadata quality, but also the assessment of metadata workflows, specifically with regard to the sharing of metadata through the ISSN Register. The next several articles focus on the assessment of efficient and effective metadata workflows. Leigh Billings, Nerea Llamas, Beth Snyder, and Yunah Sung discuss the assessment of cataloging workflows in a large, complex academic institution in "Many Languages, Many Workflows: Mapping and Analyzing Technical Services Processes for East Asian and International Studies Materials." Emily Flynn and Erin Kilkenny take a look at how to achieve efficiencies in e-book cataloging within a consortium in "Cataloging from the Center: Improving e-Book Cataloging on a Consortial Level." The assessment of metadata workflows within an institutional repository is addressed by Ayla Stein, Kelly Applegate, and Seth Robbins in "Achieving and Maintaining Metadata Quality: Toward a Sustainable Workflow for the IDEALS Institutional Repository."

It is my hope that these studies will help catalogers, metadata specialists, managers, and administrators think through how they might approach assessment of cataloging and metadata services at their own institutions. Every library is unique, with different challenges and concerns, and there are many ways to address those challenges through a methodical approach to assessment. Whether you choose to assess productivity, quality, workflows, impact, or some other aspect of cataloging and metadata services, there are many tools that can be applied to your efforts. You might try surveys, focus groups, interviews, observational analyses, workflow analyses, methodologies borrowed from the business world, or in-depth reviews of specific metadata fields. I hope that the articles in this special issue provide inspiration and guidance to help you in your assessment efforts.

# Defining, Assessing, and Rethinking Quality Cataloging

Karen Snow (iD)

**ABSTRACT**
Definitions of "quality cataloging" may differ from cataloger to cataloger and from institution to institution. If an objective definition of quality is elusive, how can an institution assess the quality of cataloging work? This article discusses definitions of quality cataloging in the literature and different ways it has been evaluated and measured. Academic library catalogers' perceptions of quality cataloging will also be explored, as well as how these perceptions are formed. The article concludes by suggesting ways cataloging departments can approach the creation and evaluation of quality cataloging in an ethical manner.

## Introduction

Defining "quality cataloging" has been likened to defining art and pornography.[1] When used in casual conversation and cataloging literature, there is some general agreement about what this concept means. However, scratch below the surface and "quality cataloging" is harder to pin down. Is it adherence to specific standards? Ensuring that catalog records accurately represent the item in-hand and are free of typographical errors? How quickly resources are described, processed, and available to users? The ability of a user to find the information he or she needs in the catalog? Or is it some, all, or none of these things?

In cataloging literature, "quality cataloging" has been defined in the following ways:

- Accurate bibliographic information that meets users' needs and provides appropriate access in a timely fashion.[2]
- What library users say it is.[3]
- Level of content (AACR2 level of description, inclusion of subject classification or subject headings, authority control of headings, etc.)...accuracy of content (in transcription from the item, in conformity with the standards applied)...fitness for purpose.[4]
- We define quality for support staff by percentage error rate in the following: selection or suitability of OCLC record as a match for item cataloged;

correcting typographical errors in the following fields: 100, 245, 260, 300, 5xx; making appropriate edits to bibliographic and holdings records; accurate creation of item and holdings records; recognizing cataloging problems and bringing them to the attention of a supervisor. For cataloging librarians: quality is defined by excellent original cataloging based on AACR2 full-level standards; name authority records created to standards set by NACO; effective supervision of support staff, including timely resolution of questions and problems; a reasonable turnaround time for materials so that a backlog is not created or growing; responsiveness to needs of internal and external patrons; completeness, efficiency, responsive to queries and complaints.[5]

There are certainly some common threads in these definitions, but the focus and level of specificity found in each differ quite dramatically. If the cataloging community cannot agree upon a universal definition of quality cataloging, how are libraries supposed to assess the quality of cataloging work?

This article explores quality cataloging definitions primarily from the viewpoint of catalogers in academic libraries and how it has been viewed over time. It considers how catalogers develop their ideas of what quality cataloging means, as well as the problems associated with trying to nail down a standardized and actionable definition of this concept. Finally, the article provides suggestions for creating and evaluating quality cataloging in an ethical manner.

## Cooperation and a crisis

In 1870, Charles A. Cutter was hired as the editor of the Boston Athenaeum catalog and quickly noticed something amiss with the catalog work already completed:

> Sometimes they took the title from the back of the book, sometimes from the title-page, sometimes from the half-title, and sometimes, apparently, from their own imaginations. They omitted freely, of course, and they altered the order of words for the purpose of omitting, and of the words which they retained they abbreviated the greater part to the verge of unintelligibility. They spent no time on the investigation of authors' full names or in the discovery of the authors of anonymous and pseudonymous books, nor did they trouble themselves about cataloguing rules.[6]

Cutter's comments are unique because it is rare to find such pointed criticisms of cataloging practice during this time period—a time when cataloging rules were far from standardized. However, Cutter's concerns about standardization and accuracy were not unusual. Cutter and other librarians of the late nineteenth century (such as Melvil Dewey, creator of the Decimal Classification) felt that standardization of cataloging practice was important for achieving another, more significant goal: cooperative cataloging on a national scale. The idea of cooperative cataloging was praised as a means of achieving greater "accuracy, method, and uniformity" through the sharing of catalog copy, but also criticized for similar reasons.[7] There was concern that cooperative cataloging would take away too much local control and force standardization on disparate libraries. Frederic

Vinton, a librarian at Princeton University, asserts that "co-operative cataloguing (by which each librarian shall have the least possible writing to do) is unfavorable to good librarianship" because it is the "supposed drudgery of cataloguing" that allows the librarian to become good at his job.[8] R.R. Bowker, writing in the 1883 *Library Journal*, argues in response to the demand for cooperative cataloging that

> [i]t chiefly behooves us, building a fair basis for the future, not to attempt and to expect too much; to make haste slowly; not to rashly ignore and put aside the old in planning for the new; and to remember that cooperation does not mean rigid uniformity, and that, among many varieties of situation and circumstance, the best way is often a relative term.[9]

The implementation of the Library of Congress card distribution program effectively sealed the (positive) fate of cooperative cataloging, but the concern that "rigid uniformity" could lead to problems within the cataloging community did not fade.

*The Crisis in Cataloging*, Andrew Osborn's infamous rebuke of the cataloging community's inclination toward legalism, paints cataloging as "elaborate, highly technical, a skill too often existing in and for itself" due to the increase of and focus upon cataloging rules by catalogers working in the early part of the 20th century.[10] Osborn recommends that catalogers focus less on strict adherence to standards and more upon how to adapt rules and practices in ways to best meet the needs of their library's users. Osborn argues that "[t]he quality of cataloging in such libraries is satisfactory because it has been developed with the practical needs of the library constantly in mind."[11] "Quality cataloging" for Osborn is not a static, objective notion, but one that is limited by local necessity and constantly evolving as "the taste or the needs of the time" frequently change.[12]

## The rise of cooperative networks

The rise of cooperative cataloging networks, such as the Ohio College (later Online Computer) Library Center (OCLC) and Research Libraries Information Network (RLIN), during the 1970s parallels the increase in the number of articles and studies in library science literature that mention quality cataloging specifically. This surge in discussion was due to two main issues: (1) any library belonging to a network could input and copy records, introducing records from a variety of institutions that may not all adhere to the same local standards; and (2) some networks (OCLC in particular) allowed the input of records of what many felt were of dubious quality in order to increase the number of records in the network as quickly as possible. For these reasons, the increase in cooperation among institutions was seen as a boon and a bane.

Separate doctoral dissertations by Luquire and Schoenung found that quality was a major issue for OCLC participants, but not all participants in their studies viewed quality through the same lens.[13] Luquire, whose dissertation was about library staff perceptions of using automated systems, was surprised that participants felt so strongly that many OCLC records were flawed. Digging further into participants' reasons for feeling this way, he finds that "what is called quality may not really be absolute quality but rather local practices and needs which are often not met by contributed copy."[14] Schoenung observed a similar sentiment among his study participants. He notes that OCLC member-contributed copy sometimes lacked the quality of Library of Congress records, but most of the differences were ones of style (punctuation, capitalization, etc.) rather than substance (incorrect access points, typographical errors, etc.). Schoenung concludes that "the concept of quality cataloging is most meaningful within the context of a particular library," echoing the conclusions that Osborn had reached forty years earlier.[15]

The idea that cataloger perceptions of quality (or *not* quality) are heavily influenced by local priorities and preferences was a common theme in articles published in the late 1970s and throughout the 1980s. Christian Boissonnas, who worked at the Cornell Law Library (CLL) in the 1970s, found that quality in the OCLC database "is a continuing source of controversy for catalogers."[16] Consequently, Boissonnas decided to compare records from CLL against Library of Congress (LC) and OCLC records to understand the differences between the records. At CLL, they constructed what they called an "authoritative record" that captured what they believed was a quality record for their users, where all applicable fields were completed and little, if any, modifications were made to cataloging copy (only the 049 MARC field, the Cutter within a call number, and series information were touched).[17] Boissonnas found that LC records resembled their authoritative records more closely than OCLC records and have fewer errors that negatively impact access. Nonetheless, Boissonnas concluded that the degree of impact is dependent upon the standards of the individual institution. Boissonnas writes:

> Quality or the definition of an authoritative record, is a very subjective notion. Because of the standards and procedures followed at CLL, a substantial amount of work is generated which another library would not consider doing. Its records would not be less correct than CLL's; they would merely be different.[18]

Separate studies in the 1980s by Intner and Davis, also concluded that the quality of records in OCLC was not necessarily bad according to their metrics, and the perception of OCLC as a "dirty database" had more to do with preference for certain ways of transcribing the information at the local level rather than finding errors that truly inhibit access.[19]

## Quality cataloging at the Library of Congress

A series of decisions by the Library of Congress in the late 1970s and the 1990s designed to reduce the major backlogs at the institution resulted in more discussion in the literature about cataloging quality at the Library of Congress, which was generally acknowledged as producing the highest quality cataloging work. The introduction of minimal level cataloging (MLC) in 1979 and the Whole Book Cataloging

Project in 1990 were meant to decrease the amount of time LC catalogers spent processing resources and therefore reduce backlogs. At the time of initial implementation, MLC records consisted of only the author, title, Library of Congress card number, edition, publication/distribution information, physical description, a series statement, and notes, but little or no subject analysis and authority work were performed.[20] The goal of the Whole Book Project was to merge the separate subject and descriptive cataloging divisions, a workflow partition that had been in place at the Library of Congress since the 1940s. The Librarian of Congress at the time, James Billington, believed that having fewer steps in the cataloging process would reduce the amount of time resources spent in technical services and thus help decrease arrearages. Both decisions incited much discussion about quality cataloging inside and outside the Library of Congress because many institutions faced some of the challenges LC did, particularly in regard to growing backlogs.[21] There was also great concern that increasing the speed of cataloging and decreasing the amount of information included in records would lead to less cataloging quality, even if it meant getting resources into the hands of users faster.

Cataloging quality was a common theme in the newly created Library of Congress Cataloging Forums that were held from 1991–1996. Of the six publications that resulted from these forums, cataloging quality was the focus of four.[22] Many definitions of quality cataloging were suggested at these forums and subsequently published in opinion papers. In the fourth opinion paper published in 1993, Lavon Avdoyan creates a lengthy list of quality cataloging attributes, but ultimately concedes:

> [a]s with the person who cannot define art but knows it when he sees it, I cannot completely define a good cataloguing record, but I know it when I retrieve it. And is that not the ultimate test? If you cannot retrieve it, what good is it?[23]

In the sixth opinion paper, Barbara Tillett compiled the definitions of a large number of LC employees and devised the following definition of quality cataloging: "accurate bibliographic information that meets users' needs and provides appropriate access in a timely fashion."[24] Though certainly a more specific description of quality cataloging than "I know it when I retrieve it," Tillett's definition still lacks actionable details: what does "accurate" mean exactly? Which "users" does she mean—Library of Congress users? All library users? How do catalogers know what constitutes "appropriate access"? How quickly must resources be processed for the cataloging to be considered "timely"? Within a day? A week? A year? One could argue that although Tillett's definition is a good starting point for discussion of quality cataloging, there is much more that should be considered in order to apply it in a practical way.

## Measuring quality cataloging

Beginning in the 1990s, more effort was expended to study what, exactly, constituted quality cataloging and how to measure it within the context of the library catalog. Formed in 1995, the Program for Cooperative Cataloging (PCC) is a collective of primarily academic and research libraries with a goal of promoting "the creation of unique original cataloging according to a mutually agreed upon standard in a timely and cost-effective manner."[25] Shortly after its formation, the PCC promoted the use of a core record that contained "reliable, accurate, and authoritative access points," but not necessarily subject access or notes.[26] A full-level record was soon adopted that included subject access fields as well, but the core and full-level dichotomy was superseded by the BIBCO standard record (BSR) in 2009. According to the PCC, the BSR is a "'floor' record that promotes an essential set of fields and codes that are sufficient for user tasks" and essentially made the full-level record the minimum standard for PCC records.[27] It was believed that libraries that followed the PCC BSR guidelines would produce quality records. It should be noted that the PCC does not take into account the needs of various types of libraries, but instead focuses on what it feels are the baseline bibliographic record needs of its members, who are largely academic libraries.[28] However, research by El-Sherbini confirmed that "the quality of PCC-produced bibliographic records is high, as defined by the parameters" of the study.[29] El-Sherbini focused solely on access point fields and determined that most of the errors found in BIBCO standard records (primarily errors of punctuation and spacing) did not impact indexing or retrieval within the catalog.[30]

In the first decade of the 2000s, several researchers endeavored to produce an audit tool for determining error rates of poor quality metadata. However, these researchers largely focused on creating a measurement tool for a specific library as opposed to developing a tool that could be used in any library. In 2002, Chapman and Massey created an audit tool that attempted to measure the accuracy of bibliographic records in the University of Bath library catalog. They focused on eleven specific areas that they identified as being the most important for determining quality. The areas, based on the *International Standard Bibliographic Description* (ISBD), were title, material description, statement of responsibility, author headings, edition information, physical description, imprint, series, classmark/shelfmark, subject headings, genre/category, and location (or branch).[31] Within those areas, Chapman and Massey looked for particular errors, such as missing fields, typographical mistakes, and incomplete data. The authors stressed that even though the audit tool could be used in different libraries in a general way, it is essential to modify the tool based upon the library's collections and user needs. Therefore, the audit tool is not necessarily an objective standard for measuring cataloging quality, but a means of evaluating "accuracy in the library's own terms."[32]

MacEwan and Young attempted a similar audit for the British Library, but primarily using Tom Delsey's mapping of Machine-Readable Cataloging (MARC) data elements to the *Functional Requirements for Bibliographic Records* (FRBR) user tasks.[33] They felt that focusing on the elements that best helped users find, identify, select, and obtain information would ensure quality cataloging, but ultimately they could not come to any definite conclusions due to the small sample size (30 records) of the audit. However, they felt their system of using the FRBR user tasks, and then weighting data elements according to the importance of the user task to British Library users, was a significant first step. On the other hand, it is important to keep in mind that the creators of FRBR did not conduct user studies when they developed the conceptual model and user tasks.[34]

In order to construct a quality cataloging measurement tool that was based more on evidence of user needs and preferences, Hider and Tan conducted multiple studies and used multiple tools to examine the validity of "expert opinion" of quality cataloging, as well as what data elements users want and are actually using in the library catalog, specifically in public libraries in Singapore.[35] In order to test the reliability of expert opinion on what constitutes quality cataloging, they asked seven cataloging experts to rank the same five bibliographic record sets of Library of Congress full-level records from best to worst in terms of quality. Each of the seven experts ranked the record sets differently. The authors also conducted interviews, distributed surveys, and carried out "think-aloud sessions" with patrons of the National Library Board public libraries in Singapore. The purpose of these data collection methods was to determine which data elements the users found most helpful in the identification and selection of items at the public library. Hider and Tan then used the data to create a record quality measurement tool that weighted the data elements according to user preferences. For example, a misspelling in the title proper (MARC field 245$a) would be weighted more heavily than a misspelling in the physical description field (MARC field 300) because users identified the title field as one of the most important data elements.

Hider and Tan note that the creation of such a quality cataloging measurement tool is time-consuming, expensive, and highly localized in its effectiveness. However, they emphasize that empirical research at the local level is essential for understanding what quality cataloging means for the individual library since standardized measurement of quality cataloging will not necessarily fit the needs of all users in every library.[36]

In addition to exploring how to create standardized measurements for quality cataloging, several groups and researchers have attempted to define dimensions of metadata quality. Instead of focusing on, for example, which MARC fields are needed in a quality record, the developers of these efforts sought a general framework for data quality that can be adapted to any information environment, not just library cataloging departments. Statistics Canada, for example, created the *Quality Assurance Framework* that focuses on the characteristics of information important for measuring quality: relevance, accuracy, timeliness, accessibility, interpretability, and coherence.[37] Bruce and Hillmann developed their own set of characteristics based on Statistics Canada's framework that are "better adapted to the growing number of large-scale projects in which metadata from multiple source providers is aggregated into a unified metadata resource."[38] These characteristics are: completeness, accuracy, provenance, conformance to expectations, logical consistency and coherence, timeliness, and accessibility.

These frameworks could be viewed as too general to be useful across libraries and user populations, but Bruce and Hillmann insist that starting with a mutually agreed upon framework is essential for productive dialogue about quality at the local level, even if details are lacking.

## Exploring quality cataloging definitions

Frameworks are certainly useful as a starting point for quality cataloging discussions, but what about specific definitions? What can we learn from how others have defined quality cataloging? What aspects of the cataloging process and product are discussed most often in quality cataloging definitions? What are the common themes, if any? Quality cataloging definitions found in the literature discussed above and through dissertation research by Snow contained descriptions that fell largely into four major categories: the technical details of the bibliographic record, adherence to standards, the cataloging process, and the impact of cataloging on users.[39] Definitions that contained attributes from the first category, the technical details of a bibliographic record, typically would include how accurately bibliographic data describes a particular resource, the existence of typographical errors, and the presence of enough information to identify a resource. When definitions included attributes from the second category, adherence to standards, they referred to following local, national, professional, and/or network standards such as *Resource Description and Access* (RDA), Machine-Readable Cataloging (MARC), Library of Congress Subject Headings (LCSH), Library of Congress and the Program for Cooperative Cataloging's Policy Statements (LC-PCC-PS), and best practices guides. The third category, the cataloging process, includes the pace of workflow and existence of backlogs, administrative support, and the training and performance of staff. The fourth category, the impact of cataloging on users, includes how well users are able to find and access resources through information provided in the catalog.

Note that definitions do not always specifically address the contents of bibliographic records; process and impact of cataloging work are seen as part of the quality equation as well. In addition, quality cataloging definitions often did not fall exclusively into a single category. More often than not, definitions would mention one or more attributes from these categories. For example, if someone defined quality cataloging as adherence to RDA and ensuring that users can find a resource in the collection, then this definition would count in both the "adherence to standards" and the "impact of cataloging on users" categories. Moreover, attributes of these categories are not mutually exclusive. For example, typographical errors (an attribute of the "technical details of the bibliographic record" category) will likely have an impact on a user's ability to find a record in the catalog (an attribute of the "impact of cataloging on users" category). Nonetheless, grouping quality cataloging definitions into these broad categories can be helpful when trying to determine what aspects of cataloging catalogers focus on most when defining quality cataloging and applying this understanding to their cataloging work.

Snow's research found that catalogers who perform original cataloging in academic libraries define quality cataloging in terms of the "technical details of the bibliographic record" more often than the other categories.[40] Ensuring that a bibliographic record contains enough information to identify and assess the resource, as well as the accuracy of the transcription, were the most important parts of quality cataloging for study participants. The "impact of cataloging on users" and "adherence to standards" categories were a close second and third place, followed by the "cataloging process." However, most participants in the study used attributes in their definition that fall into more than one category, indicating that most view quality cataloging as multi-faceted.

When asked to rank predetermined attributes from "Very Important" to "Not Important," study participants ranked attributes in the "technical details of the bibliographic record" category as "Very Important" most often, but the top three "Very Important" attributes chosen by participants fell under the "impact of cataloging on users" category (the three attributes are: "creating a bibliographic record that is helpful/useful to the user," "enough access points are included so that the record can be found," and "The user is able to find records in the catalog efficiently").[41]

## Accurate and complete

A word frequency analysis conducted on the definitions in the Snow study revealed the usage of many of the same (or very similar) words. *Accurate* and *Complete* (including variations of these terms, such as *accuracy* and *completeness*) are two of the most common terms used to describe quality cataloging.[42] If one assumes that the terms *correct* and *correctness* can be used synonymously with *accurate* and *accuracy*, then the occurrence of *accurate* and its synonyms is almost double the frequency of the next most frequently used term describing quality cataloging. These terms were often used on their own, but it was not uncommon to find them paired with other words, such as *information, description, access point*, or *subject heading*. In addition, it was sometimes unclear how the person providing the definition was using the term because most participants did not define the terms they used within their quality cataloging definition. However, some participants did define certain terms and the definitions differed from participant to participant. For example, one participant defined *accuracy* as "the record adequately identifies the item in hand" and another participant defined it as "conforming to cataloging standards."[43] How can catalogers use *accuracy* as a way to define and assess cataloging quality when it can refer to different ideas?

Graham, in an article devoted to examining the meaning of quality cataloging, defines *accuracy* as "correctness of what is provided," but qualifies that definition by dividing accuracy into two main areas: mechanical and intellectual.[44] Mechanical accuracy is about typographical and transcription precision, and intellectual accuracy is how well the description of a resource matches the resource itself. Bruce and Hillmann define accuracy in largely the same way as Graham. They state that accuracy is "[m]inimally, the information provided in the values needs to be correct and factual. At the next level, accuracy is simply high-quality editing: the elimination of typographical errors, conforming expression of personal names and place names, use of standard abbreviations, and so on."[45] Both Graham and Bruce & Hillmann note that adherence to standards may be considered part of the definition of *accuracy*, but it is not an essential part; it is useful, but still a luxury.[46] Graham points out that describing resources using agreed-upon standards does not always guarantee that user needs are met. As mentioned earlier, the developers of cataloging standards have largely neglected to study users as part of the development process and therefore current standards may not accurately reflect the needs of modern library users.[47] Therefore, accuracy through adherence to cataloging standards may demonstrate cataloging quality within the cataloging community, but how crucial this particular aspect of accuracy is for library users' sense of quality cataloging is unclear.

Defining *complete*, on the other hand, involves more judgment on the part of the cataloger and individual institutions. In the Snow study, participants often describe *complete* or *completeness* as including all information necessary for identifying a resource or required according to specific standards.[48] However, some participants define *complete* or *completeness* as going beyond core descriptions, "including as much information as possible" or "not meeting a floor standard, but full-level cataloging at least."[49] According to several study participants, minimum standards are good, but they do not necessarily produce *quality* cataloging. Graham discusses completeness in terms of *extent*: "how much information is provided in the record," but the extent of the information needed for a "quality" record is a subjective notion that can be viewed differently for a variety of reasons.[50] Bruce and Hillmann explain that:

> [m]etadata should be complete in two senses. First, the element set used should describe the target objects as completely as economically feasible…Second, the element set should be applied to the target object population as completely as possible; it does little good to prescribe a particular element set if most of the elements are never used, or if their use cannot be relied upon across the entire collection.[51]

The idea that *completeness* should be measured in regard to what is "economically feasible" and how suitable the metadata is for a particular user population is something that the cataloging community has been grappling with for some time. Boissonnas (who wrote about the Cornell Law Library's "authoritative record" in the 1970s) muses that quality is frequently determined by economic realities: "Given our resources and the current standards, how much quality can we afford to provide?"[52] David Bade returns to this theme in 2008 in an article criticizing the disingenuous use of the phrase "the perfect record" by those who view cataloging as too focused on unimportant details and not enough on users.[53] Instead of using perfection as a straw man to dismiss genuine quality concerns, Bade insists on an honest discussion about what information is most useful and also financially achievable at the local level.[54]

Even though monetary considerations are certainly important when assessing quality cataloging at the institutional level, catalogers' views of the completeness and accuracy of cataloging are often influenced by other factors and these views have a great impact on their cataloging work.

## How quality definitions are formed: Cataloging as a community of practice

How catalogers think about quality cataloging is influenced heavily by experience and external forces, such as the work and words of other catalogers, the type of institution and user population they serve, and the specific demands of their position (for example, if they have administrative duties). It is generally recognized that knowledge of cataloging standards and practices, as well as the refinement of a cataloger's judgment, is gained not by simply studying cataloging in school, but by on-the-job experience. The experience gained in internships, and paraprofessional and professional positions lays the groundwork for the formation of cataloger perception of "quality" and "not quality" cataloging.

In the dissertation research by Snow, study participants refer to various influences that have shaped their thinking about quality cataloging, their cataloging work, and, in many cases, department policies and procedures. These influences include experience, conference and webinar attendance, cataloging email discussion lists (such as AUTOCAT), speaking with colleagues at his/her institution, as well as simply looking at other catalogers' records.[55] The learning and practice of cataloging display many of the characteristics inherent in situated learning theory and communities of practice. Situated learning theory, developed in the early 1990s by educational theorists Jean Lave and Etienne Wegner, is an offshoot of social learning theory that stresses that the skills and knowledge of a particular practice can only be learned effectively by engaging in actual practice and by interacting with others who take part in the same practice.[56]

Within situated learning theory is the idea of communities of practice. Communities of practice are established formally or informally by practitioners to discuss and learn about their practice. Lave and Wenger explain that joining communities of practice implies "participation in an activity system about which participants share understandings concerning what they are doing and what that means in their lives and for their communities."[57] Using various methods of communication, either in-person or at a distance, communities of practice are formed around a desire to interpret existing standards and negotiate their meaning. This negotiation, in turn, shapes the ideas of individuals within the practice, as well as the practice itself. It is likely that this is the reason why there are only a few common categories in which quality cataloging definitions tend to fall; even though there may be disagreements over the details, overall catalogers tend to gravitate towards certain ways of thinking about what makes cataloging quality.

Understanding that cataloging is a community of practice and that catalogers learn about and find meaning in their work from engaging in the cataloging community of practice can be helpful in many ways. First, encouraging novice, experienced, and soon-to-be catalogers to engage more fully in the cataloging community of practice benefits both the cataloger and the community. Through formal (e.g., conference attendance) or informal (e.g., email discussion lists, social media) community of practice activities, novice catalogers and library school students have multiple avenues of learning more about their profession, its expectations, and the tools of the trade. These avenues also help shape a cataloger's judgment, whether the cataloger works in a large department or is the lone cataloger at his/her institution. Experienced catalogers have multiple avenues to influence novice catalogers, voice their concerns, and learn about new developments in the community.

In addition, a greater understanding of how catalogers navigate, communicate, and learn within their community of practice may help cataloging practitioners and educators gain insight into the ways catalogers utilize the various activities to learn about their practice and interact with other practitioners. This may lead to more effective ways of engaging with, and educating the community on, topics that cataloging practitioners and educators feel are important.

## Rethinking quality cataloging

Quality cataloging definitions are shaped in individual minds largely through experience and engagement in the cataloging community of practice. As previously discussed, most of these definitions fall into at least one of four categories: the technical details of the bibliographic record, adherence to standards, the cataloging process, and impact of cataloging on the user. But are these categories *sufficient* for defining quality cataloging? Do definitions need to be more specific? Should certain categories be emphasized or *de*emphasized? Is there more that needs to be considered? These categories, as well as the quality frameworks provided by Statistics Canada and Bruce and Hillmann, and the quality cataloging definitions mentioned above, are good starting points for discussion within an institution. It is important for catalogers at individual libraries to come to a general agreement on what quality cataloging looks like for their institution and user population, perhaps designing an audit tool like the ones suggested in studies by Hider & Tan and Chapman & Massey.

At the same time, library catalogers should rethink certain assumptions about what makes cataloging *quality*, like the idea that rigorously following standards will produce quality data in all library environments. Catalogers need to look beyond catalog data and, more importantly, the catalog record when they reflect upon what quality cataloging means to them. This is not to say that the data are unimportant, but they should not be the cataloger's sole focus. In addition to the data and the record, catalogers need to pay more attention to the library user's overall discovery experience. Francis Miksa maintains that early cataloging education emphasized the construction of the catalog as a whole, not just individual records and fields: "bibliographic system making as a total concept... [rather than] cataloging as the preparation of entries."[58] In the late 19th- and early 20th-centuries, cataloging courses taught future catalogers:

> the best way to display bibliographic data, how thoroughly names should be established and written, the relative merits of different sizes and thicknesses of cards, the design and arrangement of card catalog furniture, problems in handwriting (or typing) bibliographic data, and, with respect to item files, the merits of closely classified, relative position systems.[59]

Even though many of these topics are irrelevant in the age of electronic cataloging, the idea that catalogers should learn about, and be more involved in, the design of the cataloging system should be revisited. Discovery layers have certainly made the online public access catalog more user friendly, but more could be done. Considering that leaders in the development of cataloging standards are focusing more on allowing greater flexibility for resource description via *Resource Description and Access* (RDA) and encouraging greater sharing of bibliographic data on the web using linked data and other web-compatible standards, the time is ripe for catalogers to broaden their ideas of what quality cataloging can and should be at the local level.

While standardization of bibliographic data remains important (especially now since machines need to read and act upon this data on the web), standardization without concern for user needs does not produce quality cataloging. Gretchen Hoffman's research highlights the difficulties catalogers face while trying to meet user needs without fully knowing who their users are, as well as being discouraged from adapting cataloging copy even if user needs are known.[60] She insists that this is an ethical issue since the *Statement of International Cataloguing Principles* states that the "convenience of the user" is the highest principle of cataloging and many catalogers, knowingly or unknowingly, are unable to determine and meet the needs of the user population they serve.[61] Hoffman suggests that instead of continuing to believe that cataloging standards (if followed) magically meet user needs and that "one size fits all," the ethical path for the cataloging community is to study user needs directly—not individual users, necessarily, but *domains* of users, and produce standards congruent with those needs.[62] This domain analytic approach, originally proposed by Birger Hjørland, would help catalogers evaluate groups of users who have common information needs, such as academic or public library users in a broad sense, or more subject-specific groupings: humanities majors or chemistry students, for example.[63] Two recent studies do just this.

Maurine McCourry's study of the catalog information needs of music students in small, academic libraries provides a blueprint for using domain analysis to determine elements of description that users actually want to see in a library catalog.[64] After surveying and interviewing students *away* from the library catalog, McCourry finds that "only 52% of the elements of information identified by these students as needed in a library catalog are elements likely to be included in these catalogs."[65] Jihee Beak did not mention domain analysis specifically in her study, but nonetheless focused on a particular domain to learn more about its information needs. Beak studied the information needs of primarily elementary-aged (or younger) children and exposed the disconnect between how children think about library resources and what attributes of these resources library cataloging standards tell catalogers to focus on. For example, catalog records frequently include title, author, and publisher information, but young children rarely remember this type of information when searching for resources. Instead, they focus more on unique physical characteristics of resources, such as the shape of a book, or if there are holes or fur inside. If these attributes are included in the record at all, they tend to be placed in note fields, which are typically not indexed and make such unique attributes more difficult to search and browse.[66]

By deliberately studying these specific domains of users away from existing cataloging standards and systems, McCourry and Beak were able to gain a better understanding of what information these users truly want in a library catalog and not just what the cataloging community *thinks* they want. Not only are more studies like these needed for different user groups, but their findings need to be incorporated into cataloging standards and best practices guides. Quality cataloging can be defined in many ways, but ultimately, whichever framework is used to create and evaluate cataloging work, clearly defined user needs should be part of the equation. Existing quality cataloging definitions demonstrate that catalogers do care about the impact of their work upon users, but there needs to be a greater awareness of what that impact actually means for different types of users. Simply stating that quality cataloging should be *accurate* and *complete*, or should follow specific standards, is not enough, practically or ethically.

Quality cataloging will continue to be elusive and unfairly assessed as long as the cataloging community continues to ignore actual user information needs. Therefore, the following action plan is recommended.

(1) First of all, each cataloger should think about what quality cataloging means to him or her and then externalize that discussion within a cataloging quality conversation at the department-level. Use the frameworks discussed earlier (from the Snow study, Statistics Canada, or Bruce and Hillmann) to inform the conversation, but do not be afraid to identify quality attributes that may fall outside these frameworks.

(2) Conduct a study of user information needs to determine what information is important to users at your institution and try to accommodate those needs in a way that is financially feasible, as suggested by Bade.[67] Furthermore, do not simply focus on what data are included in your local catalog, but also explore the user's experience using the catalog. Study the user experience and work to improve it.

(3) The cataloging community should conduct more studies that attempt to address the actual information needs of users, particularly domains of users, as suggested by Hoffman.[68] There are many domains to explore, from

those interested in specific subjects (religion, engineering, business), genres (romance, mystery, self-help), audiences (young adults, professors, caregivers), and resource types and formats (graphic novels, kits, audiobooks).

(4) The results of these user studies should be incorporated into cataloging standards, such as RDA and best practices guides, but even user-informed cataloging standards should not carry the entire weight of the user discovery experience. Catalogers must become more open to the idea of allowing user-contributed metadata, circulation statistics, and other outside information sources to enhance the catalog. This is already done to a certain extent in many catalogs, but this should be commonplace rather than an exception to the rule.

(5) Finally, cataloging needs a heavy dose of design thinking. In short, design thinking is human-centered exploration that seeks to address problems by privileging the cyclical approach of design rather than the linear approach of the scientific method.[69] It is, according to Steven J. Bell, "fully understanding the problem before thinking about possible solutions," and then attempting to solve the identified problems with a fresh perspective and a passion for providing the user a positive and memorable experience.[70] Cataloging is ripe for innovative approaches and solutions, but first the cataloging community of practice must acknowledge and identify problems in order to work towards more user-centric solutions. Design thinking can help the cataloging community do this.[71]

Jesse Shera once said that "because the catalog is not built for a day, a year, or even a decade, but for at least a generation, the catalog suffers most from the dead hand of tradition."[72] It's time to rethink quality cataloging, not to reject all that the catalog has become, but in order to imagine and believe that it can be so much more.

## ORCID

Karen Snow (iD) http://orcid.org/0000-0003-4763-4695

## Notes

1. Art, see Levon Avdoyan, "The Good Cataloguing Record, or, When Cataloguing Records Go Bad," in *Cataloging Quality Is…Five Perspectives: Opinion Papers, no. 4* (Washington, D.C.: Library of Congress Cataloging Forum, 1993), 3–6. Pornography, see Thomas R. Bruce and Diane I. Hillmann, "The Continuum of Metadata Quality: Defining, Expressing, Exploiting," in *Metadata in Practice*, ed. Diane I. Hillmann & Elaine L. Westbrooks (Chicago: American Library Association, 2004), 238–256.
2. *Cataloging Quality: A Library of Congress Symposium: Opinion Papers, no. 6* (Washington, D.C.: Library of Congress Cataloging Forum, 1995), 28.
3. Lydia W. Wasylenko, "Building Quality that Counts into Your Cataloging Operation," *Library Collections, Acquisitions, and Technical Services* 23, no. 1 (1999): 102. Note that the definition, though recorded by Wasylenko, is actually from featured speaker Karen Calhoun.

4. Andrew MacEwan and Thurstan Young, "Quality vs. Quantity: Developing a Systematic Approach to a Perennial Problem," *Catalogue & Index* 152 (2004): 2.

5. Primary Research Group. *Academic Library Cataloging Practices Benchmarks*. (Rockville, MD: Primary Research Group, 2008),136.

6. Boston Athenaeum and Charles A. Cutter, *Catalogue of the Library of the Boston Athenaeum. 1807-1871. Part IV*. (Boston: Boston Athenaeum, 1880), 3399.

7. R.B. Pool, "[Letter to the Editor]," *Library Journal* 1, no. 8 (1877): 290.

8. Frederic Vinton, "Hints for Improved Library Economy, Drawn from Usages at Princeton," *Library Journal* 2, no. 2 (1877): 53.

9. R.R. Bowker, "The Work of the Nineteenth-Century Librarian for the Librarian of the Twentieth," *Library Journal* 8, no. 9/10 (1883): 250.

10. Andrew D. Osborn, "The Crisis in Cataloging," *Library Quarterly* 11, no. 1/4 (1941): 395, http://www.columbia.edu/cu/libraries/inside/units/bibcontrol/osmc/crisis.pdf.

11. Ibid, 401.

12. Ibid, 399.

13. Wilson Luquire, *Selected Factors Affecting Library Staff Perceptions of an Innovative System: A Study of ARL Libraries in OCLC* (Doctoral dissertation, Indiana University, 1976); James Schoenung, *The Quality of Member-Input Monographic Records in the OCLC On-line Union Catalog* (Doctoral dissertation, Drexel University, 1981).

14. Luquire, *Selected Factors Affecting Library Staff Perceptions of an Innovative System: A Study of ARL Libraries in OCLC*, 62.

15. Schoenung, *The Quality of Member-Input Monographic Records in the OCLC On-line Union Catalog*, 83.

16. Christian Boissonnas, "The Quality of OCLC Bibliographic Records: The Cornell Law Library Experience," *Law Library Journal* 72 (1979): 80.

17. Ibid.

18. Ibid, 82.

19. Sheila S. Intner, "Much Ado About Nothing: OCLC and RLIN Cataloging Quality," *Library Journal* 114, no. 2 (1989); Carol C. Davis, "Results of a Survey on Record Quality in the OCLC Database," *Technical Services Quarterly* 7, no. 2 (1989); "dirty database" from Davis, "Results of a Survey on Record Quality in the OCLC Database," 43.

20. Andrea L. Stamm, "Minimal Level Cataloging: Past, Present, and Future," in *Technical Services Management, 1965–1990: A Quarter Century of Change and a Look to the Future: Festschrift for Kathryn Luther Henderson*, ed. Linda C. Smith and Ruth C. Carter (New York: Haworth Press, 1996): 193.

21. See, for example, Ryburn Ross and Linda West, "MLC: A Contrary Viewpoint," *Journal of Academic Librarianship* 11, no. 6 (1986): 334–336, Sue Rhee, "Minimal-level Cataloging: Is it the Best Local Solution to a National Problem? *Journal of Academic Librarianship* 11, no. 6 (1986): 336–337, and Thomas Mann, "Cataloging Quality, LC Priorities, and Models of the Library's Future," in *Opinion Papers 1* (Washington, D.C.: Library of Congress Cataloging Forum, 1991).

22. The six published opinion papers that were the result of the Cataloging Forums (all published by the Library of Congress) are: *Cataloging Quality, LC Priorities, and Models of the Library's Future* by Thomas Mann (1991; no. 1); *A Perspective on Cataloging Simplification* by David A. Smith (1991; no. 2); *Nonromanization: Prospects for Improving Automated Cataloging of Items in Other Writing Systems* by James Agenbroad (1992; no. 3); *Cataloging Quality is…: Five Perspectives* (1993; no. 4); *Cataloging and Classification Quality at the Library of Congress* by Thomas Mann (1994; no. 5); and *Cataloging Quality: A Library of Congress Symposium* (1995; no. 6).

23. Avdoyan, "The Good Cataloguing Record, or, When Cataloguing Records Go Bad," 5.

24. *Cataloging Quality: A Library of Congress Symposium: Opinion Papers, no. 6*, 28.
25. Sarah E. Thomas, "Quality in Bibliographic Control," *Library Trends* 44, no. 3 (1996): 499.
26. Thomas, "Quality in Bibliographic Control," 500.
27. Library of Congress, "Frequently Asked Questions: Implementation of the BSR for Printed Books." Last modified December 18, 2009. https://www.loc.gov/aba/pcc/bibco/documents/BSR_FAQ.pdf
28. Library of Congress Program for Cooperative Cataloging. *LC Acquisitions and Bibliographic Access Directorate Program for Cooperative Cataloging Statistics – NACO/BIBCO/CONSER/SACO. Annual Compilation FY2016 (October 1, 2015 - Sept 30 2016)*. Last modified December 1, 2016. http://www.loc.gov/aba/pcc/stats/AllProjectsAnnual.pdf
29. Magda El-Sherbini, "Program for Cooperative Cataloging: BIBCO Records: Analysis of Quality," *Cataloging & Classification Quarterly* 48, no. 2 (2010), 235.
30. Ibid.
31. Ann Chapman and Owen Massey, "A Catalogue Quality Audit Tool," *Library Management* 23, no. 6/7 (2002): 316.
32. Ibid, 322.
33. MacEwan and Young, "Quality vs. Quantity: Developing a Systematic Approach to a Perennial Problem." See also Tom Delsey, *Functional Analysis of the MARC 21 Bibliographic and Holdings Formats*. Last modified April 6, 2006. http://www.loc.gov/marc/marc-functional-analysis/functional-analysis.html
34. Gretchen L. Hoffman, "Meeting Users' Needs in Cataloging: What is the Right Thing to Do?" *Cataloging & Classification Quarterly* 47, no. 7 (2009).
35. Philip Hider and Kah-Ching Tan, "Constructing Record Quality Measures Based on Catalog Use," *Cataloging & Classification Quarterly* 46, no. 4 (2008).
36. Hider and Tan, "Constructing Record Quality Measures Based on Catalog Use."
37. Statistics Canada. *Statistics Canada's Quality Assurance Framework*. Last modified 2002. https://unstats.un.org/unsd/industry/meetings/eg2008/AC158-11.PDF
38. Bruce and Hillmann, "The Continuum of Metadata Quality: Defining, Expressing, Exploiting," 243.
39. Snow, *A Study of the Perception of Cataloging Quality Among Catalogers in Academic Libraries* (Doctoral dissertation, University of North Texas, 2011).
40. Ibid.
41. Ibid, 117.
42. Snow, *A Study of the Perception of Cataloging Quality Among Catalogers in Academic Libraries*.
43. Ibid, 172.
44. Peter S. Graham, "Quality in Cataloging: Making Distinctions," *Journal of Academic Librarianship* 16, no. 4 (1990): 214.
45. Bruce and Hillmann, "The Continuum of Metadata Quality: Defining, Expressing, Exploiting," 243.
46. Graham, "Quality in Cataloging: Making Distinctions".
47. Hoffman, "Meeting Users' Needs in Cataloging: What is the Right Thing to Do?".
48. Snow, *A Study of the Perception of Cataloging Quality Among Catalogers in Academic Libraries*.
49. Ibid, 175.
50. Graham, "Quality in Cataloging: Making Distinctions," 214.
51. Bruce and Hillmann, "The Continuum of Metadata Quality: Defining, Expressing, Exploiting," 243.
52. Boissonnas, "The Quality of OCLC Bibliographic Records: The Cornell Law Library Experience," 80.

53. David Bade, "The Perfect Bibliographic Record: Platonic Ideal, Rhetorical Strategy or Nonsense?," *Cataloging & Classification Quarterly* 46, no. 1 (2008): 109–133.

54. Bade, "The Perfect Bibliographic Record: Platonic Ideal, Rhetorical Strategy or Nonsense?," 129.

55. Snow, *A Study of the Perception of Cataloging Quality Among Catalogers in Academic Libraries.*

56. Jean Lave and Etienne Wenger, *Situated Learning: Legitimate Peripheral Participation.* (Cambridge: Cambridge University Press, 1991).

57. Ibid, 98.

58. Francis Miksa, "Cataloging Education in the Library and Information Science Curriculum. In *Recruiting, Educating, and Training Cataloging Librarians: Solving the Problems,* ed. Sheila S. Intner and Janet Swan Hill (New York: Greenwood Press, 1989), 291–292.

59. Ibid, 285.

60. Hoffman, "Meeting Users' Needs in Cataloging: What is the Right Thing to Do?".

61. International Federation of Library Associations and Institutions, *Statement of International Cataloguing Principles.* Last modified 2016. http://www.ifla.org/publications/node/11015

62. Ibid, 637–638.

63. Ibid.

64. Maurine McCourry, "Domain Analytic, and Domain Analytic-Like, Studies of Catalog Needs: Addressingthe Ethical Dilemma of Catalog Codes Developed with Inadequate Knowledge of User Needs," *Knowledge Organization* 42, no. 5 (2015).

65. Ibid, 342.

66. Jihee Beak, "Where is Childrens' Voice in KO?" *Knowledge Organization* 42, no. 5 (2015): 285.

67. Bade, "The Perfect Bibliographic Record: Platonic Ideal, Rhetorical Strategy or Nonsense?"

68. Hoffman, "Meeting Users' Needs in Cataloging: What is the Right Thing to Do?".

69. Rachel Ivy Clarke, "Beyond Buildings: A Design-Based Approach to Future Librarianship." In *Leading the 21st-Century Academic Library: Successful Strategies for Envisioning and Realizing Preferred Futures,* ed. Brad Eden. (Lanham, MD: Scarecrow Press, 2015).

70. Steven J. Bell, "Design Thinking," *American Libraries* 39, no. 1/2 (2008): 45.

71. In addition to the Rachel Ivy Clarke and Steven J. Bell works cited above, the following works on design thinking are recommended: Lisa Peet. "The Future of Futures: Designing the Future." *Library Journal* (September 13, 2016) http://lj.libraryjournal.com/2016/09/future-of-libraries/the-future-of-futures-designing-the-future/; IDEO's Design Thinking for Libraries website: http://designthinkingforlibraries.com/; and Don Norman, *The Design of Everyday Things. Revised & Expanded Edition.* (New York: Basics Books, 2013).

72. Jesse Shera, "On the Teaching of Cataloging," *Journal of Cataloging & Classification* 12, no. 3 (1956): 130.

# A Librarian-Centered Study of Perceptions of Subject Terms and Controlled Vocabulary

William N. Schultz, Jr. and Lindsay Braddy

**ABSTRACT**

Controlled vocabulary and subject headings in OPAC records have proven to be useful in improving search results. The authors used a survey to gather information about librarian opinions and professional use of controlled vocabulary. Data from a range of backgrounds and expertise were examined, including academic and public libraries, and technical services as well as public services professionals. Responses overall demonstrated positive opinions of the value of controlled vocabulary, including in reference interactions as well as during bibliographic instruction sessions. Results are also examined based upon factors such as age and type of librarian.

## Introduction

The use of subject headings and controlled vocabulary can sometimes be considered almost passé, particularly in circles outside of technical services, catalogers, or metadata librarians. Librarian reactions to their use may also depend on what terminology is used to describe or discuss controlled vocabulary. If one utters the word "metadata" when associating it with Library of Congress subject headings, those headings can suddenly take on the aura of being fresh and cutting edge, particularly to the uninitiated. In fact, the value and power of controlled vocabulary in information discovery has been proven through a variety of studies that are included in the literature review of this article. One might also assume that cataloging and metadata librarians are particularly partial to these tools by the nature of their work. The authors of this article wanted to explore how librarians in general currently feel about the value of subject headings and controlled vocabulary. Is there a difference between the opinions of public librarians and academic librarians? Is there a difference between the opinions of technical services librarians and public services librarians? Even more specifically, are librarians actually using controlled vocabulary, and if so, in what situations? Do reference librarians use or teach students about clickable subject heading links? Finally, is the value and proper use of subject headings or controlled vocabulary being taught in library instruction sessions? The authors conducted a survey in the fall of 2015 which attempted to uncover answers to some of these questions.

## Literature review

In his 2008 article, "Search Engine User Behaviour: How Can Users Be Guided to Quality Content?", Dirk Lewandoski suggested that the major problem in web searching was the same as it was ten years prior: search result relevance to information that is being sought.[1] Today, it is not hard to argue that relevance is still a major problem. This is the case in broad-based web searching as well as with library catalogs and databases. Often, libraries are seduced by the siren song of the "one search box" that Google presents. However, libraries are not Google, nor should they strive to be. Lewandoski stresses that it is not only about libraries *offering* great collections, but being able to point users to them.[2] Controlled vocabulary is one of the means that we have to point users to our high-quality content.

Of course there are nuances and potential problems that controlled vocabularies such as Library of Congress subject headings can pose. Sevim McCutcheon points out that on the one hand, sub-headings attached to primary topics that a person has already searched may provide options that he or she may not have been aware of until that point.[3] In contrast, controlled vocabulary requires time to develop, so items described by more obscure terms or older terms, or conversely, items about cutting-edge developments, might be found most effectively with keywords that may not be contained within headings. McCutcheon reminds us that, "The goal of both indexers and catalogers is to facilitate easy findability by imposing consistency on search terms, disambiguating synonyms and homonyms, and by ensuring accuracy."[4]

In 2005, Tina Gross and Arlene Taylor conducted a study that investigated the appearance of keywords in subject searches of catalog records and found that in many cases at least one third of successful results from keyword searches would be lost if not for the existence of keywords *within* a subject heading.[5] This illustrates that in addition to headings functioning strictly as subject headings, they clearly serve a purpose in keyword searching as well, in that they produce real results. A similar but improved study was conducted by Gross, Taylor, and Joudrey ten years later. Included in this new study—designed to reflect developments in catalog records—were records that had been enhanced with table of contents and summaries. As the presence of tables of contents and summaries could theoretically de-emphasize the importance of subject headings, this is a significant shift. One of the results from the study found that even with tables of contents and summary notes, 24.8% of keyword search hits still would have been lost without the presence of subject headings in the catalog records (compared to 35.9% in 2005 without them).[6]

In their 2014 article "Teaching the Use of Library of Congress Subject Headings as a Research Strategy for Undergraduate Students," Debra Spidal and Lara Ursin

Cummings conducted a survey to determine if subject headings or controlled vocabularies are still being taught as a part of library instruction. Although similar to our inquiry, their approach was more targeted, focusing on library instruction. Of the 389 responses they received, 33% said they never or rarely mentioned subject headings when they taught, 29.2% said sometimes, 21.9% answered often, and 14.5% responded they always did.[7] In using online tutorials, either alone or in conjunction with face-to-face instruction, 87% acknowledged having a section on keyword searching, and 40.4% with a component on LCSH. Spidal and Cummings also found that many librarians who responded felt that one-shot sessions (usually about 50 minutes) were too short to include controlled vocabulary. Other respondents began teaching with keyword searches, and then pointed out clickable links. Other responses spoke to the perceived importance of subject headings or controlled vocabulary, including a statement from one respondent that "keyword searching isn't adequate for serious research."[8]

## Methodology

In the Fall 2015, the authors of this article constructed a 16-question survey using Qualtrics as the dissemination tool. The survey was sent out to a number of national and regional electronic discussion lists. The authors strove to get participation from both public services and technical services librarians as well as academic and public librarians. One question ("Are you currently in library school?") was contingent on the respondent answering "no" to the preceding question that asked whether the respondent had a master's in library science. This was automated by Qualtrics. Because the authors are a part of the Illinois library community (Eastern Illinois University and the Skokie (Il) Public Library), the survey was sent out to the Consortium of Academic and Research Libraries in Illinois (CARLI) Public services discussion list, the CARLI instruction discussion list, CARLI technical services discussion list, the Illinois Library Association (ILA) Reference Services Forum, and the Reaching Across Illinois Library System (RAILS) discussion list. RAILS is one of two multi-type regional library systems in Illinois, whose membership includes academic, public, school, and special libraries. On the national level, the survey was sent to Autocat, an electronic discussion list geared towards technical services librarians, particularly catalogers and metadata librarians. Although the survey did reach a variety of librarians, the authors recognize that the responses do constitute a convenience sample due to the ease and voluntary nature of the survey.

## Findings

The 170 respondents to the 16-question survey represented a mix of public and academic librarians (about 34% and 55%, respectively), as well as public services and technical services librarians in very similar proportions (33% and 53%, respectively). Fifty-three percent of the respondents also reported either being engaged in library instruction or working at a public services desk between 0 and 6 hours per week, and another 22% serving between 7 and 12 hours per week. Fourteen percent reported spending between 13 and 30 hours per week, and 11% reported 24 or more a week with instruction or on a service desk. Basic awareness that respondents had of subject analysis and headings, and related recent developments was gauged by responses to a pair of statements. One was "I am aware that changes have occurred in recent years to make some headings more user-friendly; examples include changing "cookery" to "cooking," and "violoncellists" to "cellists." (Yes/No) and "My grasp of the concept of subject analysis could be described as one of the following:" (Excellent, Very good, Good, Fair, Poor). Respondents in general reported a notable awareness that changes have occurred, with 86.5% answering "yes" to this statement. In a related expression of familiarity, 63% of responding librarians reported having at least a "very good" grasp of the concept of subject analysis.

One phenomenon we observed was the relationship between work with the public, and how prevalent the use of subject headings and controlled vocabulary is in these circumstances. Of those who reported working with the public in their positions, a 61.5% majority reported using subject headings at least often. The remainder reported 27% for sometimes, and only 3% reported never using them (see Figure 1). Within the venue of actual library instruction sessions, more than three quarters of the respondents (76.1%) reported teaching about subject headings at least sometimes (see Figure 2).

Tangentially, it is worth noting that there were a fair number of technical services librarians who reported working with the public or engaged in library instruction. For example, in filtering for respondents who reported technical services as being his or her "primary job duties, or primary professional interest" who also were engaged in public services, 22.4% reported spending at least 7 hours, and up to 24 hours per week either at a public service desk or engaged in library instruction.

As the above illustrates, the authors were also interested in separating out the attitudes of librarians with respect to certain factors such as age or type of librarian with regard to title or responsibilities (e.g., public services, technical services). In the case of using controlled vocabulary in library instruction, there was a particular interest in comparing public service librarians to technical services librarians who engaged in library instruction. The study found that 76.6% and 63.4% of librarians (technical services and public services, respectively) taught about subject headings during instruction sessions. Although this finding represents behavior that librarians engage in, it does not necessarily translate into representation of attitude. In seeking to get a sense of corresponding attitudes about the value of subject heading searches, a breakdown by public services and technical services librarian responses to survey item 10 (The ability to perform subject searches is a necessary function of my Online Public Access Catalog (OPAC) or discovery layer) was also examined. These results reveal that of 53 self-identified public services librarians (75%) at least agree with the statement, and of 86 self-identified technical services

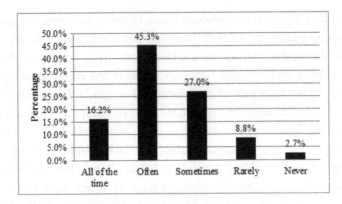

**Figure 1.** Use of subject headings when assisting patrons.

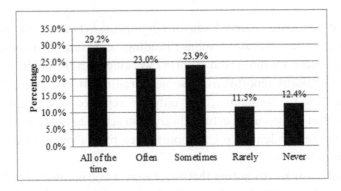

**Figure 2.** Teach the use of subject headings when engaged in instruction.

librarians (94.2%) at least agree. In contrast to this when examining responses of the entire sample of survey responses (despite the type of librarian) only 4.3% disagree that the ability to perform subject searches is a necessary function, and no respondents strongly disagreed with the statement.

The authors were also interested in finding if attitudes varied across other distinctions besides public services and technical services librarians. These

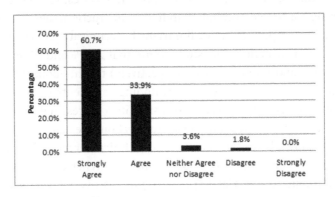

**Figure 3.** Agreement that the ability to perform subject searches is a necessary OPAC function (academic librarians).

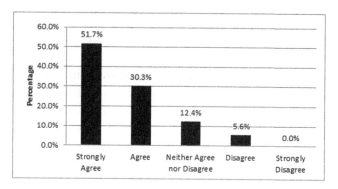

**Figure 4.** Agreement that the ability to perform subject searches is a necessary OPAC function (public librarians).

distinctions included generational gaps and academic librarians contrasted with public librarians. High-perceived value and importance of subject headings and controlled vocabulary among older and younger librarians was evident for each, despite what professional area or type of library they worked in. Both groups largely either agreed or strongly agreed that subject headings are valuable resources. Among respondents who reported being 46 years old or older, 94.8% agreed or strongly agreed that subject headings are valuable discovery tools, and an even larger majority (97.3%) of respondents 18–35 years old either agreed or strongly agreed with that statement.

The authors were also interested in uncovering any distinctions between academic librarians and public librarians when they were asked about subject search capability being "a necessary function of my Online Public Access Catalog (OPAC) or discovery layer" (see Figures 3 and 4). In this analysis, an overwhelming majority of both groups of respondents either agreed or strongly agreed that they are a necessary function, although the public librarian opinion did not have quite the conviction of the academic librarians (94.6% of academics and 82% for public librarians). This sentiment was mirrored in overall responses to that statement, with more than 86.4% of all respondents agreeing that subject search capability is a necessary function.

## Discussion

The survey results were notable for the respondents' across-the-board expression of respect for, and perception of the value of controlled vocabulary and subject headings. Furthermore, there were fewer differences than one might have expected between the opinions and attitudes of public services librarians and those of technical services librarians. It may go without saying that Catalogers or Metadata Librarians probably tend to have more familiarity with subject headings. For example, if a university student is seeking analyses of the writings of a particular novelist, knowing to implement the subheading "criticism and interpretation" is a powerful tool that can be used to target such scholarship. This knowledge may be an advantage that librarians who are more technical services or metadata oriented tend to have.

As with any study of this type, we recognized over time some things that we might have liked to have done differently, to have added in, or stripped out. For example, in retrospect, we realized that although we ascertained the age of respondents through the survey, we neglected to ask respondents about their gender. Although this was not at the crux of the type of information we were seeking, including the element of gender into the study may have produced additional results of interest. Also, we recognize that although respondents answered a question about holding a degree in library science, being more specific with regard to exactly what type of degree may have been valuable.

## Conclusions and suggestions for future research

What does all of this information tell us? On the one hand, the results of the survey demonstrate that librarians do indeed recognize the value and importance of what controlled vocabularies such as subject headings can do for patrons in terms of uncovering resources that are highly relevant to their searches. But how can patrons most effectively be exposed to these tools, and encouraged to regularly use them? Singer et al. mention that users "seldom use help pages…but automatic contextual help may be useful in supporting users in achieving their search goals."[9] Implementing contextual assistance may indeed be one way to help. Particularly in academic settings, it is easy to assume in this technological age, that students are savvy about using technology-related search tools; thus, teaching about them feels redundant or like a waste of time. In the experience of the authors of this article, demonstrating the use of controlled vocabulary in the context of constructing searches, in addition to teaching the simple act of locating and clicking on them, can certainly open up doors of discovery that may not have been recognized. The implications from the results of this survey are that despite what type of library or what types of librarianship backgrounds people come from, most librarians agree with that notion.

However, tangential factors may prohibit librarians from putting these tools and techniques into practice as much as they might like to. These may include the limitation of time to cover these more advanced search strategies (e.g., one-shot instruction sessions), a challenge that librarians reported in Spidal and Cummings' study mentioned earlier.[10] Perhaps librarians may also assume that patrons already have a familiarity with them or can figure it out for themselves. Further study that examines the knowledge, opinion, and use of controlled vocabulary tools by library patrons, and perhaps students in particular from the undergraduate as well as graduate levels would be valuable. Is there a difference between these two groups? Are there any trends that can be distinguished as a student progresses through their academic careers that demonstrate increased awareness and use of clickable subject strings or controlled vocabulary? Are there any significant differences distinguishable by academic major? Having more of this type of information could help librarians consider how aggressively these tools should be taught, and what teaching strategies might contribute to a higher prevalence of use in patron research habits.

The themes from this survey reveal generally positive information about how librarians from a variety of professional backgrounds feel about subject headings and controlled vocabulary. As a whole, librarians who responded to this survey recognize the value of them and have a high level of agreement on several particular sentiments, including that subject searches are a necessary function of library OPACS (for example). Along with the information gathered here about librarian attitudes, there is also important evidence through other research that controlled vocabulary and bibliographic features like clickable subject headings can increase discoverability.

This research is useful to librarians in demonstrating that even in a world that seems to be dominated by Google and Google-like searches, one can argue that there is an increased need for targeted searching that takes advantage of the power of controlled vocabulary. Implications are that this may be particularly pertinent as interest in linked data increases. This phenomenon will bring more and more information and unknown directions into the fold that will benefit from being anchored to elements of stability like controlled vocabulary.

## Notes

1. Dirk Lewandoski, "Search Engine User Behaviour: How Can Users Be Guided to Quality Content?" *Information Services & Use* 28, no. 3/4 (2008): 262.
2. Lewandoski, "Search Engine User Behaviour," 267.
3. Sevim McCutcheon, "Keyword vs Controlled Vocabulary Searching: The One with the Most Tools Wins," *The Indexer* 27, no. 2 (2009): 63.
4. McCutcheon, "Keyword vs Controlled Vocabulary Searching," 62.
5. Tina Gross and Arlene G. Taylor, "What Have We Got To Lose? The Effect of Controlled Vocabulary On Keyword Searching Results," *College & Research Libraries* 66, no. 3 (2005): 220.
6. Tina Gross, Arlene G. Taylor, and Daniel N. Joudrey, "Still a lot to Lose? The role of Controlled Vocabulary in Keyword Searching," *Cataloging & Classification Quarterly* 53, no. 1 (2015): 30.
7. Debra Spidal and Lara Ursin Cummings, "Teaching the Use of Library of Congress Subject Headings as a Research Strategy for Undergraduate Students," *College & Undergraduate Libraries* 21, no. 2 (2014): 165.
8. Spidal and Cummings, "Teaching the Use of Library of Congress Subject Headings as a Research Strategy for Undergraduate Students," 167.
9. Georg Singer, Ulrich Norbisrath, and Dirk Lewandowski, "Ordinary Search Engine Users Carrying Out Complex Search Tasks," *Journal of Information Science* 39, no. 3 (2013): 354.
10. Spidal and Cummings, "Teaching the Use of Library of Congress Subject Headings as a Research Strategy for Undergraduate Students," 167.

**Appendix: Survey questions**

1. **If you work with the public, do you make use of subject headings in assisting patrons with questions?**
   (a) All of the time
   (b) Often
   (c) Sometimes
   (d) Rarely
   (e) Never

2. **If you engage in library instruction, do you use or teach about subject headings when doing library or bibliographic instruction?**
   (a) All of the time
   (b) Often
   (c) Sometimes
   (d) Rarely
   (e) Never

3. **Approximately how many hours per week do you spend either at a public service desk or engaged in library instruction?**
   (a) 0–6
   (b) 7–12
   (c) 13–20
   (d) 20 or more hours

4. **Subject headings are valuable tools that help to discover resources.**
   (a) Strongly agree
   (b) Agree
   (c) Neither agree or disagree
   (d) Disagree
   (e) Strongly disagree

5. **Controlled vocabulary/subject headings are useful for patrons in helping to group similar resources, particularly through clickable links.**
   (a) Strongly agree
   (b) Agree
   (c) Neither agree or disagree
   (d) Disagree
   (e) Strongly disagree

6. **Patrons at my library make use of subject headings (intentionally or unintentionally) by activities such as clicking on heading links, using headings from search results as keywords in more searches, etc.**
   (a) All of the time
   (b) Often
   (c) Sometimes
   (d) Rarely
   (e) Never

7. **I am aware that changes have occurred in recent years to make some headings more user-friendly; examples include changing "cookery" to "cooking," and "violoncellists" to "cellists."**
   (a) Yes
   (b) No

8. **My library uses local subject headings or statements to intellectually gather or connect specific collections of materials for the public.**
   (a) Frequently
   (b) Occasionally
   (c) Not at all

9. **My grasp of the concept of subject analysis could be described as one of the following:**
   (a) Excellent
   (b) Very good
   (c) Good
   (d) Fair
   (e) Poor

10. **The ability to perform subject searches is a necessary function of my Online Public Access Catalog (OPAC) or discovery layer.**
    (a) Strongly agree
    (b) Agree
    (c) Neither agree or disagree
    (d) Disagree
    (e) Strongly disagree

11. **What best describes your primary job duties, or your primary professional interest?**
    (a) Public services
    (b) Technical services
    (c) Other (please explain)

12. **What best describes the type of library you work at, or have interest in?**
    (a) Academic library
    (b) Public library
    (c) School library
    (d) Special library
    (e) Other (please explain)

13. **Do you have a Master's degree in library science?**
    (a) Yes
    (b) No

14. **Are you currently in library school?**
    (a) Yes
    (b) No

15. **How many years have you been a librarian, or worked in libraries?**
    (a) 0–5
    (b) 6–10
    (c) 11–20
    (d) 21–30
    (e) 31+
16. **What is your age range?**
    (a) 18–25
    (b) 26–35
    (c) 36–45
    (d) 46–55
    (e) 56+

# Initiating Cultural Shifts in Perceptions of Cataloging Units through Interaction Assessment

Andrea Payant ⓘ, Becky Skeen ⓘ, and Liz Woolcott ⓘ

**ABSTRACT**

Points of contact formulate the culture of any organization and shape the perceptions of decision makers and colleagues alike. This research project investigated the interactions between Cataloging and Metadata Services staff and other library employees by analyzing interactions. This article summarizes the results of data gathered from interaction assessments and compares them with surveys about the current perceptions of the cataloging unit at the Utah State University Libraries. It discusses the ways these results have influenced existing unit workflows to enhance awareness of cataloging and metadata contributions to the library and posits possible ways to continue such initiatives moving forward.

## Introduction

As is likely the case with many cataloging and metadata units within academic libraries, the Cataloging and Metadata Services (CMS) unit at Utah State University has confronted the challenge of shrinking staff and changing roles over the last decade. Catalogers and technical services, in general, are sometimes under-valued as contributors to the field of librarianship due to the complex and "behind-the-scenes" nature of the work they do. This labyrinthine work, dependent on a mosaic of bewildering standards and rules and more visible for its failures than successes, is easily trivialized as unnecessary, excessive, or outsourceable. For example, a common mistake is the assumption that implementing shelf-ready has eliminated most of the work that catalogers do, without much thought to providing access for original material (whether archival collections or the budding field of data and institutional research products) or the current shift to batch loading work that moves and manipulates records in previously unimaginable quantities. Just as often, the value of cataloging is hampered by the caricature of the "cataloger" as individuals who prefer to work alone, who are dogged perfectionists, inflexible, uncompromising, and unnecessarily overcomplicate everything. Separating the work of the cataloging unit from the rest of the library allows for efficiencies in labor division, but ultimately engenders long-term isolation that leads to dwindling resources, staffing, and sometimes even respect, particularly in a field abuzz with words such as "collaboration" and "cross-departmental." A variety of proposed ways to combat this trajectory have focused on the cataloging unit moving outward to incorporate more with the library, such as working public service desk shifts. Some have even looked at drawing colleagues in by job shadowing or training. Both of these examples are well worth considering.

This research project, however, aimed to develop a new data-centric approach by recording and mapping out interactions between CMS unit members and the rest of the library staff. The end goal of the process was to test if proving the value of cataloging was really a matter of education or communication. The interaction mapping was compared against a survey of the perception of the CMS unit to test if there were correlations between frequency of interactions and positive views of the unit. Outlining the topography that defined the CMS unit's impact identified key areas of strengths and deficits in communication and interaction. The data even supported that many of the long-held stereotypes of catalogers do not hold up to scrutiny. Overall, it allowed the CMS unit to develop data-driven strategies to increase engagement with the library.

## Literature review

A survey of existing literature revealed that no significant measures have been taken to assess specific interactions between catalogers and other library staff. Despite the apparent lack of this kind of assessment, a number of notable articles provide valuable insight into different attitudes toward cataloging. Some of the literature seeks to demonstrate the value of cataloging services while others identify established perceptions of catalogers and cataloging work and advise on how to change possible misconceptions. Other recent themes concentrate on roles, or evolving roles of catalogers, which have been necessitated by the implementation of RDA and recent developments involving Linked Data and the slow progression away from traditional MARC cataloging. Generally, these works appear to be congruous with no apparent opposition to the observations or assertions made by the authors.

There is a consistent theme in the literature showing evidence that the cataloging profession is greatly undervalued. Authors have made efforts to bring this fact to light and offer suggestions for solving this problem. For instance, Borie, MacDonald, and Sze observe that "...catalogers have a unique challenge to overcome in demonstrating the value of their services...[and] the better they are at performing their work...the more invisible their efforts are to users and administrators."[1] They assert that since catalogers work out of the public view that they are often not "...conceptualized as a public service, even within libraries."[2] Miksa offers parallel remarks on the difficulties catalogers must face in that they "...often have to endure misunderstanding of their jobs from colleagues, patrons, and administrators."[3] CannCasciato[4] and Borie, MacDonald, and Sze[5] refer to a statement titled "The Value of Cataloging Librarians," published in 2007[6] with the sole purpose of assisting managers in describing the crucial need for cataloging librarians. CannCasciato observes "...there appears to be no similar existing statement for other specializations in librarianship."[7] This suggests that other library professions are not likely burdened with the obstacle of defending their worth.

Among the relevant literature that addresses perceptions of catalogers, we find that there are generally negative sentiments associated with the profession and individuals employed therein. For example, Banush discusses long-held stereotypes connected to academic catalogers. He relates how they are often seen as back-room hermits, surrounded by books, and as unwavering perfectionists unconcerned with the library outside their cubicle or office.[8] He states that this "...image has long been a misrepresentation of the actual contributions of catalogers to library users...[and] its persistence suggests that even as it becomes increasingly incongruous with reality, it remains a powerful force, one which influences the perceived importance of catalogers' work while also limiting their potential for contributing to a more holistic view of librarianship."[9] Hoerman echoes this assertion and frankly describes witnessing "...a great deal of disparagement of cataloging..." and that there is "...distaste for cataloging among library school students, experienced librarians, and administrators."[10] Unfortunately, there seems to be no clear explanation as to why these stereotypes continue, but all the authors concur that opportunities for catalogers to take part in the broader purpose of the library are abundant. They also conclude that catalogers need to make the extra effort to participate more actively to change these false perceptions and work to find ways to expand beyond traditional roles.

In addition to these difficulties, it is clear that catalogers are also expected to adapt and evolve as quickly as changes occur in the cataloging, metadata, and library fields. For example, Boydston and Leysen discuss findings of a 2011 study regarding changing cataloging roles and responsibilities.[11] They conclude that cataloger librarians will be required to develop or expand their skills, especially at a higher technological level, if they expect to "...be a part of emerging trends and communicate with internal and external partners and communities."[12] Banush also emphasizes the same point as he describes how the role of catalogers has evolved at the Cornell University Library. He writes about how the most traditional cataloging roles are currently being carried out by "...highly-trained non-MLS staff [while] MLS-holding catalog librarians have in turn taken on significant roles in other library activities."[13] Other authors, like Folsom, discuss some potential roles for catalogers and technical services librarians. The focus of Folsom's research seeks to address how catalogers can transition into roles in public services and relates how they bring valuable qualities to this aspect of librarianship. Folsom lists catalogers' high level of technical skill, knowledge of database structure and design, and overall understanding of technical services as having particular value in a public services role.[14] Likewise, Turner and Nann explore the possibilities of technical services librarians playing a role in teaching information literacy. They explain the need for these groups to be part of the academic conversations and that technical services librarians have an "…intimate knowledge of workflow in their own department that may impact the library's efforts in information literacy."[15]

Most of the authors mentioned previously offer helpful insight into possible solutions for addressing the issues of misconceptions, underestimated value, and changing roles of cataloging librarians. Based on their observations, one can easily conclude that the best solution lies on the shoulders of the catalogers themselves. For example, one recommendation is to "…learn to communicate in the language of administrators and users, using approaches of broad appeal that speak within and beyond the cataloging community."[16] Similarly, they advise improving communication so that administrators are made aware of the effects of an investment, or lack thereof, to employ catalogers by demonstrating the need for their expertise in providing the highest level of service.[17] Others encourage thinking broadly about roles and not being limited by a specific job description,[18] or they suggest exploring new ways to provide access to library information.[19]

## Interaction logs

Understanding the current interactions that build the foundations of library relationships should provide insight into the perpetuation of cultural perceptions about catalogers and cataloging work. The Cataloging and Metadata Services unit at Utah State University developed a methodology to analyze the frequency, format, and purpose of the interactions that occurred between the unit and the rest of the library. This assessment metric was used to formulate an overall understanding of the communication patterns in order to identify deficits and areas of growth or potential outreach.

The CMS unit staff ("staff" being a term all USU Library employees are called, regardless of position or faculty/non-faculty status) were asked to track their interactions on a weekly log. Throughout the week, unit staff would track each meeting, phone call, email, or interaction during his or her normal work hours with any non-CMS library employee. Interactions within the unit were not counted as part of this process. Interaction tracking continued for four weeks and the information from the physical tracking sheets was entered into a spreadsheet at the end of each week. The options and layout of the log sheet were vetted over a two-week trial run prior to the official tracking period. Data collection for the interaction logs took place for 18 workdays over 4 weeks, totaling one month. (Note: The University was closed two days during the assessment period. The data outputs described below were weighted to exclude the days that no interaction was expected.)

The interaction log was designed to not only collect the data needed, but also to fit easily into the daily work of the CMS staff to ensure consistent, timely use

| Week 1 Cataloging Interaction Log for _____ | | | | | | | |
|---|---|---|---|---|---|---|---|
| **Legend for "Reason for interaction":**  a = Database questions (Sierra, CONTENTdm, etc.); b = Request assistance; c = Procedures/Workflow questions or issues; d = Drop off /Pickup of materials; e = Meetings, Committees, Projects, or Training; f = General Library issues; g = Social (either inside or outside the workplace); h = Patron-driven questions; i = Reference desk; j = Other (please explain in notes area) | | | | | | | |
| Date | Time | What Dept is the other person from? | Who initiated (CIRCLE ONLY ONE) | **Method of Interaction/Communication** a=In Person b=Email c=Phone d=Other (please explain) | **Length of Conversation** a=5 min or less b=5-15 mins c=15-30 mins d=30 mins or more (CIRCLE ONLY ONE) | **Reason for interaction** [SEE LEGEND ABOVE] (CIRCLE ALL THAT APPLY) | Notes |
| | | | Me  Them Both  N/A | a   b   c d _____ | a   b   c   d | a  b  c  d  e f  g  h  i  j | |
| | | | Me  Them Both  N/A | a   b   c d _____ | a   b   c   d | a  b  c  d  e f  g  h  i  j | |

**Figure 1.** Example of weekly interaction log.

without interrupting workflows. The log sheet was constructed to track: name of the recorder; date and time of interaction; name of the library department interacted with; who initiated the interaction; method of interaction and communication; length of conversation; reason for interaction; and a notes field for any comments the author might want to make about the encounter. Whenever possible, multiple-choice answers were utilized to facilitate the speed of data capture and provide standardized categories. In typical logbook fashion, the form was set up with column headers and legends for the multiple-choice answers. The log was structured to have one entry (i.e., interaction) per row with the optional note field available at the end when more information was needed for that particular log entry (see Figure 1).

## Structure of the Cataloging and Metadata Services Unit at USU

Before investigating the results of the interaction log, a brief outline of the organizational structure of the CMS unit will be necessary to understand the dynamics in the data. The unit is one of four units belonging to the Technical Services division. At the time, the interaction logs and survey were conducted, the unit was composed of 5.5 full-time equivalent (FTE) professional catalogers, 3 FTE paraprofessional cataloging assistants, and 1 department head, with a total number of 10 individual people in the unit. All CMS unit staff are located in the same physical space on the second floor of the library, with the exception of one professional cataloger who resides full time in the Special Collections & Archives unit, but reports to the CMS unit.

While each professional cataloger has a specialty, there is considerable cross training that allows them to move fluidly between specialties in response to the influx of collections and projects. For instance, the General Cataloger is responsible for cataloging foreign language material, as well as collections for regional campus libraries, the children's library, and Special Collections material, in addition to database maintenance tasks such as authority changes and withdrawals. The

Metadata Coordinator aids with cataloging for regional campus libraries and foreign language material, in addition to managing the metadata creation for the digital library and providing guidance on metadata schemas for research outputs. The Government Documents and Special Formats cataloger does the original or complex copy cataloging for the Government Documents while also handling the individual title cataloging for electronic resources, all of the specialty formats (maps, audio visual, etc.), and contributes to the Special Collections cataloging efforts. The Serials Cataloger is the only professional that concentrates almost entirely on one specific cataloging activity, but she also oversees the authority control work for the unit. Each of the three cataloging assistants is cross-trained for traditional MARC cataloging and Dublin Core metadata assignments. One cataloging assistant helps with audio-visual formats, and regional campus libraries, general research collection cataloging, and metadata assignment for the Digital Library. The remaining two cataloging assistants copy catalog for Special Collections and assign metadata for the Digital Library.

### Analysis of interaction logs

To completely understand existing perceptions of the Cataloging and Metadata Services unit, it is important to know which library units the CMS staff interact with the most. Analysis of this information found that the top five library units that the CMS staff were in contact with the most were:

1) Special Collections & Archives (SCA) - 33%
2) Library Administration - 16%
3) Digital Initiatives - 10%
4) Collection Development - 8%
5) Acquisitions - 8%

These five units accounted for 75% of all the interactions logged in this research project. Of that 75%, almost half of the exchanges were with Special Collections & Archives staff. There are a few possible reasons that may contribute to the high frequency of interactions with SCA, the most obvious being that the cataloger embedded in the SCA unit likely has more interactions with Special Collections staff on a daily basis because of its location. Another explanation for the high interaction rate is the library's continued emphasis on digitizing and creating metadata for the unique materials found in SCA. Finally, half of the Cataloging and Metadata Services staff provide weekly reference assistance at the SCA public service desk, which opens up the opportunity for more interactions between the two units.

What proved to be the most surprising trend was the relative infrequency of interactions within the Technical Services division in which the CMS unit resides (see Figure 2). This division is also composed of the Collection Development unit, the Materials and Acquisitions unit, and the Resource Sharing and Document Delivery unit. With Collection Development and Acquisitions comprising just 8%

**Figure 2.** Library unit and number of interactions. Number of records refers to the number of times the interaction was recorded on the log sheet.

of interactions each, and Resource Sharing and Document Delivery comprising just 2% of interactions, the question arose—what reasons lead us to interact more with other divisions than our own? This was even more striking considering that the Cataloging and Metadata Services unit resides in the same physical space as the Collection Development unit and next door to the Acquisitions unit. While one cataloger working in the Special Collections unit might drive up the number of interactions with that unit, shouldn't the remaining nine members of the CMS unit residing with, and next to, two other units do the same? This suggests that much of the communication differences were related to workflow rather than proximity. Further investigation of this question warrants a deeper dive into the reasons CMS staff were interacting with the rest of the library. The unit staff were asked to record the reason for their interaction with library staff outside of the Cataloging unit, with the available options being:

- database questions
- drop-off/pickup materials
- general library issues
- meetings, committees, projects, or trainings
- patron-driven question
- procedures/workflow issues
- public service desks
- request assistance
- social
- other

When compiled, the most common reason for interaction was unexpected. Contrary to the stereotypical view of the quiet and withdrawn cataloger, the most common reason a CMS staff member interacted with library colleagues was for social reasons. Almost a quarter of interactions were defined as "social." When further broken down by who initiated the interaction, social interactions were also twice as likely to be initiated by the CMS unit member as by non-CMS library colleagues (see Figure 3).

The next most common reason for interaction was for "Meetings, Committees, Projects or Training." (Please note this category was broadly constructed to

## Reason for Interaction

| Reason for Interaction | | Number of Records |
|---|---|---|
| Database questions | 17 | 2 ▇▇▇▇▇ 140 |
| Drop off/pickup materials | 40 | |
| General library issues | 58 | |
| Meetings, Committes, Projects, or Training | 125 | |
| Patron-driven question | 4 | |
| Procedures/workflow issues | 65 | |
| Reference desk | 31 | |
| Request assistance | 29 | |
| Social | 140 | |
| Other | 61 | |
| Not supplied | 2 | |
| Grand Total | 572 | |

**Figure 3.** Reason for interaction. Number of records refers to the number of times the interaction was recorded on the log sheet.

facilitate log sheet entry because defining the differences between committee meetings, project meetings, training meetings, etc. proved subjective and varied widely in the testing phase.) Both the social interactions and the meetings were significantly more prominent than any other reason for interaction, almost doubling that of "Procedures/workflow issues," which was the third highest recorded reason for interaction. This demonstrated an active engagement in the general work and operations of the library, apart from the traditional "backroom" perception. Figure 4 demonstrates the reasons for interaction with specific units in the library, which revealed interesting trends. As previously discussed, the most frequently reported interactions were with the Special Collections & Archives unit, located two floors down from the Cataloging and Metadata Services unit. And as the overall trend displayed above, the most common reasons for interaction were typically social (29%), meetings (22%), public service desk (11%), procedures and workflow issues (11%), or picking up or dropping off material (10%). Overall, it appeared that the general work of the CMS overlapped significantly with the SCA unit.

Interactions with the Library Administration unit were the next most common division, but the reasons for interaction differ from the overall model, with "General Library Issues" accounting for 30% of the interactions. This is not surprising considering that the Library Administration is more concerned with overall library issues than with specific projects. Committees and

**Figure 4.** Reason for interaction by division and department. Numbers are presented as percentages of the interactions recorded on the log sheets for each specific unit.

meetings accounted for 22% of the interactions, and "Other" accounted for 21% of the interactions.

For the Technical Services division as a whole, social interactions cumulatively comprised 44% of the interactions and were over twice as common as procedure and workflow questions, which accounted for 20% of the interactions. Meetings and projects totaled just 8% of all interactions with our fellow division units. This may be due to impromptu discussions about day-to-day work happening between the members of the division, rather than regularly scheduled project or meeting-based work. It might also be indicative of a workflow that remains fairly constant over time, without requiring a lot of meetings or committees to maintain or update the process. Ultimately, however, these numbers appear to indicate a larger shift in Technical Services work away from conventional, labor-intensive workflows towards batch loading and large-scale maintenance of mainstream research collections, which is increasingly handled in USU library's Systems unit. This unexpectedly low number of interactions highlighted the need to re-analyze the larger patterns of the division workflows and the role of the CMS unit within them. Acknowledging and embracing the changing information ecosystem presents the unit with the opportunity to retool itself for a new model of content demand and information delivery. While the need for traditionally cataloged material is still very much present in the library, there appears to be a significant shift in demand for access to original content owned by the library. Up until now, this has been a niche concern, with minimal staffing thrown its direction upon request. The information gathered in this assessment demonstrated a need to retool the unit's skill set and re-assign dedicated duties to focus on original content description in multiple cataloging languages.

Figure 5 outlines the reasons that each of the CMS unit members had interacted with non-CMS library colleagues. As interactions with the Special Collections & Archives division (composed of the Special Collections & Archives unit, Art Book Room, Digital Initiatives unit, and Government Documents unit) accounted for 45% of the total interactions, it was unsurprising that the three of the 4 primary catalogers for SCA material (the Special Collections Cataloger, the Metadata Coordinator, and the General Cataloger) recorded the most frequent interactions (with the exception of the CMS unit head, whose interactions were heavily driven by meetings.)

Reason for Interaction by Position Type and Title

| | Position Type / Position Title | | | | | | | | | | | |
|---|---|---|---|---|---|---|---|---|---|---|---|---|
| | Cataloger | | | | | | | | Cataloging Assitant | | | Number of Records |
| Reason for Interaction | Department Head | Special Collections Cataloger | Metadata Coordinator | General Cataloger | Gov Docs and Special Formats Cataloger | Special Collections and Batchloading Cataloger | Serials Cataloger | Total | Cataloging Assistant | Total | Grand Total | 1 … 88 |
| Social | | 18 | 8 | | 15 | 9 | | 129 | 11 | 11 | 140 | |
| Meetings, Committes, Projects, or Training | | 7 | 23 | 1 | 3 | 1 | | 123 | 2 | 2 | 125 | |
| Procedures/workflow issues | 3 | 2 | 11 | 2 | 2 | 5 | 6 | 65 | | | 65 | |
| Other | | 2 | 4 | 6 | | 4 | 4 | 59 | 2 | 2 | 61 | |
| General library issues | 3 | 14 | | | 3 | 2 | 1 | 58 | | | 58 | |
| Drop off/pickup materials | 1 | 3 | 2 | 4 | 2 | | | 36 | 4 | 4 | 40 | |
| Public service desk | 11 | 12 | | | 25 | 4 | | 31 | | | 31 | |
| Request assistance | 4 | 6 | 5 | | 1 | 7 | 4 | 27 | 2 | 2 | 29 | |
| Database questions | 8 | 4 | 1 | 1 | | 2 | | 16 | 1 | 1 | 17 | |
| Patron-driven question | | 2 | 1 | | | | | 3 | 1 | 1 | 4 | |
| Not supplied | | | 1 | | | 1 | | 2 | | | 2 | |
| Grand Total | 261 | 67 | 61 | 59 | 49 | 35 | 17 | 549 | 23 | 23 | 572 | |

**Figure 5.** Reason for interaction by position type and title. Number of records refers to the number of times the interaction was recorded on the log sheet.

The data also highlighted the lack of interactions between the CMS cataloging assistants and the rest of the library staff. While their work is more day-to-day and less of the planning or project management focused work, the three cataloging assistants showed a surprising paucity of every kind of interaction, including social. This demonstrated a need to create more opportunities for the cataloging assistants to engage with colleagues in other parts of the library. Work silos exist for more than just the library professionals or project managers in a unit. Compartmentalization creates divisions between units that can ripple into other, daily aspects of library work and cause cultural misunderstandings within a library, a lack of value for the work done in a different unit, and also a lack of understanding of how the workflows in a different unit impact one's own unit.

In order to understand more about how interactions between CMS unit members and other units occurred, it was necessary for the interaction logs to identify and relate information about the origin of contact and the methods by which communications were established. Differentiations between those who initiated contact were made by including the option for those logging interactions to identify either party, both parties, or cases when identification was not applicable to any given situation. The methods of communication were tracked in the logs by including the following categories: in-person, e-mail, phone, and other (which usually described interactions achieved through social media platforms or text message) (see Figure 6).

Overall, analysis of parties initiating contact showed that exchanges driven by Cataloging and Metadata unit members were the most common, but also that those initiated by others were at an almost equal percentage, with both factors adding up to 70% of the total. The data also showed that exchanges originating equally from both parties, or not initiated by either party, were at an equal percentage as well with both factors adding up to 30% of the total. The nearly equal percentages, shown respectively by the data, imply that there is a very balanced level of communication among all parties. One can, in turn, assume that this balance is evidence of an equal inclination for initiating interactions, which contradicts the "withdrawn and introverted cataloger" stereotype and further suggests a highly cooperative work environment.

This trend away from the outmoded cliché of shy catalogers holds true when looking at the methods of interaction, which showed that the vast majority of exchanges were made in person. This indicates that in-person interaction is likely

Method vs. Who Initiated

| Method of Interaction | Null | Both | Me | N/A | Them | Grand Total |
|---|---|---|---|---|---|---|
| Null | | 1 | | | | 1 |
| a-In person | 7 | 62 | 117 | 84 | 102 | 372 |
| b-Email | 2 | 20 | 63 | | 70 | 155 |
| c-Phone | | | 3 | | 13 | 16 |
| d-Other | | 2 | 19 | 1 | 6 | 28 |
| Grand Total | 9 | 85 | 202 | 85 | 191 | 572 |

**Figure 6.** Methods of interaction by initiator. Number of records refers to the number of times the interaction was recorded on the log sheet.

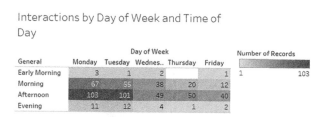

Interactions by Day of Week and Time of Day

| General | Day of Week | | | | | Number of Records | |
| --- | --- | --- | --- | --- | --- | --- | --- |
| | Monday | Tuesday | Wednes.. | Thursday | Friday | | |
| Early Morning | 3 | 1 | 2 | | 1 | 1 | 103 |
| Morning | 67 | 55 | 38 | 20 | 12 | | |
| Afternoon | 103 | 101 | 49 | 50 | 40 | | |
| Evening | 11 | 12 | 4 | 1 | 2 | | |

**Figure 7.** Interactions by day of week and time of day. Number of records indicates the number of times an interaction was recorded on the log sheet. No interactions were recorded on Thursdays in the early morning.

the most effective and useful mode of communication across units. It also suggests that meeting in person is essential for accomplishing work tasks and therefore the high level of face-to-face contact is warranted.

A more detailed investigation of the methods of contact revealed that email interactions were the second most common mode of communication. Email exchanges, added together with the in-person interactions, made up 92% of the total. Working under the assumption that email exchanges were made mostly between two individuals, it is apparent that one-on-one communication is more prevalent than interactions involving groups. This suggests that cross-departmental communication may be driven by specific purpose and focused on individuals' expertise and skill set.

When considering the days of the week that most interactions occur, the results strongly indicated that communication and engagement are 2–3 times more likely to take place on Mondays and Tuesdays (see Figure 7). Similarly, most interactions take place in the afternoons, with intermittent interactions in the early morning (before 8 am) or in the evenings (after 5 pm).

The date and time of interactions data were useful in deciding how to approach new services that the CMS unit offers, particularly what times of the day were most important for unit members to be available to answer questions, participate in meetings, and receive or deliver library acquisitions (see Figure 8).

## Developing initiatives

The Cataloging and Metadata Services unit explored potential strategies to increase the utility and visibility of the unit to the rest of the library. While many possibilities were presented by the data and discussed by the unit staff, it was felt that workloads and project due dates required a measured approach to developing more interactions with the library staff. The unit members valued putting forward a couple of manageable initiatives, measuring the effectiveness of those initiatives, improving them based on the feedback, and then exploring more options once the initial projects were completed or in place. The two exploratory initiatives decided on were a single service point model for quickly addressing issues in the library catalog and a series of infographics to educate about and trumpet the work of the unit.

Reason for Interaction by Time of Day

| Reason for Interaction | Early Morning | Morning | Afternoon | Evening | Grand Total |
|---|---|---|---|---|---|
| Social | 4 | 41 | 87 | 8 | 140 |
| Meetings, Committes, Projects, or Training | | 43 | 75 | 7 | 125 |
| Procedures/workflow issues | 1 | 29 | 32 | 3 | 65 |
| Other | 1 | 29 | 27 | 4 | 61 |
| General library issues | 1 | 14 | 40 | 3 | 58 |
| Drop off/pickup materials | | 13 | 27 | | 40 |
| Reference desk | | 7 | 23 | 1 | 31 |
| Request assistance | | 8 | 17 | 4 | 29 |
| Database questions | | 5 | 12 | | 17 |
| Patron-driven question | | 2 | 2 | | 4 |
| Not supplied | | 1 | 1 | | 2 |
| Grand Total | 7 | 192 | 343 | 30 | 572 |

Number of Records: 1 — 87

**Figure 8.** Reasons for interaction by time of day. Number of records indicates the number of times an interaction was recorded on the log sheet.

### Single service point initiative

Under the CMS unit's old service model, when a library staff member had a cataloging or metadata related question, they would consult a large "Go-To" chart posted in the entrance of the unit featuring 80 options that outlined each cataloger's expertise. The CMS unit streamlined this process with the aforementioned initiative, referred to as the single service point model, by designating the most experienced cataloging assistant to act as the starting point for all questions. When approached with a question, the single service point coordinator would investigate the issue and address any concerns that were within his purview, referring higher-level issues to the appropriate cataloger, if needed. The single service point model was advertised to all of the library staff using library-wide emails and visits to other library unit meetings to highlight the purpose of the service and distribute the name and contact information for the cataloging assistant they should consult. This model met internal needs for streamlining unexpected work brought to the department and also met the data-identified needs for increasing interactions between the cataloging assistants in the unit and the rest of the library staff.

### Infographics and education initiative

The second initiative was an education and awareness push using data visualizations. Infographics were created to exhibit the accomplishments and work of the CMS unit. Annual statistics, information about new processes the unit had innovated, and scholarly contributions to the field were translated into infographic visualizations, such as the example presented in Figure 9.

The infographics displayed data including facts about catalogers' knowledge of standards and formats, their service on committees, memberships in local and national library organizations, fluency with specific computer programs, and their years of combined service to the library. Additional infographics included timelines for completed large-scale projects, explanations of common obstacles that

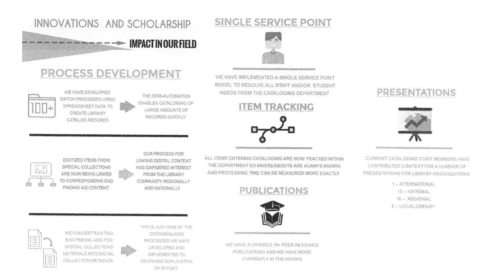

**Figure 9.** Example of one infographic used to visualize innovations and scholarship within the CMS unit.

catalogers face when describing resources, and items from library collections that were particularly unique or difficult for our department to catalog. These were featured to further illustrate the cataloging contributions made to our institution.

The infographics were printed using a large format printer and posted on walls and cubicles around the CMS office. Library administration members were invited to a luncheon in the Cataloging and Metadata Services area to view these accomplishments by the CMS staff and additional metadata and cataloging volunteers from around the library. With a heavy emphasis on casual conversation, the luncheon was an open house style that utilized the displayed visualizations as a focal point for generating discussion between the library administration and the CMS staff. The primary goal of the process was to both demonstrate the value of the cataloging work accomplished and to build relationships through face-to-face interactions. After the luncheon, the infographics were housed on the walls of the Technical Services conference room and displayed on the department blog.[20]

## Measuring effectiveness

Following the implementation of the single service point and the infographics, the Cataloging and Metadata Services unit created a survey to investigate the effectiveness of the two new initiatives and also more accurately define the library's cultural perceptions and expectations of the unit. Using a Qualtrics platform, the survey questioned respondents about their perceptions and assessments of the CMS unit. Forty-six respondents (49% of the employees in the library) completed the entire survey, with a handful of partially finished

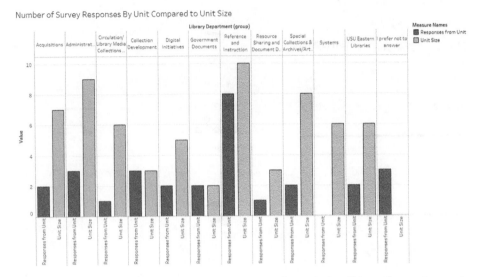

**Figure 10.** Number of survey responses by unit compared to unit size. Value refers to the number of responses and the number of individual, salaried employees in each unit.

responses. Responses were received from almost all of the eleven main library units and regional campus libraries in the USU Libraries organization, with only three respondents indicating a preference to not identify the unit to which they reported. The largest number of survey responses came from the Reference and Instruction unit (which is also the largest library unit), accounting for just over a quarter of all responses. 100% of the personnel in the Collection Development and Government Documents units (the two smallest units) answered the survey. The rest of the departments averaged around 30% percent of their staff as respondents, with just the Systems unit having no respondents (see Figure 10). The survey asked respondents about the frequency and reasons for their interactions with the CMS unit members, how the unit facilitated their (respondent's) day-to-day work, what the unit could do better, what skills CMS unit members should have, their (respondent's) understanding and attitude toward new services and initiatives the CMS unit provided, and the name of their (respondent's) own unit. No question other than the agreement to the terms and conditions of the survey was required and every multiple-choice question provided an option for "I prefer not to answer." Therefore, the number of responses for each question varied.

### Perceptions of the unit

To fully understand current library staff perceptions of the Cataloging and Metadata Services unit, respondents were asked to describe the ways the unit assisted them in their day-to-day work. In response, a vast majority answered that the unit made library materials accessible to patrons and staff. Although a seemingly obvious answer to the question, it validated the importance of this crucial step in the workings of the library. The second most common answer was database mainte-nance. These two activities provide the backbone for the CMS unit and can be summarized best by the following survey quotations:

> They provide a necessary part of the process of making new materials available and trou-bleshooting access to existing resources.

> Their work is essential for mine. Reference isn't possible without good metadata.

Other activities that aided them in their work included the willingness of CMS staff to not only help patrons find what they need directly, but also to explain and share their knowledge and expertise with other staff members so they can better serve patrons as well. The respondents were also impressed with the CMS unit's continual review and updating of workflows and procedures in response to the ever-changing atmosphere of the Library.

While the answers were all extremely positive, several mentioned that CMS members have "behind the scenes work," but they were not sure what that work entailed. This appears to support the literature assertions and highlights the need to educate other library staff about the overall work of the unit and the additional job responsibilities unit staff perform outside of cataloging materials.

Building upon the foundation of how the CMS unit assists library staff in their day-to-day work, the next step was to ask a free-response question about what skills CMS staff members should have to be effective in their positions. Not surprisingly, the top answer by far was the ability to catalog library materials, including metadata creation. Many answers were even more definitive and included knowledge of cataloging and metadata rules and standards, subject headings and classifications, and how to catalog different formats of materials. This basic knowledge was followed by the desire for good communication skills which, according to the survey, should predominantly focus on keeping other staff in the library aware of changing rules and standards and how that affects their work as well as how those changes impact library users. Subsequent profi-ciencies in diminishing order included the need to be detail oriented, capacity to bal-ance quality work with sufficient quantity of work to meet library demands, good analytical and technical skills, ability to keep up with the ever-changing library and cataloging fields, and realizing how patrons use our materials in order to enhance access to those items. Finally, library colleagues also listed such aptitudes as being a self-moti-vator, having supervisory experience, familiarity with project management, and under-standing how cataloging and metadata workflows fit into the larger picture for the Library and the University as a whole.

The final question given to gauge perceptions of the CMS unit was whether library coworkers felt that the work done in the Cataloging and Metadata Services unit contributed to the scholarship in the field of library and information science. Approximately two-thirds responded with a resounding yes. Furthermore, many answered that they were also familiar with specific examples of scholarship work done by members of the CMS unit staff. Most of the remaining respondents were unsure if Cataloging staff were involved in scholarship in the library field. This left only a couple of respondents who answered that they were not knowledgeable enough to know if the unit staff members did scholarship activities or published anything other than Cataloging standards.

Overall, the perceptions of the unit were very positive, with a recognition of the central role of cataloging in making library collections accessible. This deviates from many of the perceptions portrayed in the literature, which may possibly be explained in different ways. Library staff members will understandably be loath to criticize colleagues in a survey that will be analyzed by those same colleagues, even with anonymity. A third-party analysis of the data, or even an aggregated survey that combined more than one institution would likely get more accurate accounts of perception. This would be an intriguing study to pursue in the future. However, even considering this, the perceptions of the catalogers in general are probably not as dire as much of the literature has made out. While some negative perceptions of (albeit stereotypical) traits of catalogers may persist, they often co-exist with a strong positive regard for the work that is done by cataloging and metadata librarians, as well as the personnel that performs them. Reductions in cataloging staff over time and frictions between different librarian roles are often the result of internal struggles for resources to support the ceaseless onslaught of new library projects and services as libraries continue to expand their roles, looking to find once again that "sure footing" as the respected information professional in a digital age of immediate information.

### *Feedback on services*

Survey respondents were asked "What can the Cataloging and Metadata Services do better to help you?" in order to solicit direct information about ways the CMS unit could improve existing services or meet demands. Twenty-one survey respondents replied to this question, 20% of whom indicated that they were wholly satisfied and could not think of anything else to suggest. The remaining 80% touched on multiple topics in their response, including communication, education and advocacy, and speed.

The largest number of respondents indicated a combination of issues that highlighted the need for more communication between the CMS unit and other library units. The surprising element in these responses was the stronger emphasis on receiving cataloging or metadata education rather than miscommunication regarding workflows or procedures. Many respondents indicated that they would like to know more about what the unit does and how it operates, such as:

> It might be nice simply to be more educated on the work CMS does, what is and is not cataloged, under what systems–basically to have more people understand the scope of our collections and different strategies for meeting patrons' needs.

Others wanted the unit to advocate more on its own behalf and brag about the accomplishments of its members, such as this response:

> They do a lot to help the library, but I think they need to publicize more of what they do.

The majority of requests for more education and advocacy demonstrated the potential for rethinking what was meant by this request. Education may not mean training how to catalog in MARC or batch load records, although this information would be incredibly useful. Many of the comments mentioned wanting to know *what* the unit did, rather than *how* the unit did it. In fact, the responses about perceptions of the unit demonstrated that many respondents already knew *what* the unit did—at least at a high level. Perhaps these units wanted a mid-level understanding of the work done in the unit—something between making material accessible and understanding the intricacies of SuDoc classification. The CMS unit will look at developing middle of the road trainings to help other library staff understand the day-to-day work of the unit without necessarily training library colleagues to do that work.

Additionally, three other comments reflected a lack of understanding about the division of labor in the department and the status of current projects. Comments ranged from questions about who to contact for specific tasks to requests for specific projects to be completed. This highlighted the need to make the work of the department more transparent for library colleagues.

Four responses (19% of the total responses) included an element relating to the speed of the work done in the CMS unit. Comments ranged from mentioning specific projects the respondent wished were addressed more quickly to simple general statements such as "Be faster." Of the requests for faster turnaround times for cataloging workflows and projects, 50% came from the Collection Development unit, 25% from Special Collections and Archives and Art Book Room unit, and 25% preferred not to indicate their unit.

### *Feedback on initiatives*

#### *Single service point initiative*

Survey respondents were asked, "Have you used the single service point model that Cataloging has put in place?" to determine awareness and usage of the service. They were also asked "Has the single service point model worked for you—why or why not?" to gather feedback on the strengths and weaknesses of the program.

The majority of respondents were not aware of or not sure they had used the single service point model, which was evident by respondents' confusion about the terminology used to describe the service. This outcome suggests a need for better branding of the single service point model, as well as a more targeted advertising and education about the system in general. A minority of respondents answered that they had not used the service, and working under the assumption that these individuals knew about it but did not have cause to use it, indicates that there is not a necessity among all staff to engage with the Cataloging department to report issues or request assistance. The commentary provided by individuals who did not use the service echoed the need to increase awareness of the program.

The remainder of respondents, about one-third, indicated that they had used the service. Among those individuals, the commentary was highly positive. Generally, the service seems to have improved the process of troubleshooting and fixing problems in the catalog, and has done so in a quick and efficient manner. Those who had used the service also reported that it was very helpful to have only one person to go to instead of being required to search for assistance among several staff members. Respondents' only criticism was not knowing what to do in the case the single service point person was not available when needed.

### Infographics and education initiative

Respondents were asked, "Have the infographics developed by the Cataloging and Metadata Services department impacted your view of the work done in the Cataloging Department? If so, how have they impacted you?" to determine if the information related to them using these infographics improved their perceptions of the work done by the department. Most of the respondents indicated that they had seen the infographics and that they did affect their view.

Those who responded that the infographics influenced their view mostly reported that the information was educational and increased their understanding of what cataloging work entails. They also liked the method and ease of disseminating the information using bright, colorful, and succinct posters to highlight important facts and indicated being inspired to do the same for their own departments. Among the few individuals who responded that the infographics did not impact them, all related that they already knew about the department's work and achievements so were naturally not influenced by the information. Overall, the use of infographics to inform and celebrate achievements was highly successful, considering the encouraging feedback received from library staff outside the department.

## Comparing the data

Both the interaction assessment and the survey provided valuable quantitative and qualitative data points about the perceptions of the CMS unit and its services. From an internal perspective, the unit's ability to map out the prevailing patterns of communication using data instead of anecdotal feedback helps in strategically addressing communication deficits and capitalizing on communication strengths. It also permits a better visualization of the ways in which our colleagues' perceptions of their own communication patterns with the CMS unit differed from the quantified data. When comparing the results of both the perceptions survey and the interaction assessment to one another, a few interesting trends emerged.

The first trend involved the frequency of interaction between the CMS unit and other library units. The library units with the greatest accuracy in perceiving their interaction with the CMS unit were also the ones with which the unit interacted the most. Overall, other library units tended to underestimate the amount of interaction they had with the CMS unit.

When the interaction logs were parsed, the data was graphed to show the percentage of days, weeks, and months that interactions occurred in the allotted assessment period, which, as mentioned previously, comprised 18 days over 4 weeks during 1 month. Figure 11 shows the percentage of days, weeks, and months where interactions occurred with each department. It contrasts those recorded interactions with the expected rate of interaction reported by other library unit members in the survey.

In the survey, respondents were asked, "On average, how frequently do you interact with a Cataloging and Metadata Services staff member?" Options included Daily, Weekly, Monthly, Intermittently, or Never. Four units had at least one respondent who indicated that they interacted daily with the CMS unit. Overall, the most common response was "weekly." Only two units had at least one respondent who reported meeting only monthly with the CMS unit staff; and three units had at least one respondent who reported meeting only intermittently with CMS unit staff. No respondents expected to never interact with the CMS unit, so this option is excluded from the data graphs (see Figure 11).

When comparing these expected interactions against the recorded data, four units were fairly accurate: Administration, Circulation, and Library Media Collections and Reserves (hereafter called Circulation), Digital Initiatives, and Special Collections and Archives and Art Book Room (SCA). Administration staff members perceived their interactions with the unit to be either daily or weekly. The Associate Dean for Technical Services, the direct supervisor for the CMS unit, is considered

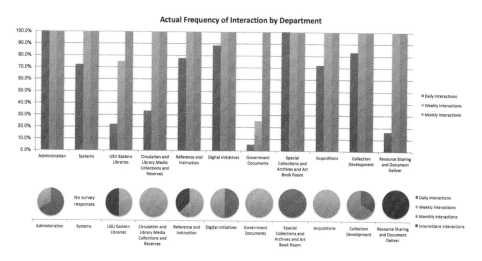

**Figure 11.** Actual versus expected frequency of interaction. Actual interactions were recorded as part of the Interaction Assessment logs kept by the CMS unit staff and are measured as a percentage of the total possible for each category (daily, weekly, or monthly). Expected interactions were gathered using the survey taken by other library units and are measured as a percentage of the total responses for each unit. Please note that not all staff members of every unit responded to the survey.

part of the Administrative unit so daily interactions with that unit are not unexpected. Daily interactions between the SCA unit and the CMS unit were expected by the respondents from SCA and aligned with the recorded unit interactions.

With the exception of Collection Development, all of the units with daily interactions with the CMS unit had an accurate perception of their interactions. Daily interactions with Collection Development happened over 80% of the days recorded in the interaction logs, but only 33% of the Collection Development unit (1 individual) perceived meeting daily with CMS unit staff. The other two-thirds of the unit indicated only interacting monthly. Due to anonymity measures taken in both the survey and the interaction logs, it is unknown if this individual respondent is responsible for the majority of these interactions. However, as stated previously, the Collection Development unit shares a space with the CMS unit, so considering their close proximity as well as the over 80% daily interaction rate recorded, the expectations contrast significantly with the recorded interactions.

Respondents from the Acquisitions unit were unanimous in expecting weekly interactions, but considering the over 70% rate for daily interactions, it appears odd that more respondents did not expect interactions more frequently than weekly. The same holds true for the Reference and Instruction unit, which had interaction numbers that resembled the Acquisitions unit. Respondents from the Reference and Instruction unit expected weekly, monthly, and intermittent interactions, but the recorded data showed over 70% daily interactions.

On the opposite side of the spectrum, the Government Documents unit, 100% of whose staff responded to the survey, unanimously anticipated weekly interactions with the CMS unit staff, but only interacted 25% of the weeks during the interaction log assessment. The Resource Sharing and Document Delivery (RSDD) unit anticipated only intermittent interactions, which is striking because the RSDD unit interacted with a CMS unit staff 100% of the weeks involved in the interaction log. However, RSDD had only one respondent to the survey ($^{1}/_{3}$ of their staff members), so the perceived frequency of interaction may not be accurate for the unit as a whole.

Comparing the recorded reasons for interaction against the perceived reasons for interactions presents a second series of interesting trends (see Figure 12).

**Recorded vs. Perceived Reasons for Interactions**

| | Acquisitions | | Administration | | Circulation / Library Media Collections | | Collection Development | | Digital Initiatives | |
|---|---|---|---|---|---|---|---|---|---|---|
| | Recorded | Perceived | Recorded | Perceived | Recorded | Perceived | Recorded | Perceived | Recorded | Perceived |
| Database questions | 0.0% | 0.0% | 0.0% | 66.7% | 0.0% | 0.0% | 2.1% | 33.3% | 12.3% | 100.0% |
| Drop off/pickup materials | [illegible] | 0.0% | 3.7% | 0.0% | 14.3% | 100.0% | 10.8% | 66.7% | 3.5% | 0.0% |
| General library issues | [illegible] | 0.0% | [illegible] | 100.0% | 21.4% | 0.0% | 14.9% | 33.3% | 0.0% | 50.0% |
| Meetings, Committees, Projects, or Trainings | [illegible] | 0.0% | 25.7% | 100.0% | 14.3% | 0.0% | 14.9% | 33.3% | 31.6% | 100.0% |
| Patron-driven questions | 0.0% | 50.0% | 0.0% | 33.3% | 0.0% | 0.0% | 0.0% | 33.3% | 0.0% | 50.0% |
| Procedures/workflow issues | [illegible] | 100.0% | 6.3% | 100.0% | 14.3% | 0.0% | 14.9% | 100.0% | 7.0% | 100.0% |
| Public service desks | 0.0% | 0.0% | 0.9% | 33.3% | 21.4% | 0.0% | 0.0% | 33.3% | 5.3% | 0.0% |
| Request assistance | 2.2% | 100.0% | 5.5% | 66.7% | 7.1% | 0.0% | 4.1% | 66.7% | 7.0% | 50.0% |
| Social | [illegible] | 50.0% | 11.0% | 66.7% | 7.1% | 0.0% | [illegible] | 33.3% | 28.1% | 100.0% |
| Other | [illegible] | 0.0% | 18.4% | 0.0% | 0.0% | 100.0% | 4.5% | 0.0% | 5.3% | 0.0% |
| Not supplied | 0.0% | 0.0% | 0.0% | 0.0% | 0.0% | 0.0% | 0.0% | 0.0% | 0.0% | 0.0% |
| Total Categories | 7 | 4 | 8 | 8 | 7 | 2 | 5 | 9 | 8 | 7 |

| | Government Documents | | Reference and Instruction | | Resource Sharing and Document Delivery | | Special Collections and Archives and Art Book Room | | Systems | | USU Eastern Libraries | |
|---|---|---|---|---|---|---|---|---|---|---|---|---|
| | Recorded | Perceived | Recorded | Perceived | Recorded | Perceived | Recorded | Perceived | Recorded | Perceived | Recorded | Perceived |
| Database questions | 0.0% | 50.0% | 0.0% | 37.5% | 0.0% | 0.0% | 1.6% | 50.0% | 12.9% | 0.0% | 0.0% | 0.0% |
| Drop off/pickup materials | 0.0% | 50.0% | 5.6% | 12.5% | 0.0% | 0.0% | 10.1% | 100.0% | 5.6% | 0.0% | 0.0% | 0.0% |
| General library issues | 0.0% | 0.0% | 0.0% | 0.0% | 8.3% | 0.0% | 7.9% | 50.0% | 0.0% | 0.0% | 0.0% | 0.0% |
| Meetings, Committees, Projects, or Trainings | 50.0% | 50.0% | 13.9% | 50.0% | 50.0% | 0.0% | 22.2% | 100.0% | 25.0% | 0.0% | 0.0% | 0.0% |
| Patron-driven questions | 0.0% | 0.0% | 2.8% | 75.0% | 0.0% | 0.0% | 1.6% | 0.0% | 13.5% | 0.0% | 0.0% | 0.0% |
| Procedures/workflow issues | 0.0% | 100.0% | 2.8% | 0.0% | 33.3% | 100.0% | 11.1% | 100.0% | 0.0% | 0.0% | 0.0% | 50.0% |
| Public service desks | 0.0% | 0.0% | 8.3% | 37.5% | 0.0% | 100.0% | 11.1% | 0.0% | 8.3% | 0.0% | 0.0% | 0.0% |
| Request assistance | 50.0% | 100.0% | 8.3% | 25.0% | 0.0% | 100.0% | 3.2% | 50.0% | 25.0% | 0.0% | 0.0% | 50.0% |
| Social | 0.0% | 50.0% | 2.8% | 50.0% | 0.0% | 0.0% | 28.6% | 50.0% | 3.6% | 0.0% | 0.0% | 0.0% |
| Other | 0.0% | 50.0% | [illegible] | 0.0% | 8.3% | 0.0% | 2.7% | 0.0% | 2.8% | 0.0% | 100.0% | 50.0% |
| Not supplied | 0.0% | 0.0% | 2.8% | 0.0% | 0.0% | 0.0% | 0.0% | 0.0% | 0.0% | 0.0% | 0.0% | 0.0% |
| Total Categories | 2 | 7 | 8 | 7 | 4 | 3 | 10 | 7 | 8 | 0 | 1 | 3 |

**Figure 12.** Recorded versus perceived reasons for interactions. Recorded reasons for interaction are represented as a percentage of all of the reasons for interacting with a specific library unit. The perceived reasons for interaction represent the percentage of respondents from a library unit who selected that reason for interaction on the survey.

Similar to the frequency of interaction trend, the perceived reasons for interactions were often under-reported by other library units and no single unit was 100% accurate in identifying all of the categories for interactions that occurred. The more discerning units were those that interacted with the CMS unit the most. Lastly, what do the two categories of interactions that were the most over-perceived (database questions and patron-driven questions) mean for the CMS unit?

There were ten categories used to group reasons for interactions in both the survey and the interaction logs: database questions, drop off/pick up materials, general library issues, meetings, patron-driven questions, procedures and workflow issues, public service desks, requesting assistance, social, and other. Overall, the CMS unit averaged 6.45 interaction categories with each library unit. However, the units who took the survey tended to under-anticipate their interactions with the CMS unit, averaging 5.7 interaction categories per unit.

When compared with the data collected in the interaction logs, those units with the most insight into their reasons for interacting with CMS staff were: Administration, Collection Development, Reference and Instruction, and Special Collections & Archives. Three of the four units indicated that they interacted daily with the CMS unit, which provides further evidence that perception of regular interaction improves the understanding of the role the CMS unit plays in the day-to-day work of other library units. For the purposes of this evaluation, perceptions seen as accurate were those where an interaction was perceived and also recorded. This evaluation did not compare the percentages for the recorded or perceived reasons for interaction because those percentages measure two different values. For recorded interactions, the percentages indicate what portion of all of the interactions that category encompassed for each unit. For the perceived interactions, the percentage indicated what portion of the respondents in a given unit selected that category in the survey. Respondents were not asked to weigh how often that interaction occurred, just whether or not they felt they interacted with a CMS staff member for the reason presented.

Most interesting of all was how often other library units anticipated that their interactions with the CMS unit would involve a question about a database or soliciting an answer on behalf of a patron. Six units selected "Database questions" and five units selected "Patron-driven questions" as reasons for interacting with the CMS unit. Although the unit prides itself on maintaining a robust working knowledge of the library catalog and the digital library (the two databases it regularly contributes to), the only other units who actually interacted with the CMS unit about those databases also have an active part in maintaining them: Systems and Digital Initiatives. This led the CMS unit to question why this was the case. The obvious answer is that the Systems and Digital Initiatives were conferring with the CMS unit about an issue in the databases rather than asking a question outright. For the rest of the library units, either the databases rarely caused problems or those issues were not making it to the CMS staff. From this data, the unit identified the need to re-examine the single service point initiative to determine if a more effective method could be employed.

Likewise, patron driven questions were likely answered in other units before getting to the CMS unit. With the exception of a select few instances during the interaction log assessment time period, other units asked very few questions on behalf of a patron. In previous years, patron driven questions mostly revolved around investigations into the status of a book and when it would be ready for checkout. A change in this type of interaction can be due to a number of external and internal factors: shelf-ready workflows that bypass the CMS unit, increasing patron demand for e-resources instead of print material, or even streamlined rush cataloging procedures that have reduced the amount of issues that keep patrons waiting for material.

## Implementing what we have learned

The process of tracking interactions, developing new service initiatives, and surveying the landscape of library peer perceptions provided a valuable self-reflection exercise for the Cataloging and Metadata Services unit. In many ways, it encouraged the unit to begin to reimagine itself and its role in the larger framework of the library. The data, admittedly, only illustrates the communication patterns of the CMS staff and could benefit from greater context, seeing how it compares to the broader interaction trends among all library staff. This possibility is outside the purview of the unit, but would be an intriguing study to undertake in the future. The immediate takeaways, however, provided an ideological foundation for redeveloping the unit outreach model, including: (1) understanding the importance of regular interaction and (2) using education as advocacy.

### *Recurring interaction as a priority*

Every interaction is an opportunity to develop a personal connection to library colleagues. The reasons to create personal connections go well beyond making friends or having an enjoyable work environment, although these are admirable goals in their own right. Regular interactions create small but important opportunities to exchange ideas and gain insight into what is happening in other parts of the library, as well as giving those units an idea of what is happening in the world of cataloging and metadata. Over time, these interactions and discussions build on one another and form the perceptions and impressions that shape how units regard and appreciate the work that is done around the library. In these interactions, it is as important to gain an understanding of the work and personnel in other units, as it is to generate interest in the work of one's own unit. Valuing the work that is performed in other units provides not just a feel-good work environment, but also the ability to see how cataloging and metadata skills can actively benefit and animate the work done in other library units.

Taking this into account, the CMS unit identified other key library units where actual or perceived interactions were the lowest and invited representatives from those units to work with our single service point coordinator to redevelop the service. The cross-departmental team was charged with analyzing the best possible model to meet the needs of the rest of the library. They were also given the responsibility for branding the service, advertising, and even recommending possible changes to the physical layout of the CMS unit space. This provided an ongoing reason for interaction with groups underrepresented in the interaction assessment while also seeking out feedback and input from the intended users of the single service point initiative. The group was also encouraged to work together to develop a presentation or scholarly deliverable to further invest participants in developing a positive program and provide a longer lasting connection between the units. While the work of this group is still in progress, the potential outcomes are numerous: increase communication with units where a deficit was detected, create interaction opportunities for members of the CMS unit who are not in contact with other units frequently, develop a service that will meet the needs of the other units in the library, increase awareness of that service, and engage library colleagues by inviting them to be stakeholders in the work and functionality of the CMS unit.

The unit also arranged for opportunities to train with other library peers in collaborative professional development settings. Typically, the cataloging and metadata staff has sought out training specific to the work of the unit. In the interest of increasing interactions, the unit went outside these traditional areas and explored more universal topics, such as leadership and communication styles, or current library trends, such as open educational resources and data management, as a joint venture with library colleagues from other units. The last two topics, in particular, provide a platform to explore the commonalities shared by each library discipline, allowing CMS staff to discuss the impact of cataloging and metadata standards in each of these areas and, vice versa, allowing other units to discuss the application of these issues in their fields.

Less attractive, but still vitally important, the CMS unit re-examined some of the more common interaction potentials mentioned at the beginning of the article: service desk opportunities and committee service. The unit adjusted committee appointments to more evenly spread duties among the staff and provide more opportunities for interaction. A few, but not all, members felt comfortable enough to assume new public service desk duties. Additionally, some also began observing Reference and Instruction Librarians as they worked in the classrooms demonstrating databases and resources for students.

There are other possibilities for improving and increasing interactions with other units in the library. For instance, occasionally attending other unit's meetings to observe processes and learn about broader topics or issues that are being addressed in the library. Doing this may help increase the visibility and accessibility of the unit's skills and open up new ways they can be utilized elsewhere in the library. The CMS unit will also explore ways in which our research and scholarship intersect similarly with other staff efforts to possibly conduct more comprehensive studies and assessment of library services.

### Education as advocacy

Interpreting and implementing requests for more information and education about the work of the CMS unit was more challenging than developing interaction opportunities. Educating library colleagues on the work of the unit could range from full-blown training on cataloging and metadata standards and workflows to simply talking more about the projects and issues that keep the unit busy. Finding the right tone and level of information is tricky, especially as expectations differ between other library units and colleagues. The CMS unit identified three potential areas to meet the education and advocacy recommendations elicited from the survey: cataloging and metadata training, project visibility, and pushing out communications. The overall purpose of these outreach and education initiatives was not necessarily to cross train library colleagues, but rather to develop a foundation for understanding the principles that drive the work of the unit.

This emphasis on developing a common language and understanding of information architecture is an essential piece of the education component. The CMS unit identified the need to create short, digestible trainings on metadata and cataloging concepts that could be presented periodically—either in the regular meetings of other departments or the library's biweekly all-staff "table talks" gatherings. These bite-sized educational pieces should explain cataloging and metadata concepts through the lens of the work done in other library units. For instance, a short demonstration and hands on exercise about how indexing works in the discovery layer can be used to facilitate the work of the Reference and Instruction unit or anyone working at a service desk. A few test tutorials and exercises are currently in development in the CMS unit, but a field-wide collaboration to build and share micro-lessons such as these could capitalize on the general knowledge of the field and expand the collective impact of cataloging units.

From the survey, the term education was also used to mean a general understanding of the projects the unit is working on and the current progress made on those projects. In the survey, library units that requested this type of communication were not involved in the regular workflow of the CMS unit and therefore did not have a forum for knowing what projects were tying up the staff and time of the unit. To address this communication deficit, the unit developed a shared working space in a cloud based storage system utilized by the library. These shared spaces were used to visibly document any projects that the unit worked on, including project charters, time and cost estimates, and procedures. In addition, the unit compiled an overarching tracking spreadsheet that listed and ranked every project in order of priority to the library. Units wanting to know where their project stood in the queue can consult that spreadsheet at any time. Units that simply want to know what the CMS unit is working on can likewise see the priorities, current projects, and the estimated time to complete the backlog. This ongoing cumulative estimate for backlogs has been instrumental in helping the unit make the case for continued staffing and additional student help.

While the existence of a project tracking spreadsheet has been helpful to refer other library units to, it does not take the place of broadcasting information about the unit. Additional steps have been identified to push out information about the unit on a more regular basis, including ideas such as crafting a quarterly e-newsletter to feature the projects completed or underway in the unit, as well as recent accomplishments and scholarship done by unit members. This same kind of content would also be transferred to the unit's blog, where it shares information about workflows used in the unit.

There are a number of other ways to advance education efforts. For example, continuing to use infographics to distill and disseminate information about the CMS unit's activities and accomplishments. Placing them more strategically throughout the library will likely yield the same positive results as they have already, but on a larger scale. Determining central locations where other units, students, and faculty frequent will further promote cataloging as a public service to the university. Together with infographics, the CMS unit's efforts can be published online and openly accessible using websites, blogs, and newsletters. Sharing workflows, procedures, and innovations will not only garner more attention to the CMS unit's contributions to the field, but also help other technical services units follow suit.

## Conclusion

The Cataloging and Metadata Services unit at USU recognized a clear need to promote our services and advocate for better understanding of our impact in the library and in the larger scope of librarianship. In this effort, we sought to determine the source of commonly held perceptions and ways to proactively shift these views to truly reflect the reality of the public service we offer. Data gathered from interaction assessment revealed a few surprising results. First, most interactions were of a social nature and therefore contradicted established stereotypes. Second, interactions with other technical services units were comparatively rare which suggests a possible need to engage with these other units more directly. Third, regular interactions yield better understanding of the role and work of the unit.

As a result of conducting this survey research to determine perceptions and measure the effectiveness of our services, we found that opinions of the CMS unit were much more positive than expected. Moreover, despite a highly praised effort to educate using infographics, there were expressed desires to know more about cataloging work. Feedback also revealed a lack of understanding about some of our services, which reiterated the need to continue our education efforts.

Moving forward, building upon previous endeavors to educate others about cataloging scholarship, innovation, and impact in the library, efforts will be made to implement what has been learned from this interaction assessment. The strategy for doing so includes: increasing our level of collaboration, celebrating our achievements in a more visible format, utilizing opportunities to promote services to staff and administration, publicizing existing partnerships that directly meet user needs, enhancing physical space to encourage use of the single service point model, developing task-based micro tutorials to demonstrate cataloging and metadata concepts, and growing our online presence by sharing workflows, procedures, and scholarship.

## ORCID

Andrea Payant (iD) http://orcid.org/0000-0001-9873-1538
Becky Skeen (iD) http://orcid.org/0000-0002-0215-6936
Liz Woolcott (iD) http://orcid.org/0000-0002-6017-1392

## Notes

1. Juliya Borie, Kate MacDonald and Elisa Sze, "Asserting Catalogers' Place in the 'Value of Libraries' Conversation." *Cataloging & Classification Quarterly* 53, nos. 3–4 (2015): 352.
2. Ibid.
3. Shawne D. Miksa, "You Need My Metadata: Demonstrating the Value of Library Cataloging," *Journal of Library Metadata* 8, no. 1 (2008): 23.
4. Daniel CannCasciato, "An Essay on Cataloging," *Library Philosophy and Practice*. Paper 468 (2010).
5. Borie, MacDonald and Sze, "Asserting Catalogers' Place," 355.
6. ALCTS, "Value of Cataloging Librarians," *Associations for Library Collections & Technical Services*, June 13, 2006, http://www.ala.org/alcts/resources/org/cat/catlibvalue (accessed February 27, 2017).
7. CannCasciato, "An Essay on Cataloging," 2.
8. David Banush, "Stepping Out: The Expanding Role of Catalogers in Academic Libraries and Academic Institutions," *Cataloging & Classification Quarterly* 45, no. 3 (2008): 81–82.
9. Ibid., 81.
10. Heidi Lee Hoerman, "Why Does Everybody Hate Cataloging?," *Cataloging & Classification Quarterly* 34, no. 1–2 (2002): 30.
11. Jeanne M. K. Boydston and Joan M. Leysen, "ARL Cataloger Librarian Roles and Responsibilities Now and in the Future," *Cataloging & Classification Quarterly* 52, no. 2 (2014): 229.
12. Ibid., 244.
13. Banush, "Stepping Out," 84.
14. Sandy L. Folsom, "Out of the nest: the cataloger in a public services role, Library Collections," *Acquisitions, and Technical Services* 24, no. 1 (2000): 67–68.
15. Laura Turner and Alejandra Nann, "Venturing from the 'Back Room': Do Technical Services Librarians Have a Role in Information Literacy?" *Proceedings of the Charleston Library Conference* (2014): 397.
16. Borie, MacDonald and Sze, "Asserting Catalogers' Place," 364.
17. Miksa, "You Need My Metadata," 34–35.
18. Banush, "Stepping Out," 89.
19. Hoerman, "Why Does Everybody Hate Cataloging?," 37.
20. "USU Cataloging & Metadata Services," last updated February 23, 2017, https://usucataloging.wordpress.com/ (accessed March 3, 2017).

# Failure Modes and Effects Analysis (FMEA) for Cataloging: An Application and Evaluation

Jennifer Meekhof ⓘ and Amy B. Bailey ⓘ

**ABSTRACT**

Failure Modes and Effects Analysis (FMEA) is a proactive assessment tool originally created for quality assurance in manufacturing industries. FMEA involves the assignment of rankings for frequency, severity, and detection of errors within a process. Catalogers at ProQuest undertook an innovative project to use FMEA to evaluate MARC record production. This article provides an overview of FMEA for process evaluation and summarizes an application for cataloging. It considers the tool's value for error-proofing in MARC record creation and how FMEA might be applied more effectively in a variable environment.

## Introduction

ProQuest produces MARC bibliographic records in one of its metadata teams to support its Research Collections products. These records are distributed without ongoing maintenance, so it is essential that records are error-free at the time of distribution to customers. An established step in the quality control process had been proofreading created records by a second cataloger, a costly but effective step. As an endeavor to possibly remove the proofing component while still ensuring quality records, the team creating bibliographic records for these products undertook a review of the MARC record creation process using Failure Modes and Effects Analysis (FMEA). The purpose of the analysis was to identify steps in the process that result in record errors and to prioritize the need to improve those steps.

FMEA is a preventative risk management tool used to anticipate and identify process or design failures and their causes, and to identify ways to resolve issues related to those failures before they reach the customer. FMEA results can be used to prioritize efforts for process improvements and to reduce failures and associated risks. FMEA is about identifying causes and effects, attributable to various conditions. Through FMEA, users can anticipate and prevent problems, reduce costs, shorten product development or production times, and achieve safe and reliable products and processes. Simply put, FMEA answers questions such as: what can go wrong? how likely is an error to occur? and if an error does occur, what are the consequences of that error? There are versions of FMEA for both the *process* to create a product (PFMEA) and the product *design* (DFMEA), with DFMEA also applying to services (a variant of product).

The library profession has long assessed the cataloging end-product for its ability to serve user needs. These assessments have inspired the introduction of new MARC fields, changes to descriptive standards, and even a vision for leaving the MARC record data model altogether. This application of FMEA was not to address possible errors in the design of the product (a DFMEA), but rather to analyze the process that can result in a flawed version of the intended product (a PFMEA). This article presents a case study of the ProQuest team's PFMEA application and an evaluation of the effectiveness of utilizing PFMEA for the cataloging process.

## Literature review

This application of PFMEA, to identify, prioritize, and address process steps with failure risks, is novel to the library environment. Studies on quality assurance initiatives for processes, such as authority control in the cataloging process, have been documented extensively, but no published articles discuss a technique to identify, prioritize, and address process steps with failure risks, as is accomplished with PFMEA. The authors did, however, identify three published resources related to manufacturing process applications in libraries and cataloging process assessment techniques that are relevant to cataloging work.

Hsieh, Chang, and Lu[1] presented a review of quality management tools and techniques for libraries and information services, with a section specific to "quality by process control." They note that improving the process to avoid errors is more efficient than inspections to detect and then fix them after the fact. They emphasize the need for ongoing process improvement and describe a cycle for planning, carrying out, studying the effect, and further improving the process. While some specific tools are mentioned for process improvement, they do not reference FMEA. The FMEA tool is included, however, in their "quality by design" section, a DFMEA application. The article exposes some manufacturing-based models and techniques for possible use in libraries, with the valuable note in the conclusion that a re-focus for an application in a new sector may be necessary.

Hunt[2] described specific process improvement tools and techniques for cataloging and other technical services processes, based on practical experience discussed at improvement workshops at the University of Warwick. Noting that "there is very little research that has been undertaken that applies to process improvement techniques to cataloging,"[3] he presents seven improvement tools and techniques developed in manufacturing that can be useful for discussions of process improvement for libraries. FMEA was not included.

Nelson's article "Using Six Sigma and Lean in the Library"[4] presents Six Sigma and related Lean techniques and tools from the manufacturing and business disciplines that have been used in libraries. She summarizes studies on their application to improve process efficiency such as reducing the time for acquisitions teams to obtain overseas purchases and another to reduce the time required to process incoming materials. Nelson then discusses ways in which libraries might successfully incorporate the proven process improvement techniques from the business world. In that discussion, she describes FMEA as a "powerful tool" to expose likely failures and to address them by improving the process or detection methods. While she recommends the use of PFMEA, she does not reference any known applications.

## Introduction to FMEA

FMEA was first developed in the 1950s to study malfunctions of military systems.[5] Since then, use of the tool has expanded to analyze designs and processes in aerospace and defense industries in the 1960s, automotive companies in the 1970s,[6] to an everyday Lean Six Sigma practitioner's tool[7] today. FMEA builds on the assumption that a failure is possible, and the FMEA team must establish how and when the failure might occur and what the resulting impact would be.[8]

A FMEA team starts with a process chart that provides an overview of the complete production process.[9] The chart is used to help identify quality characteristics to be discussed in the FMEA error matrix, where the bulk of the FMEA work is done. The error matrix is a table that lists all process steps and all anticipated ways in which the step can go wrong (failure modes) with corresponding ratings for severity, occurrence, and detection. The ratings for those three factors are traditionally on a scale of 1–10, as shown in Figure 1.

**FMEA Scales for Severity, Occurrence, and Detection**

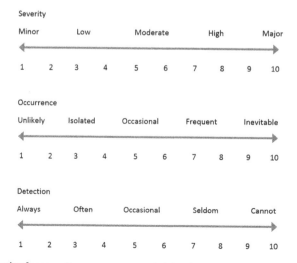

Figure 1. Rating scales for severity, occurrence, and detection.

The team begins the error matrix by listing potential errors that could occur during the current production process. Then the team brainstorms and lists potential effects of each failure in the next column,[10] followed by a column for the corresponding Severity rating. Potential causes of the error are considered and listed in the next column followed by the corresponding Occurrence rating. Then current controls are listed followed by the corresponding Detection rating.[11] A risk priority number (RPN) is calculated for each step by multiplying the three ratings together.[12] This number is intended to indicate the seriousness of the quality issues.[13] The higher the number, the greater the importance.

Once the RPN is calculated, a final column in the error matrix is used to suggest corrective action to reduce the severity of the error, to reduce the frequency of occurrence, or improve the detection, with an overall goal of reducing the RPN. For the errors that are prioritized for further action, the corrective action steps are transferred to a control plan where the team lists the actions to implement, assigns responsibility for each action, and states appropriate checks on actions and potential future actions.[14]

## Case study

The ProQuest metadata team creates full, "I" level MARC records in a process similar to librarians cataloging in more traditional library settings, using OCLC Connexion and Library of Congress tools such as Cataloger's Desktop and Classification Web. The team approached the PFMEA process looking for ways to create MARC records with minimal errors and to increase speed to market. The investigation focused on records created for ebooks in a variety of Western European languages. At the time of this PFMEA project, records were created according to *Anglo-American Cataloguing Rules, 2nd Edition* (AACR2) standards, with authorized access points when available in the NACO authority file. Catalogers did not contribute new NACO records but formulated the needed text strings for those fields according to NACO standards.

The project kicked off with a team meeting to discuss quality control vs. quality assurance, PFMEA, and the major task of completing an error matrix. In preparation for the meeting, the project coordinator consulted professional literature addressing errors in vendor records, to determine the greatest concerns of the customers. During the meeting, catalogers discussed MARC error categories, the PFMEA error matrix and other steps for the project. The team identified three main categories of errors to use for evaluating potential failures in the FMEA model: errors affecting access (access errors), errors preventing records from being loaded into an ILS or ProQuest databases (critical errors), and errors unlikely to affect access or loading (other errors).[15] A second consideration for categorizing errors came from questions within the group regarding objective vs subjective "errors." The cataloging process was outlined by creation method (original or derived) and field type (fixed, variable, and constant data), which were added to the error matrix as consideration for categorizing errors.

To fill out the error matrix, the team first identified potential failure modes in any given MARC field and the potential effects of each error. The effects were assigned a rating for Severity. Ratings for severity were scored high or low based on the seriousness of the perceived impact on the customer, on a scale of 1–10 (see Figure 1). Errors like incorrect notation of chief source were rated lower than missing name authority fields, given a library patron is less likely to have difficulty finding a resource based on a 588 note than a missing name. Next, potential causes of the error were identified, and those causes were assigned a rating for Occurrence (how likely it was to occur). Lower ratings were assigned for errors that are less likely to occur and higher ratings for common errors. Then current controls were identified that might catch that error, and a corresponding Detection rating was assigned. For the detection category, lower numbers were assigned when a cataloger would know that an error occurred. Specifically, a rating of 1 was only used for errors that could always be detected through automation, while a rating of 2 was used for errors frequently caught through manual detection. For each error, the Severity, Occurrence, and Detection ratings were multiplied together to get a Risk Priority Number, used to determine the multiplicative effect of each error. Errors with the highest RPN were considered a priority for process improvement investigation.

## Results

The team organized the identified failure modes into three major components of a MARC record: constant data, fixed fields, and variable fields. A second grouping was assigned based on the type of data contained in each field: local unit information, company information, codes, matching fields, title and publication information, access/authority data, and notes. Using these categories, the team found the majority of failure modes existed in variable fields. Figure 2 shows the number of possible errors identified for each field category during the project. The team found

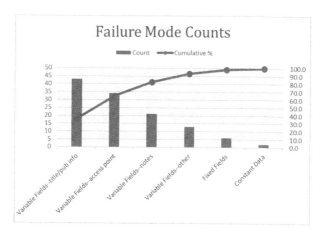

**Figure 2.** Failure modes counts.

the highest number of potential errors in title and publication information, followed by access point fields for a close second in potential errors.

While the failure mode counts reflect opportunities for errors within each MARC field category, the RPNs indicate the assigned risk for errors that occur. This part of the FMEA process involved discussion among the team members of how the error might impact the end user of the MARC record, the potential ways in which an error could occur, and the ways in which the error might be detected if it should occur.

For example, an incorrect 050 field resulted in one of the mid-to-lower RPNs. The severity of the error was not critical because it would not prevent a record from loading. Because these were e-book records, the team determined that a call number error would not be as severe as for a book on a shelf, but the error could prevent the record from correctly appearing in a call number browse feature or impact collection evaluation based on classification ranges. Potential Causes for the error were recorded as the cataloger simply making a typographical error or being distracted, or the cataloger needing more training on using Classification Web or the Cutter table. For the rest of the Error Matrix fields, the team recorded "manual proofing" for Current Detection Controls and "documentation" as Current Prevention Controls, which received moderate ratings. For the Control Plan, the team suggested more training on call numbers and using the tool Classification Web, as an opportunity to reduce the Occurrence value going forward.

An example that received a higher RPN is a missing 650 field. The potential error was not critical because it would not prevent a record from loading, but it would be an access error. In the Error Effects field, the team determined the error would prevent the item from appearing in a subject search result or subject browse. Potential Causes for the error were recorded as a cataloger's lack of subject familiarity or poor authority searching skills. The team recorded "manual proofing" for Current Detection Controls, "documentation" and "training" as Current Prevention Controls. For the Control Plan, the team suggested additional training available through continuing education programs in the profession.

The MARC fields that returned the highest RPNs were the 1XX and 7XX fields followed by other access point fields that might be incorrect or missing. The next highest grouping of errors included almost every possible title entry error and then publication fields. The team assumed the major errors in a title field were based on incorrect transcription from the chief source of information. Most of the comments related to errors in access point fields were based on browse and search indexes that use that metadata. Figure 3 shows the average RPN for the MARC field categories.

The top-rated error was the 111 meeting name main entry field, at an RPN of 324. Other top errors include 100/110 wrong form of name, missing series title and subject headings, incorrect and missing title field data, and incorrect diacritics. The lowest rated errors were missing $e in the 1XX and 7XX fields and general 500 notes missing, both with a rating of 1. Other low-rated errors included note field

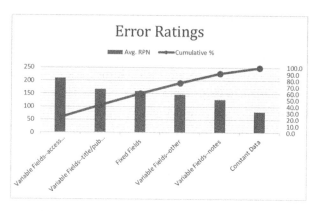

**Figure 3.** Average RPNs for MARC field categories.

indicators and missing 511 fields for video records. At this point, the team had not switched from AACR2 to *Resource Description and Access,* (RDA), so the impact of included or missing RDA elements in an AACR2 record were unclear. Therefore, ratings were not applied in situations where a 33X field might be missing (for example), as the team did not know or understand the impact of those fields.

The team conducted extensive discussions of possible causes for errors, how errors were detected, how errors were prevented, and actions taken upon finding an error in the control plan. Some possible causes included oversight, misinterpretation of rules, language barriers, unintentional typos, or general confusion. Detection method results were largely manual proofing by another cataloger, looking at a record field by field and comparing it to the item being cataloged. Some errors were caught by the validation tools built into the cataloging utility. The team's method of prevention was largely through cataloging documentation for the product and the initial training a new cataloger goes through when first starting on the team. Other detection methods relied on tools within the cataloging utility to verify field contents. Access point field errors could often be detected and corrected by controlling name and subject headings. Actions for correcting errors were typically resolved by a proofer noting the error and the cataloger fixing it. The project coordinator asked several times why the proofer couldn't fix the errors. The reason the team found against it was due to errors that were considered subjective and that the cataloger would be more likely to reduce mistakes after receiving the error feedback from the proofer. Actions for correcting subjective errors were noted as "Proofer notes error, cataloger evaluates and decides if it should change."

## Discussion

The final step of the error matrix was brainstorming ideas to prevent future errors. Suggestions offered during the error matrix discussion were copied to create the control plan. Many suggestions revolved around better training up front or review of standards for all catalogers. A few suggestions resulted in changes to the constant data used to begin creation of MARC records and researching new tools that might aid in the proofing process. As an end result, the team added information to constant data, such as an underscore to the 856 field, which triggered a validation fail if a cataloger forgets to add URL information. Catalogers set derive record settings to exclude 856 fields from used records. The catalogers searched for additional macros to use during cataloging, created new documents to be used as a guide for higher rated errors (foreign language information, titles with numbers and parts, and/or meeting main entry field creation), and updated existing documentation for best practices. The catalogers implemented use of a new quality control tool, to add some automation to the manual proofing process. The catalogers now go through annual group meetings to review and edit documentation, making alterations based on changing current standards and interpretations. In general, the catalogers opt for a continuous improvement approach to their process, including education and training opportunities and new tools and techniques for improving the quality and efficiency of the cataloging process.

## Evaluation of PFMEA for cataloging

The PFMEA team identified specific areas to address process improvement initiatives, based on this application of PFMEA for cataloging. Although the tool had the aforementioned beneficial outputs, some caveats and suggestions for improved applications for cataloging are worth noting. These can be grouped into categories related to making appropriate preparations before starting the project, considering the traditional application of RPNs vs. how RPNs can be applied outside of traditional manufacturing processes, and understanding the time involved in completing the FMEA process.

### *Prepare for the project*

Achieving successful FMEA results begins with understanding the fundamentals, definitions and procedures of FMEA, selecting the right FMEA projects, and completing preparation steps.[16] A key preparation step that the team identified for cataloging was defining an error. The project coordinator at ProQuest provided the team with a brief presentation of the differences between quality assurance and quality control and a general overview of creating the PFMEA error matrix, which the group then began to populate. The concept of errors, however, had not been well established, and as the team worked to identify the failure modes for the cataloging process, it became clear that the concept of an error was inconsistent. While some metadata entered in a MARC field is unquestionably wrong (e.g., an invalid indicator or a typographic error), sometimes it is the lack of metadata that was perceived as an error. For a clearly stated series title on the piece that was not included in the record, the team interpreted that as an error. But during manual proofing process, a reviewer might "correct" a record that lacks an appropriate and useful subject heading even if other valid subject headings had been assigned. This is something the catalogers later decided to categorize as a "subjective error" (based on cataloger judgement) and did not consider it a failure mode. In support of that concept, a study that audited completed MARC records in a catalog did not investigate note fields because they found that they contained too much variation, and different may not be incorrect.[17] The definition of an error should be stipulated at the beginning of the PFMEA to render the extensive rating process as simple and consistent as possible.

The team occasionally lost focus on what the intended product was, and began speculating on possible failure modes for RDA records (as they were creating AACR2 records at that time), or what the severity of an error might mean for metadata mapping to a linked data model. Preparing for the PFMEA should involve a clear explanation of what an error-free product is, and having that posted in view of the team as a constant reminder while working through the error matrix would have helped the team to stay on task.

The members of the project team should represent a range of experience because different perspectives will result in different rating assignments. A small group of people who all do the same thing may not be aware of the things they don't know.[18] This team was composed only of vendor catalogers, none of whom had a background at an institution that loaded vendor records into a local system. Although the team tried to imagine the severity of an error from the customer's perspective, they had no specific knowledge of how different catalog systems or record-loading processes might be impacted by particular errors.

### RPNs and what they really mean

The concept of the RPN creation, the multiplication of the Severity, Occurrence, and Detection ratings, is not supported by evidence that such a calculation is the best way to compare the error risks.[19] As an example, a one-point difference for one factor at the high end can result in an RPN difference of 100 ($10 * 10 * 10 = 1000$ vs. $10 * 10 * 9 = 900$), while a one-point difference for one factor at the low-end results in an RPN difference of only 1 ($1 * 1 * 1 = 1$ vs. $1 * 1 * 2 = 2$). The two RPNs at the high end of the scale seem significantly different, while those at the low end seem about the same. To remove the biased perception from the multiplicative nature of the RPN, the results could be assigned a corresponding ordinal number, which for a 10-point scale would result in the high-end example having RPNs of 119 and 120 and the low-end example having RPNs of 1 and 2, showing that their difference is the same.[20]

The Risk Priority Number is not a consistent measure of real risk, rather a rating of how the team considers the risk,[21] and to account for this another proposed revision of the RPN calculations involves weighted sums.[22] That calculation allows different team members to assign different values, which the developers of the weighted sums calculation believe are better suited for an uncertain environment. If different perspectives mean different value assignment, then the resulting value should reflect those differences rather than requiring one that everyone agrees on.[23] The rethinking of RPN calculations can involve complex mathematical formulas, but what is of particular interest is how users have been able to adapt the RPN to allow FMEA to better suit different scenarios and desired outcomes.

For cataloging, the ratings for Occurrence are also based on impressions rather than solid data. For this team, the Occurrence ratings came primarily from experience in creating MARC records and proofing each other's records. Relying on error occurrences that are generated from database error reports might seem more appropriate, but there are errors that could not be detected by machine generated data.

After completing a PFMEA that used the traditional RPN calculation, the catalogers questioned whether the three factors should be considered equally. Following the traditional RPN, the three factors are equally weighted, and different combinations of values for Severity, Occurrence, and Detection would result in the same RPN. As the team reviewed the RPNs of the project, it became clear that this is too simplified a perspective, and that not all errors with the same RPN are truly equal. Though the group did not create an actual weighting factor, they felt that the errors with high Severity value should be given greater attention in the control plan, as illustrated with Figure 4.

Figure 4 shows the RPNs for errors that rate at the extreme ends for Occurrence, Detection, and Severity when applying a 10-point scale. The corner labeled A correlates to an error with high Severity but low Occurrence and Detection. This scenario could be interpreted as "errors that don't happen often, are usually detected, but have a serious impact when not caught." The region near the corner labeled B could be interpreted as "errors that happen a lot and are rarely detected, but with no significant impact." The RPN for an error at A would be 10 (ordinal value of 10) and at B would be 100 (ordinal value of 46).

The team concluded that a failure mode that involved a high Severity value should be addressed even if the calculated RPN was not high relative to other failure modes. They felt that the point at which Detection happened could be important in failure mode prioritization. There are economic consequences related to

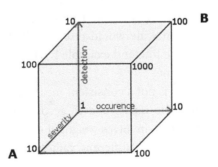

**Figure 4.** The RPN cube for a 10-point scale.

the amount of time an error goes undetected and how much effort is required to then correct the error. Detection at the time an error is made is more efficient and should result in a lower Detection value. Errors that could only be detected by manual proofing should be prioritized for improvement over those that are detected by automated validation tools.

### It can take a long time

Many who have applied the PFMEA tool have noted that it is time consuming, and possibly frustrating, even for a production process using standard parts that are assembled or enhanced in a regular, predictable way.[24] Creating MARC records involves many variables in the production parts, including the characteristics of the item to be cataloged and possible errors already in place when deriving from an existing record. There are many MARC field creation steps that had to be considered, and creating the error matrix was very involved for each of these steps. In the end, the team spent a great deal of effort on areas that turned out to be of little concern.

However, if the time and effort is not spent on the error matrix and the FMEA is not detailed enough, errors can be missed, making the process ineffective. This lack of detail would result in areas of concern with little to no definition to the problem.[25] If a team spends too little time brainstorming, solutions may be lacking and high-risk problems could remain unresolved.

This PFMEA project was designed to address every possible error in every MARC field, and the time to complete the project was much lengthier than expected. After many hours of work over several weeks, the team became less engaged in discussing and assigning values. One possible way to reduce the time needed for this process is to assign one of three rates, for Low, Medium, and High. There is evidence that reducing the rating options will minimize meaningless debate on close values[26] and will not greatly impact the results.[27] This simplified three-point rating would quickly identify the high Severity errors, which had become a priority for this application. Then the subset of highly rated errors could be further refined with a larger scale if necessary.

### Conclusions

The cataloging team's key takeaway from the PFMEA process was recognizing the need to ensure that local practices comply with external standards and support evolving metadata use. Even though additional quality management tools were added to cataloging practices, the ongoing work of reviewing points made in the control plan has kept the team in the practice of continuous improvement. Due to ongoing changes in metadata standards and the introduction of new applications of that metadata, continuous improvement is necessary for cataloging processes. Hsieh, Chang, and Lu, in their discussion of manufacturing-based models and techniques for managing quality in library and information services, conclude that a framework of quality management must be established for the library by promoting a quality culture.[28] The catalogers saw value in having ongoing quality management conversations that are not limited to managers. The FMEA team approach is useful to communicate the importance of quality production and to brainstorm improvement plans using the experience and expertise of the people doing the work.

The FMEA approach also gave the catalogers a different way of thinking of their processes. Using additional quality management tools provides catalogers with added opportunities for error detection, which should ideally happen at the time the mistake is made. Having to go back to the record as well as needing to inspect the item that was already cataloged is much less efficient. The team's suggested solution to catching errors at the time of production requires keeping basic under-standing of rules, practices, and standards at a high level. Participating in industry webinars and monitoring professional listservs are useful for ongoing education as standards continuously evolve and new cataloging tools are created. Improving means of automated detection should always be considered, because human proof-ing has its own risk of failure in addition to being less efficient.[29]

While the application of PFMEA can result in process changes that directly improve the occurrence or detection of errors, it is less likely to impact the severity of errors.[30] Changes to local cataloging processes will not change the impact of the errors, but catalogers can work to influence the development of systems that make use of cataloging metadata today or in the future. For example, reconciling MARC data for conversion to a linked data model will be impacted by errors and missing data, and the severity of those will depend on the conversion tools. The cataloging process would benefit from repeated FMEA-like analysis and related process changes, with the understanding that the original intent of FMEA was for a pro-duction environment where the end product is intended to be exactly the same every time. For industries like automotive production, that have experienced extensive FMEA work over a quarter century, the "critical few" may have already been addressed, leaving a "trivial many" that are hard to prioritize or even address.[31] However, this is not the case for cataloging where critical errors in the process are still very possible and need to be addressed. If catalogers think beyond MARC records, larger questions and potential problems arise. It can be said, in future environments, continuous improvement tools such as PFMEA will serve an ongoing need for quality metadata for libraries.

## ORCID

Jennifer Meekhof ⓘ http://orcid.org/0000-0001-8707-945X
Amy B. Bailey ⓘ http://orcid.org/0000-0003-0510-1487

## Notes

1. Pao-Nuan Hsieh, Pao-Long Chang, and Kuen-Horng Lu, "Quality Management Approaches in Libraries and Information Services," *Libri* 50, no. 3 (2000): 191–201.

2. Stuart Hunt, "Improving Performance in Cataloguing and Technical Services Workflows," *Catalogue & Index* 161 (Dec. 2010): 10–15.
3. Ibid., 10.
4. Elizabeth Nelson, "Using Six Sigma and Lean in the Library," *College & Undergraduate Libraries*, 22, no. 3–4 (2015): 312–324. DOI: 10.1080/10691316.2015.1070701.
5. TM Kubiak, "Conducting FMEAs for Results," *Quality Progress* 47, no. 6 (Jun 2014): 42.
6. Steven Kmenta, "Advanced Failure Modes and Effects Analysis: a Method for Predicting and Evaluating Failures in Products and Processes" (Ph.D. diss., Stanford University, 2001), 3.
7. Kubiak, "Conducting FMEAs for Results," 42.
8. Janet Webber, "FMEA: Quality Assurance Methodology," *Industrial Management + Data Systems* 90, no. 7 (1990): 21.
9. Lian-yu Zheng, Kwai-sang Chin, and Li Wei, "Knowledge-Enriched Process FMEA Model for Process Planning," *Asian Journal on Quality* 3, no. 1 (2000): 15.
10. William Goble, "The FMEA Method: a Powerful Reliability Tool for Data Analysis That Lasts for Decades," *Intech* March/April (2012): 17.
11. Webber, "FMEA," 21.
12. Goble, "FMEA Method," 17.
13. Zheng, "Knowledge-Enriched Process FMEA," 18.
14. Webber, "FMEA," 22.
15. Stacie Traill, "Quality Issues in Vendor-Provided E-Monograph Records," *Library Resources & Technical Services* 57, no. 4 (October 2013): 216.
16. Carl S. Carlson, "Which FMEA Mistakes Are You Making?," *Quality Progress* 47, no. 9 (2014): 37.
17. Ann Chapman and Owen Massey, "A Catalogue Quality Audit Tool," *Library Management* 23, no. 6/7 (2002): 320.
18. Carlson, "Which FMEA Mistakes," 39.
19. Yuxian Du, Xi Lu, Xiaoyan Su, Yong Hu, and Yong Deng, "New Failure Mode and Effect Analysis: An Evidential Downscaling Method," *Quality and Reliability Engineering International* 32 (2016): 738.
20. Donald J. Wheeler, "Problems with Risk Priority Numbers," *Quality Digest Magazine* (June 27, 2011), http://www.qualitydigest.com/inside/quality-insider-article/problems-risk-priority-numbers.html (accessed February 12, 2016).
21. Kmenta, "Advanced Failure Modes and Effects Analysis," 9.
22. Du et al., "New Failure Mode and Effect Analysis," 740–741.
23. Ibid., 745.
24. John J. Casey, *Strategic Error-Proofing: Achieving Success Every Time with Smarter FMEAs* (New York: CRC Press, 2009), 7.
25. Carlson, "Which FMEA Mistakes," 40.
26. Kubiak, "Conducting FMEA for Results," 44.
27. John Dawes, "Do Data Characteristics Change According to the Number of Scale Points Used?," *International Journal of Market Research*, 50, no. 1 (2008): 75.
28. Hsieh, Chang, and Lu, "Quality Management Approaches," 200.
29. Casey, *Strategic Error-Proofing*, 8.
30. Ibid., 5.
31. Ibid., 6.

# An Investigation of Title Ambiguity in the Health Sciences Literature

Dick R. Miller, Joanne Banko, Thea S. Allen, Ariel Vanderpool, and Ryan Max Steinberg

**ABSTRACT**

This research investigates what most catalogers already know—titles alone do not identify works sufficiently. Repetitive titles like "Annual Report" are just the tip of the iceberg. To explore the extent of ambiguity occurring in large sets of health science bibliographic data, the entire National Library of Medicine and Lane Medical Library catalogs and a sample from the PubMed database were analyzed. After measuring the uniqueness of titles, results were recalculated to determine the effect of appending date and/or edition. This initial evidence supports further exploration of whether such structured titles might serve as singular bibliographic identities.

## Introduction

Titles are perhaps the most important metadata element for accessing scientific literature. A well-written title represents the content found in a particular work and serves as its de facto identity. One primary characteristic of an effective title is that it be unique to prevent confusion about the identities of different works or different versions of the same work. Unique titles allow researchers to choose from multiple search results and to consider the relevance of related titles when displayed. While it is true that numeric identifiers and computer algorithms can eliminate some of the ambiguity that results when titles are not unique, they fail to delineate clearly the options available to the reader.

To assess titles' uniqueness, the research project reported in this paper represents an initial attempt at analyzing the degree and types of ambiguity occurring in large sets of scientific bibliographic data. The accessible and well-organized databases provided by the National Library of Medicine (NLM), such as PubMed and the NLM Catalog, make the health sciences literature particularly amenable to this type of analysis. The study of both cataloging and indexing data reflects the merged presentation of such data in discovery systems and increasing data reuse in various contexts.

Title identities begin with the author's naming of a work and continue with decisions made by editors. Avoiding uninformative generic titles at the outset, and devising policies aimed at addressing ambiguity could benefit library users, publishers, catalogers, indexers, and systems personnel. Particularly challenging to catalogers are questions relating to choice of title, where titles start and stop, and whether a uniform title is indicated. Regardless of these issues, title ambiguity still exists and continues to interfere with optimal data use. When considering how to disambiguate, catalogers also face variability in chronology (associated dates) and enumeration (edition statements). Opportunities to address titles as identities are great at this time when mapping data out of traditional library systems is under active consideration.

To tackle the title ambiguity problem, a group of metadata staff at Lane Medical Library compiled and inspected title data and potential disambiguators extracted from the complete NLM Catalog, the complete Lane Medical Library Catalog, and one year (2012) of PubMed data, totaling almost 2.7 million bibliographic records. The non-unique, or repeated titles, were termed ambiguous and became the target of further analysis. The primary research question for this study was "What is the extent of ambiguity (as measured by uniqueness) in scientific titles, and to what extent can ambiguity be reduced by appending chronological and enumerative data to titles?"

Lane Medical Library metadata staff propose that titles structured to provide unique identities are a step in the direction of linked data for libraries. At present, titles have numerical identifiers but not definitive identities. Many identifiers are accession numbers from various databases, for example, OCLC numbers, PubMed Identifiers (PMIDs), or locally assigned library catalog numbers. Other identifiers such as international standard book numbers (ISBNs) and digital object identifiers (DOIs) may be unique, but are not always available. Ideally, the components of the title itself should serve as its identity to help people distinguish it from other titles, in contrast to the many variations of author/title entry, title main entry, uniform title, etc., not always handled well by computer systems. Lessons learned from name authorities and name identifiers provide parallels for broader context.

## Literature review

Reducing ambiguity is not a foreign idea in library science. It is the rationale for name authority records. Most literature to date has focused on name ambiguity and the problems and confusion that arose in applying the fundamental *Functional Requirements for Bibliographic Records* (FRBR) user tasks of finding, identifying, selecting, and obtaining the information (FISO). "In the environment of shared cataloging and union catalogs, authority control becomes essential in order to avoid duplicated records and to match records contributed from various sources," states Tillett.[1] Delsey continues that "the concept of authority control ... is implicit in virtually all of the statements of principle relating to the objectives of the catalogue."[2]

As technology and the online environment have expanded, catalogers have found that they are not alone in the quest to disambiguate author names; it has also become a concern for database managers. There are articles available presenting and comparing different algorithms that try to enhance and identify correctly a particular author based on data that is "nearby" the author's name.[3,4] The focus on name authority work and records is pervasive in the literature. The problem of ambiguous names is not limited to the content currently in a database but also must address the flow of new data into it.[5] It is clear that disambiguating names is important to libraries in order to help their patrons find and identify the information they seek.

Databases, such as Open Research and Contributor ID (ORCID), Virtual International Authority File (VIAF), and International Standard Name Identifier (ISNI), were developed to provide specific identifiers that clearly and efficiently represent the unique name of a creator, which will be necessary for libraries to enter the linked data environment. Sandberg and Jin recently studied linking authors of journal articles to name identifiers from ISNI, ORCID, Scopus, and VIAF as a look at how linked data and potentially, the Bibliographic Framework Initiative (BIBFRAME) will help provide more accurate author information to users.[6] Further evidence of the value of name identifiers is the trend toward major publishers' and some research funders' requiring ORCID numbers during their submission process.[7]

Main entry is another topic of importance in the discussion of FISO. What should the main entry of a bibliographic record be, and what is its significance? When bibliographic records transitioned from print cards located in the card catalog to online public access catalogs (OPACs) the debate about whether the main entry to a record was the author or the title and the need for catalogers to continue to maintain such rigorous rules escalated. The idea that "we are not capitalizing upon computer technology's potential to enhance service to library users" and that "by retaining rules which narrowly focused on the choice of entries, they missed the opportunity to establish rules for the formulation of equal status entry points" was pointed out over forty years ago by Leonard.[8] Along those same lines, Winke states that "the concept of the main entry has outlived its practicality as the library's catalogs have evolved from book and card based systems to electronically generated formats.... Catalogers no longer have the luxury of continuing out-dated practices solely for the sake of tradition."[9] Howarth and Weihs note that the questioning of main entry began in the 1960s with the increase in cataloging of nonbook materials. The argument again arose with "automation and the increasing sophistication in computer programming ... this time not about what the main entry should be but rather whether there should be a main entry at all."[10] Snoham and Lazinger agree, stating "the main entry - both as complete cataloging record and primary access point - is a concept that served cataloging well, but which is unnecessary in an online environment."[11] Carlyle, Ranger, and Summerlin looked at how variations in cataloging quality could affect which main entry heading was assigned to a particular work by different libraries. They noted that due to the variation of cataloging quality "consistent identification and retrieval of records representing editions of works is not guaranteed."[12] Vellucci sums things up succinctly by stating that "all access points are equal. The first function of the main entry as the standard form of identifying the work, however, still appears to have validity. Whether it is called the primary, chief, or main access point is of little consequence; it is the function served that is important."[13]

The literature search also identified discussions on how best to select a title when writing. The *Publication Manual of the American Psychological Association* (APA) has an entire section on selecting a title for a manuscript. It states "a title should summarize the main idea of the manuscript simply and, if possible, with style. It should be a concise statement of the main topic and ... should be fully explanatory when standing alone." The APA further states that "the recommended length for a title is no more than twelve words."[14]

The concept of recommended title length has been further investigated. One study by Letchford, Moat, and Pries suggested that shorter titles get more citations because they "may be easier to understand, and hence attract more citations."[15] In contrast, a study of APA JOURNALS found that "the average title length in these journals increased with time" and "that title length has been steadily increasing for over a hundred years." The authors, Hallock and Dillner, question if potentially longer title lengths are needed today to help writers adequately describe article content to readers.[16] The trend toward longer titles also could point to authors hoping for better retrieval rates from among the multitude of articles that are available on the internet.

As to what makes a "good" title, the authors of this paper maintain that uniqueness is a key factor. Miller and Clarke stated that "many problems derive from the lack of a straightforward identity for works" and that "clear bibliographic identities are needed." They believe that "cataloging fails to provide a clear, unambiguous identity for most works," and go on to explain that this is an issue since "the title serves as the chief name or identifier for a work."[17] Smiraglia touches on this need for authority control at the level of the work by saying "effective authority control of works could yield richness in the catalog that would enhance retrieval capabilities."[18]

The current cataloging standard, *Resource Description & Access* (RDA), supplies rules and direction concerning title ambiguity. RDA 6.27.1.9 advises to "include additional elements in authorized access points if needed to distinguish the access point for a work from one that is the same or similar but represents a different work." For example:

The advocate (Boise, Idaho)
The advocate (Nairobi, Kenya)

Title identity relates directly to four of the eight RDA principles [RDA 0.4.3]: differentiation, sufficiency, representation, and accuracy.[19] Summarized by Weihs and Howarth: "as RDA continues toward realization, it does so—at least for the short term—with acknowledgement of the importance of structured titles for works, with additional identifying elements, as required, for differentiating one expression of a work from another."[20] In determining how best to record a title for optimal retrieval, having a unique title and adhering to RDA's principles will make finding, identifying, selecting, and obtaining the correct resource easier for information seekers.

## Methods

### *Data specification and extraction*

Lane metadata staff inspected three bibliographic databases – PubMed (2012), the NLM Catalog, and the Lane Catalog – and selected the data elements relevant to this project. One year of PubMed data was deemed sufficient because appending the year would automatically disambiguate titles over time. The year 2012 was selected as it seemed old enough to include any post-load updates, thus reducing data volatility.

For PubMed, a count of the Title and Date1 elements were generated for each repeating title. The data structure of the NLM and Lane files were kept as parallel as possible, augmented by five additional fields for the Lane data related to the 149 field, an experimental title field described later.

A Lane staff programmer extracted NLM catalog and PubMed data using Java, Entrez programming utilities from the National Center for Biotechnology Information (NCBI), and extensible stylesheet language transformations (XSLT) to transform the data into the specified output.[21] Lane Catalog data were extracted using Java and converted to MARCXML (MARC extensible markup language), followed by XSLT transformation of the data as specified. Subsequently, counts of duplicated (non-unique) titles were added to each report using Java. Finally, the data was split into two files, one of singletons (titles found one time), and one with "multi" titles (duplicated two or more times) using basic UNIX text utilities.

Metadata staff converted the resultant delimited text files to Excel spreadsheets for analysis. Excel was used because staff were already familiar with it and had limited time to investigate more sophisticated analytical tools. The resulting large file sizes tested the limits of Excel, but only the NLM Catalog singletons file at 155,216 KB exceeded them. This was resolved by splitting it into two files. Figure 1 shows the data elements extracted from the NLM multi file. Figure 2 shows a similar excerpt from the Lane multi file. A visual representation is not provided for PubMed since those files include only the data elements: Title and Date1 (which is always 2012).

| id | titleNF | title | date1 | date2 | edition | UTNF | UT | type | issuance | timesfound |
|---|---|---|---|---|---|---|---|---|---|---|
| 1.02E+08 | 0 | Psychopathology of everyday life | 1935 | | Authorized Eng. ed. | 0 | Zur Psychopathologie des Alltagsleben. | Book | monographic | 2 |
| 9414338 | 0 | Zoonoses and communicable diseases common to man and animals | 1987 | | 2nd ed. | 0 | Zoonosis y enfermedades transmisibles comun | Book | monographic | 3 |
| 1.01E+08 | 0 | Zoonoses and communicable diseases common to man and animals | 2001 | 9999 | 3rd ed. | 0 | Zoonosis y enfermedades transmisibles comun | Book | monographic | 3 |
| 1.02E+08 | 0 | Chinese acupuncture and moxibustion | 2010 | | 3rd ed. | 0 | Zhongguo zhen jiu xue. | Book | monographic | 4 |
| 1.01E+08 | 0 | Essentials of Chinese acupuncture | 1993 | | 2nd ed. | 0 | Zhongguo zhen jiu xue gai yao. | Book | monographic | 2 |
| 9424481 | 0 | Yearbook | 1988 | 1990 | | 0 | Zhongguo yi xue ke xue yuan, Zhongguo xie he | Serial | continuing | 5 |
| 1.02E+08 | 0 | Zhong yi hu li xue | 2012 | | Di 1 ban. | 0 | Zhong yi hu li xue (Zhang) | Book | monographic | 4 |
| 8105247 | 0 | Shinkyū kōatsuokyō. | 1941 | | | 0 | Zhen jiu jia yi jing. | Book | monographic | 2 |
| 8811045 | 0 | Cerebral and-spinal computerized tomography | 1989 | | 2nd rev. and enl. ed. | 0 | Zerebrale und spinale Computertomographie. | Book | monographic | 2 |
| 8310715 | 0 | Cerebral angiography | 1982 | | 2nd completely rev. ed. / by Peter Huber ; tran | 0 | Zerebrale Angiographie für Klinik und Praxis. | Book | monographic | 4 |
| 9713094 | 0 | Zensoku. | 1991 | 1994 | | 0 | Zensoku (Tokyo, Japan) | Serial | continuing | 2 |
| 7503955 | 0 | Zeitschrift für Zellforschung und mikroskopische Anatomie. | 1948 | 1974 | | 0 | Zeitschrift für Zellforschung und mikroskopisch | Serial | continuing | 2 |
| 1.01E+08 | 0 | Zeitschrift für Zellforschung und mikroskopische Anatomie. | 1934 | 1938 | | 0 | Zeitschrift für Zellforschung und mikroskopisch | Serial | continuing | 2 |
| 1.01E+08 | 0 | Zeitschrift für Sexualwissenschaft. | 1914 | 1928 | | 0 | Zeitschrift für Sexualwissenschaft (Bonn, Germ | Serial | continuing | 2 |
| 9112162 | 0 | Zeitschrift für Sexualforschung. | 1988 | 9999 | | 0 | Zeitschrift für Sexualforschung (Stuttgart, Germ | Serial | continuing | 2 |
| 1305675 | 0 | Zeitschrift für physikalische Chemie. | 1954 | 9999 | | 0 | Zeitschrift für physikalische Chemie (Frankfurt a | Serial | continuing | 2 |
| 1.01E+08 | 0 | Zeitschrift für Parasitenkunde. | 1869 | 1875 | | 0 | Zeitschrift für Parasitenkunde (Jena, Germany) | Serial | continuing | 2 |
| 8710749 | 0 | Zeitschrift für Parasitenkunde. | 1934 | 1986 | | 0 | Zeitschrift für Parasitenkunde (Berlin, Germany) | Serial | continuing | 2 |
| 1.01E+08 | 0 | Zeitschrift für klinische Psychologie und Psychotherapie. | 2000 | 9999 | | 0 | Zeitschrift für klinische Psychologie und Psycho | Serial | continuing | 2 |
| 8707913 | 0 | Zdrowie. | 1885 | 1933 | | 0 | Zdrowie (Warsaw, Poland : 1885) | Serial | continuing | 2 |
| 1.01E+08 | 0 | Zdravookhranenie. | 1995 | 9999 | | 0 | Zdravookhranenie (Moscow, Russia) | Serial | continuing | 3 |
| 9802319 | 0 | O medfūshīkom strakhovanii grazhdan. | 1997 | | | 0 | Zakon O medifūshīkom strakhovanii grazhdan v | Book | monographic | 2 |
| 1.02E+08 | 0 | Dental radiology | 2015 | | | 0 | Zahnärztliche Radiologie. | Book | monographic | 6 |
| 1.01E+08 | 0 | Yu fang ma zhen | 1960 | | | 0 | Yu fang ma zhen (Shanghai Shi wei sheng jiao yi | Book | monographic | 2 |
| 9427601 | 0 | Your health. | 2000 | 9999 | | 0 | Your health (Nairobi, Kenya) | Serial | continuing | 10 |
| 9440574 | 0 | Yōn gu nonmunjip. | 1916 | 19uu | | 0 | Your health (Cleveland, Ohio) | Serial | continuing | 10 |
| 1.02E+08 | 0 | Yoga international | 1967 | | | 0 | Yōn gu nonmunjip (Pogōn Changhakhoe (Korea | Serial | continuing | 2 |
| 1.02E+08 | 0 | Yin shi wei sheng | 2010 | 9999 | | 0 | Yoga international (2010) | Serial | continuing | 2 |
| 1.01E+08 | 0 | Yin shi wei sheng | 1965 | | | 0 | Yin shi wei sheng (Shanghai Shi wei sheng jiao y | Book | monographic | 3 |
| 8107239 | 0 | Ihō taiseiron. | 1972 | | Di 1 ban. | 0 | Yin shi wei sheng (Huang) | Book | monographic | 3 |
| 8105895 | 0 | Ihō taiseiron. | 17uu | | | 0 | Yi shu da quan. | Book | monographic | 2 |
| 8106109 | 0 | Ihō shikkai | 1688 | | | 0 | Yi shu da quan. | Book | monographic | 2 |
| 1.01E+08 | 0 | Ihō shikkai | 1728 | | | 0 | Yi fang ji jie. | Book | monographic | 2 |
| 1.01E+08 | 0 | Yellow-fever vaccine. | 1727 | | | 0 | Yi fang ji jie. | Book | monographic | 2 |
| 8700978 | 0 | Yearbook. | 1957 | | | 0 | Yellow-fever vaccine (October 8, 1957) | Serial | monographic | 2 |
| 1.02E+08 | 0 | Yearbook | 1987 | 1987 | | 0 | Yearbook (Springhouse Corporation) | Serial | continuing | 16 |
| 1.02E+08 | 0 | 4 year in evolutionary biology | 1984 | 9999 | | 0 | Yearbook (Conference of Latin Americanist Geo | Serial | continuing | 5 |
| 1.02E+08 | 0 | 4 year in evolutionary biology | 2013 | | | 0 | Year in evolutionary biology (2013) | Book | monographic | 3 |
| 1.02E+08 | 0 | 4 year in cognitive neuroscience | 2014 | | | 0 | Year in evolutionary biology (2014) | Book | monographic | 3 |
| 8303032 | 0 | 4 Year book of orthopedics and traumatic surgery. | 2013 | | | 0 | Year in cognitive neuroscience (2013) | Book | monographic | 3 |
| 1.01E+08 | 0 | Year book | 1969 | 1979 | | 0 | Year book of orthopedics and traumatic surgery | Serial | continuing | 2 |
| 1.01E+08 | 0 | Year book | 1983 | 9999 | | 0 | Year book (Australian Veterinary Association : 1 | Serial | continuing | 2 |
| 136351 | 0 | Yarbon ha-statisṭi le-Yiśra'el. | 1915 | 1952 | | 0 | Year book (1915) | Serial | continuing | 5 |
| 1.02E+08 | 0 | Yakubutsu ryōhō | 1949 | 1953 | | 0 | Yarbon statisṭi le-Yiśra'el (1949) | Serial | continuing | 2 |
| 1.01E+08 | 0 | Shinkan Kōtei daikei reisō | 2010 | | 2010-nenban, dai 3-han. | 0 | Yakubutsu ryōhō (Nihon Nyūgan Gakkai) | Book | monographic | 4 |
| 1.01E+08 | 0 | Shinkan Kōtei daikei reisō | 16uu | | | 0 | Xin kan Huangdi nei jing ling shu. | Book | monographic | 2 |
| 1.01E+08 | 0 | Shinpen zokukai Hachijūichi nangyō zu | 16uu | | | 0 | Xin kan Huangdi nei jing ling shu. | Book | monographic | 2 |
| 8905266 | 0 | Shinpen zokukai Hachijūichi nangyō zu | 1617 | | | 0 | Xin bian su jie Ba shi yi nan jing tu. | Book | monographic | 2 |
| 1.02E+08 | 0 | Xiao er tui na liao fa | 1617 | | Di 1 ban. | 0 | Xin bian su jie Ba shi yi nan jing tu. | Book | monographic | 2 |
| | | | 1975 | | | 0 | Xiao er tui na liao fa (Changsha) | Book | monographic | 2 |

Figure 1. NLM Catalog data sample.

| id | titleNF | title | date1 | date2 | edition | UTNF | UT | type | issuance | timesfound | 149alt | 149NF | 149UT | 149num | 149chrom |
|---|---|---|---|---|---|---|---|---|---|---|---|---|---|---|---|
| L312065 | 0 | Urogynecology and reconstructive pelvic surgery | 2015 | | Fourth edition. [4th ed.] | 0 | Urogynecology and reconstructive pelvic surge | Books | [digital] | 4 | 4 | | Urogynecology and reconstructive pelvic surge | 4 | 2015 |
| L311629 | 0 | Transplantation | 2014 | | | 0 | Transplantation (2014) | books | [digital] | 5 | 5 | | Transplantation | 5 | 2014 |
| L300932 | 0 | Color atlas of dermatology | 2011 | | Fifth edition. [5th ed.] | 0 | Taschenatlas Dermatologie. English. | books | [digital] | 2 | 2 | | Color atlas of dermatology | 10 | 2016 |
| L313110 | 0 | Sleisenger and Fordtran's Gastrointestinal and liver disease | 2016 | | Tenth edition. [10th ed.] | 0 | Sleisenger and Fordtran's gastrointestinal and li | Books | [print] | 3 | 3 | | Regimen sanitatis Salerni | | 1790 |
| LR4763 | 0 | Regimen sanitatis Salerni | 1790 | | | 0 | Regimen sanitatis Salernitanum, Latin. | Books | [print] | 3 | 3 | | Medicina Salernitana | | 1612 |
| LR4766 | 0 | Medicina Salernitana | 1612 | | | 0 | Regimen sanitatis Salernitanum, Latin. | Books | [print] | 3 | 3 | | Medicina Salernitana | | 1594 |
| LR4767 | 0 | Medicina Salernitana | 1594 | | | 0 | Regimen sanitatis Salernitanum, Latin. | Books | [print] | 3 | 3 | | Regimen sanitatis | | 1500 |
| LR4768 | 0 | Regimen sanitatis | 1500 | | | 0 | Regimen sanitatis Salernitanum, Latin. | Books | [print] | 3 | 3 | | Regimen sanitatis | | 1494 |
| LR4769 | 0 | Regimen sanitatis | 1494 | | | 0 | Regimen sanitatis Salernitanum, Latin. | Books | [print] | 3 | 3 | | Regimen sanitatis Salernitanum | | 1841 |
| LR4770 | 0 | Regimen sanitatis Salernitanum | 1841 | | | 0 | Regimen sanitatis Salernitanum, Latin. | Books | [print] | 3 | 3 | | Regimen sanitatis Salerni | | 1649 |
| LR4771 | 0 | Regimen sanitatis Salerni | 1649 | | | 0 | Regimen sanitatis Salernitanum, Latin. | Books | [print] | 3 | 3 | | Regimen sanitatis Salerni | | 1634 |
| LR4772 | 0 | Regimen sanitatis Salerni | 1634 | | | 0 | Regimen sanitatis Salernitanum, Latin. | Books | [print] | 2 | 2 | | School of Salernum | | 1966 |
| L155765 | 0 | The School of Salernum | 1966 | | | 0 | Regimen sanitatis Salernitanum. 1947. | Pamphlet | [print] | 2 | 2 | The | Regimen sanitatis Salernitanum | | 1947 |
| L155764 | 0 | Regimen sanitatis Salernitanum | 1947 | 1870 | | 0 | Regimen sanitatis Salernitanum, 1586, English. | Books | [print] | 2 | 2 | | Regimen sanitatis Salernitanum " | | 1871/1870 |
| L155767 | 0 | Regimen sanitatis Salernitanum " | 1871 | 1841 | | 0 | Regimen sanitatis Salernitanum. 1871. English. F | Books | [print/digital] | 2 | 2 | | Regimen sanitatis Salernitanum " | | 1902/1841 |
| Q265396 | 0 | Regimen sanitatis Salernitanum " | 1902 | | | 1 | Regimen sanitatis Salernitanum. | Components | [manuscript] | 2 | 2 | | Koran]. | | |
| L241941 | 1 | [Koran]. Fragment | 18uu | | | 1 | Qur'an, 19th cent. ? Fragment. | Books | [manuscript] | 2 | 2 | [ | Koran]. | | 1903 |
| L242006 | 1 | [Koran]. Fragment | 1771 | | [2nd ed.] | 0 | Qur'an. 1771. Fragment. | Pamphlet | [print/digital] | 2 | 2 | | Preventive medicine | | 2013 |
| L130341 | 0 | Preventive medicine | 1903 | | | 0 | Preventive medicine. | Books | [print] | 11 | 11 | | Positron emission tomography | | 1951 |
| L304386 | 0 | Positron emission tomography | 2013 | | | 0 | Positron emission tomography (Graovac) | Books | [print] | 4 | 4 | | Epitome of the Pharmacopeia of the United Sta | 9 | 1947 |
| L146066 | 0 | Epitome of the Pharmacopeia of the United States and the National formu | 1931 | | 9th ed. | 0 | Pharmacopoeia of the United States of America | Books | [print] | 5 | 5 | | Epitome of the Pharmacopeia of the United Sta | 8 | 1943 |
| L146065 | 0 | Epitome of the Pharmacopeia of the United States and the National formu | 1947 | | 8th ed. | 0 | Pharmacopoeia of the United States of America | Books | [print] | 5 | 5 | | Epitome of the Pharmacopeia of the United Sta | 5 | 1937 |
| L146064 | 0 | Epitome of the Pharmacopeia of the United States and the National formu | 1943 | | 7th ed. | 0 | Pharmacopoeia of the United States of America | Books | [print] | 5 | 5 | | Epitome of the Pharmacopeia of the United Sta | 10 | 1955 |
| L146063 | 0 | Epitome of the Pharmacopeia of the United States and the National formu | 1937 | | 5th ed. | 0 | Pharmacopoeia of the United States of America | Books | [print] | 5 | 5 | | Epitome of the Pharmacopeia of the United States and the | 5 | 1926 |
| L114567 | 0 | Epitome of the Pharmacopeia of the United States and the National formu | 1955 | | 10th ed. | 0 | Pharmacopoeia of the United States of America | Books | [print] | 3 | 3 | | Deutsches Arzneibuch | | 1926 |
| L114560 | 0 | Epitome of the Pharmacopeia of the United States and the National Form | 1926 | | 6. Aoug. 1926. | 0 | Pharmacopoea Germanica | Books | [print] | 5 | 5 | | Pediatric thoracic surgery | 2 | 2013 |
| L137110 | 0 | Deutsches Arzneibuch | 1926 | | Second edition. [2nd ed.] | 0 | Pediatric thoracic surgery (2013) | Books | [digital] | 3 | 3 | | Pediatric inflammatory bowel disease | 2 | 2013 |
| L305178 | 0 | Pediatric thoracic surgery | 2013 | | Fourth edition [4th ed.] | 0 | Pediatric inflammatory bowel disease [Springer | Books | [print] | 3 | 3 | | Pediatric endocrinology | 4 | 2014 |
| L304277 | 0 | Pediatric inflammatory bowel disease | 2014 | | Fourth edition [4th ed.] | 0 | Pediatric endocrinology (2014) | Books | [digital] | 11 | 11 | | Papyrus Ebers | | 1930 |
| L311537 | 0 | Pediatric endocrinology | 1930 | | | 0 | Papyrus Ebers. English. | Books | [print] | 2 | 2 | The | Ophthalmology | | 2014 |
| L133130 | 0 | The Papyrus Ebers | 2014 | | | 0 | Ophthalmology (Tasman) | Books | [digital] | 33 | 33 | | Nomina anatomica | 6 | 1999 |
| L307529 | 0 | Ophthalmology | 1999 | | Fourth edition [4th ed.] | 0 | Nomina anatomica. 1983. (6th ed.). | Books | [print] | 9 | 9 | | Nomina anatomica | 5 | 1983 |
| LG5321 | 0 | Nomina anatomica | 1983 | | 6th ed. | 0 | Nomina anatomica. 1980. (5th ed.). | Books | [print] | 9 | 9 | | Nomina anatomica | 4 | 1977 |
| L13364 | 0 | Nomina anatomica | 1977 | | 5th ed. | 0 | Nomina anatomica. 1977. (4th ed.). | Books | [print] | 9 | 9 | | Nomina anatomica | 3 | 1966/ |
| L8821 | 0 | Nomina anatomica | 1968 | | 4th ed. / | 0 | Nomina anatomica. 1968. (3rd ed.). Reprint. | Books | [print] | 9 | 9 | | Nomina anatomica | 3 | 1969 |
| L73662 | 0 | Nomina anatomica | 1950 | | 3rd ed., unchanged ed. lin. 2 | 0 | Nomina anatomica. 1960. (2nd ed.). Reprint. | Books | [print] | 9 | 9 | | Nomina anatomica | | 1996 |
| L73661 | 0 | Nomina anatomica | 1956 | | | 0 | Nomina anatomica. 1955. | Books | [print] | 9 | 9 | | Nomina anatomica | | 1955 |
| L31696 | 0 | Nomina anatomica | 1955 | | | 0 | Nomina anatomica. 1955. | Books | [print] | 9 | 9 | | Nomina anatomica | | 1998 |
| L30936 | 0 | Nomina anatomica | 1949 | | 4, durchgesehene Aufl. | 0 | Nomina anatomica. 1955. (NA4). 4th ed. | Books | [print] | 9 | 9 | | Nomina anatomica | 4 | 2015 |
| LG9582 | 0 | Neurovascular surgery | 2015 | | 2nd edition. | 0 | Neurovascular surgery (Thieme) | Books | [digital] | 3 | 3 | | Neurovascular surgery | 2 | 2013 |
| L314159 | 0 | Neuroeconomics | 2013 | | Second edition. [2nd ed.] | 0 | Neuroeconomics (Glimcher) | Books | [digital] | 2 | 2 | | Neuroeconomics | 4 | 2014 |
| L307087 | 0 | Microbial pathogenesis | 2013 | 2013 | | 0 | Metabolic syndrome (Beck-Nielsen) | Books | [print] | 2 | 2 | | Mitochondrial pathogenesis | | 2013/2013 |
| L307885 | 0 | The Metabolic syndrome | 1976 | | 9th ed. | 0 | Merck index. 9th ed. 1976. | Books | [print] | 9 | 9 | The | Metabolic syndrome | 9 | 1976 |
| L304436 | 4 | The Merck index | 1908 | | 8th ed. | 0 | Merck index. 8th ed. 1968. | Books | [print] | 9 | 9 | The | Merck index | 9 | 1968 |
| L2052 | 4 | The Merck index | 1960 | | 7th ed. | 0 | Merck index. 7th ed. 1960. | Books | [print] | 9 | 9 | The | Merck index | 6 | 1960 |
| L73419 | 4 | The Merck index | 1952 | | 6th ed. | 0 | Merck index. 6th ed. 1952. | Books | [print] | 2 | 2 | The | Merck index | 6 | 1952 |
| L78421 | 4 | The Merck index of chemicals and drug | 1940 | | 5th ed. | 0 | Merck index. 5th ed. 1940. | Books | [print] | 9 | 9 | The | Merck index | 9 | 1940 |
| L78420 | 4 | The Merck index of chemicals and drugs | 2013 | | 15th ed. | 0 | Merck index. 15th ed. 2013. | Books | [print] | 9 | 9 | The | Merck index | 15 | 2013 |
| L78511 | 4 | The Merck index | | | | | | | | | | | | | |
| L304299 | 4 | The Merck index | | | | | | | | | | | | | |

Figure 2. Lane Catalog data sample.

NLM data elements

| | |
|---|---|
| ID | Numeric value from: NlmUniqueID |
| TitleNF | Value 0–9 from: TitleMain/Title/Sort = "n" |
| Title | Text string from: TitleMain/Title |
| Date1 | Date, usually in form yyyy, from: PublicationFirstYear |
| Date2 | Date, usually in form yyyy, from: PublicationEndYear |
| Edition | Text string, consisting of first 25 characters only, from PublicationInfo/Edition |
| UniformNF | Value 0–9 from TitleAlternate/Title when TitleType = "Uniform" |
| Uniform | Text string from TitleAlternate/Title when TitleType = "Uniform" concatenated with Title/Alternate/OtherInformation |
| Type | Value from: ResourceInfor/TypeOfResource |
| Issuance | Value from: ResourceInfo/Issuance |

The Lane file has all the data elements of the NLM file with an additional five elements taken from the 149 field.

Lane data elements

| | |
|---|---|
| ID | Numeric value from: 035 ^9 |
| TitleNF | Value 0–9 from: 245 2nd ind |
| Title | Text string concatenation of: 245 ^anpqk in order they appear in field. |
| Date1 | Date, usually in form yyyy, from: 008 bytes 07–10 |
| Date2 | Date, usually in form yyyy, from: 008 bytes 11–14 |
| Edition | Text string, consisting of first 25 characters only, from: 250 ^a |
| UniformNF | Value 0–9 from: 130 1st ind |
| Uniform | Text string concatenation of: 130 ^adfgklnpqs in the order they appear in field. |
| Type | Value from: 655 47 ^a |
| Issuance | Value from: 245 ^h |
| 149ALT | If 149 2nd ind = 9, supply value 'Manual', else leave blank. |
| 149NF | Value from: 149 ^1 |
| 149UT | Value from concatenation of: 149 ^aklnpq in the order they appear in field. |
| 149ENUM | Value from: 149 ^s |
| 149CHRON | Value from: 149 ^d |

## Data analysis

As an initial assessment, the baseline percent ambiguity for all three data sets was calculated by dividing the number of non-unique titles by the total title count and expressing the results as percentages. Then the data from the NLM Catalog and the Lane Catalog were analyzed in more depth by appending chronology and enumeration data elements to the original titles and recalculating the percent ambiguity. NLM chronology data came from the date1 element; enumeration data came from the edition element. For the Lane analysis, the corresponding data were taken from the 149chron and 149enum elements.

### The 149 field and Lane record import program

Lane Library has developed a record import program (RIM) that processes all incoming bibliographic records to automate many metadata management requirements. Beginning in 2008, Lane records include a RIM-generated normalized title (MARC field 149), which is supplied for all incoming or updated records and retrospectively, as a batch process whenever field 149 is revised. The 149 field continues to evolve and currently consists of two second indicator values (automatic or manual), title proper subfield equivalents (245 ^anp), qualifier for disambiguation (^q), enumeration (^s), chronology (^d from fixed field dates), form (^hk), language, except English (^3), and control number (^w). This 149 field supports study of title elements without changing the record otherwise, and may be thought of as a transitional strategy.

Figure 3 shows a section of a MARC record from the Lane Catalog that includes a basic 149 field.

Before undertaking further content analyses, a comparison of the structure of NLM's 'title' data, and Lane's 'title' and '149UT' data was needed.

NLM and Lane title structure:

NLM title = textstring concatenation of subfields abnp, etc., but not subfield c

Lane title = textstring concatenation of 245 subfield anpqk

Lane 149UT = value from concatenation of: 149 subfields aklnpq

The NLM and Lane title structure are not fully parallel. Unlike NLM Locator, the NLM Catalog version includes subtitle text in its title field, while Lane omits the subtitle since it is not part of the title proper. Nonetheless, the data merited comparison. The Lane 149UT data element was selected for comparison instead of the Lane title (245) because the title part of the content was largely identical and the experimental title element already included normalized enumeration and chronology values.

```
000 01742cam a22003491a 450
001 127364
005 20150817090801.0
008 980209m18861888enka 00| 0 eng d
035 __ |9 L127364
035 __ |a (OCoLC)14805157
035 __ |a 127364
040 __ |d UPRA
100 1_ |a Gowers, W. R. |q (William Richard), |d 1845-1915. |0 Z22513
149 _8 |1 A |a Manual of diseases of the nervous system |d 1886-1888 |h [print] |w L127364
245 12 |a A Manual of diseases of the nervous system |h [print] / |c by W.R. Gowers.
260 __ |a London : |b J. & A. Churchill, |c 1886-1888.
300 __ |a 2 volumes (xv, 463 ; viii, 975 pages) : |b illustrations ; |c 25 cm
500 __ |a V. 1 is published in Philadelphia by P. Blakeston Son & Co., 1886.
505 0_ |a v.1. Diseases of the spinal cord and nerves. -- v. 2. Diseases of the brain and cranial nerves; general and functional diseases of the
        nervous system.
510 4_ |a Garrison & Morton (5th ed.) |c 4751 and 4569.
650 12 |a Nervous System Diseases |0 Z7109
```

**Figure 3.** MARC record with 149 field.

## Subtotal process

The first objective was to generate a breakdown of the quantity of titles (title count) by number of repetitions (times found) by title alone for both sets of catalog data. For example, a title count = 4, with times found = 12, means there were 4 different titles, each of which occurred 12 times in the data set.

Excel's Subtotal function supported obtaining a more granular view of the ambiguity. The process required two steps:

1) Find the Count associated with each group of duplicated titles:
   a. Copy the entire title column into a new spreadsheet (to reduce file size and speed up the subtotal calculations)
   b. Sort by title ascending
   c. Run the subtotal function on the title data. This groups the data by number of times found and produces a summary count row at the end of each group. The data displayed may be expanded to show all the titles in each group or collapsed to display only the summary count rows.
2) Find the Count associated with each set of duplicated times found:
   a. Copy the collapsed summary count list into a plain text file to strip out all the embedded content
   b. Reopen the text file from within Excel
   c. Sort by 'timesfound' ascending
   d. Run the subtotal function on the timesfound column.

Subtotals for both the NLM and the Lane results were calculated and assessed for patterns of ambiguity.

## Disambiguation experiments

To test the potential for reducing the amount and degree of title ambiguity, the subtotal process was repeated after appending chronology, then enumeration, and then both elements to the original title values.

## Chronology methodology

NLM Catalog chronology values came from the date1 column (PublicationFirst-Year element in the NLM Catalog DTD).

The title and date1 columns were concatenated with a vertical bar to provide visual separation.

Samiis' essentials in neurosurgery | 2008
Samiis' essentials in neurosurgery | 2014

Lane Catalog chronology values came from the 149chron column (value from field 149 subfield d, calculated based on values in MARC 008 bytes 6, 7–14).

Forensic emergency medicine | 2007
Cryopreservation and freeze-drying protocols | 2015/2015
Fractures in children | 1977/1955

## Enumeration methodology

To extract edition numbers, all titles having edition statements were captured: 12% for Lane (35,038 titles) and 14% for NLM (211,790 titles). In 2014, the experimental 149 field was expanded to include two-digit edition numbers in the range 01–99 as subfield "s." Figure 4 shows an example of a Lane MARC record with a basic edition statement. The 250 subfield a data is used to generate subfield s in the 149 field.

Four-digit numbers also occurred, e.g., "1969 edition," and were disregarded because they duplicated chronology. After the introduction of RDA cataloging rules, textual versions of edition numbers began proliferating. In response, in 2015, the Lane RIM algorithm was enhanced to handle English language words from one to twenty. The revised algorithm found that 98% of Lane's edition statements contained numbers. By running the same algorithm against the NLM edition statements, we found 89% contained numbers. The NLM result may be underestimated as that data contains textual values of numbers in many languages—not currently detected by the Lane software.

For the Lane data, the residue of edition statements for which numbers were not automatically detected were analyzed. Manual review of this remaining 2% (535 titles) revealed a few patterns:

- named editions (Academic edition, British edition, Clinician's ed.), recorded as title extensions (field 149 ^p)
- implied enumeration (rev. ed., new edition) recorded as "—", an enumeration place-holder
- language editions ignored as evident from text and language code
- outlier values needing cleanup

```
000 03098cam a2200493Ei 450
001 311349
005 20141203161013.0
008 120509s2012 stka x 001 0 eng d
020 __ |z 0702043168
020 __ |z 9780702043161
020 __ |a 0702051160 (electronic bk.)
020 __ |a 9780702051166 (electronic bk.)
035 __ |9 L311349
035 __ |a (OCoLC)797815510
035 __ |a 311349
040 __ |a E7B |b eng |e pn |c E7B |d OCLCO |d TEF |d YDXCP |d OCLCQ |d OPELS |d VAM |d OCLCF |d WAU
050 14 |a RD31 |b .P85 2012eb
060 _4 |a WO 100 |b P957 2012
149 _8 |a Principles and practice of surgery |s 06 |d 2012 |h [digital] |w L311349
245 00 |a Principles and practice of surgery |h [digital] / |c edited by O. James Garden [and others].
250 __ |a 6th ed.
260 __ |a Edinburgh : |b Churchill Livingstone Elsevier, |c 2012.
300 __ |a online resource (xi, 507 pages) : |b color illustrations
500 __ |a Includes index.
500 __ |a "A Davidson title".
505 0_ |a Metabolic response to injury, fluid and electrolyte balance and shock -- Transfusion of blood components and plasma products -- Nutritional
       support in surgical patients -- Infections and antibiotics -- Ethics, preoperative considerations, anaesthesia and analgesia -- Trauma and multiple
       injury -- Practical procedures and patient investigation -- Postoperative care and complications -- Day surgery -- The abdominal wall and hernia -
       - The acute abdomen and intestinal obstruction -- The oesophagus, stomach and duodenum -- The liver and biliary tract -- The pancreas and
       spleen -- The small and large intestine -- The anorectum -- Plastic and reconstructive surgery -- The breast -- Endocrine surgery -- Vasucla and
       endovascular surgery -- Cardiothoracic surgery -- Neurosurgery -- Transplantation surgery -- Ear, nose and throat surgery -- Orthopaedic surgery.
650 12 |a Surgical Procedures, Operative |0 Z19339
650 43 |a Surgery |0 Z72844
```

**Figure 4.** MARC record with 149 subfield s.

```
000 01474cam a22002891 450
001 118403
005 20150817090801.0
008 980209s1888 paua 00| 0 eng d
035 __ |9 L118403
035 __ |a (OCoLC)245529092
035 __ |a 118403
040 __ |a DNLM |c DNLM |d CStRLIN |d MnU-B |d UPRA
060 00 |a WL |b G723m 1888a
100 1_ |a Gowers, W. R. |q (William Richard), |d 1845-1915. |0 Z22513
149 _9 |1 A |a Manual of diseases of the nervous system. |p American edition |d 1888 |h [print] |w L118403
245 12 |a A Manual of diseases of the nervous system |h [print].
250 __ |a American ed. / |b issued under the supervision of the author, and containing all the material of the two-volume English ed., with some
        additions and revisions.
260 __ |a Philadelphia : |b Blakiston, |c 1888.
300 __ |a xx, 1,357 pages : |b illustrations ; |c 24 cm
650 12 |a Nervous System Diseases |0 Z7109
```

**Figure 5.** MARC record with manually edited 149 field.

Overall, the seemingly complex statements were readily reducible, e.g., "3rd American from the 2nd British ed.," could be resolved into a section title (American edition) and number (03), and an implied "based on" relationship to handle linking to the original 2nd British edition. Since resolution of enumeration problems had negligible effect on the overall results, we elected not to analyze the NLM data in this regard.

Figure 5 shows a Lane MARC record that requires the 149 field to be manually edited. This example has a named edition in the 250 field, so subfield p 'American edition' has been manually entered in the record as a qualifier. In such cases, the 149 second indicator is changed from the machine-generated 8 to 9. Otherwise, the manual change would be overwritten if the record were updated.

## Results

### Base ambiguity

Percent ambiguity was calculated for each data source by dividing the ambiguous count by the total titles figure. Initial calculations are summarized in Table 1.

### Recalculated ambiguity

Tables 2 and 3 summarize the effect on disambiguation of adding chronology or enumeration or both data elements to the original title data.

Appending chronology to the original title reduced ambiguity (% of Multiples) from 13.4% to 3.2% in the NLM Catalog, and from 18.7% to 2.5% in Lane Catalog.

Enumeration alone reduced ambiguity from 13.4% to 7.8% in NLM data, and from 18.7% to 10.9% in Lane data.

**Table 1.** Base ambiguity.

| Data Source | Total Title Count | Ambiguous Count | Percent Ambiguity |
|---|---|---|---|
| PubMed 2012 | 857,819 | 6,879 | 00.8% |
| NLM Catalog | 1,537,775 | 205,407 | 13.4% |
| Lane Catalog | 304,100 | 56,864 | 18.7% |
| | *2,699,694* | *269,150* | |

**Table 2.** Disambiguation summary - NLM Catalog.

|  | Original Totals | Original + Chronology | Original + Chronology + Enumeration | Original + Enumeration |
|---|---|---|---|---|
| Singles | 1,332,368 | 1,488,502 | 1,491,058 | 1,417,318 |
| Multiples | 205,407 | 49,273 | 46,717 | 120,457 |
| Grand Total | 1,537,775 | 1,537,775 | 1,537,775 | 153,775 |
| % of Singles | 86.6% | 96.8% | 97.0% | 92.2% |
| % of Multiples | 13.4% | 3.2% | 3.0% | 7.8% |

When combined with chronology, the effect of adding enumeration appears slight, reducing NLM data from 3.2% to 3.0% and Lane data from 2.5% to 2.1%.

Subtotals for the PubMed data were not calculated because they lack enumeration and share the same chronology (2012).

## Discussion

### *NLM and Lane Catalog comparison*

The analysis showed that considering title data alone, the most ambiguous NLM titles (times found > 2000) were generic titles such as "Annual Report" and "[Collection of Publications]." Lane's most ambiguous titles (times found > 50) included component series titles. Single-word disease names like "Hypertension" and "Tuberculosis" were also at the top of the list.

The greater ambiguity found in Lane's data (18.7% vs. 13.4%) may be due to using "title proper" subfields, which exclude subtitles. The NLM Catalog concatenates title subfields in the MARC to XML (extensible markup language) conversion, preventing a more precise comparison of the Lane and NLM catalogs in this regard.

Adding chronology and enumeration to titles left only 2.1% of Lane's titles needing manual attention (around 6,000 titles overall), and 3.0% (approximately 46,000 titles) of NLM's catalog. This does not seem like a small amount unless you consider that these totals represent over one hundred years of cataloging. On an annualized basis, this degree of manual disambiguation would appear manageable. As a pragmatic matter, Lane intends to revise its RIM software to compare incoming titles to the title index and append a local note "Problem: Potentially ambiguous title?" or similar when a conflict occurs.

**Table 3.** Disambiguation summary - Lane Catalog.

|  | Original Totals | Original + Named | Original + Chronology | Original + Chronology + Enumeration | Original + Enumeration |
|---|---|---|---|---|---|
| Singles | 247,236 | 247,484 | 296,597 | 297,815 | 270,837 |
| Multiples | 56,864 | 56,616 | 7,503 | 6,285 | 33,263 |
| Grand Total | 304,100 | 304,100 | 304,100 | 304,100 | 304,100 |
| % of Singles | 81.3% | 81.4% | 97.5% | 97.9% | 89.1% |
| % of Multiples | 18.7% | 18.6% | 2.5% | 2.1% | 10.9% |

## *PubMed data characteristics*

The extracted PubMed data matched what was anticipated based on the results of an online search. However, sorting the downloaded data by date revealed that 4.8% of titles lacked values in the date of publication field, and another 13% contained years other than 2012, both older and newer. Many of the blank cases had 2012 values in the MedlineDate and Year element of the PubDate, but due to time and other constraints we were unable to retrieve this additional data for a more thorough review.

PubMed's base ambiguity of less than 1% is understandable considering that PubMed is made up mostly of article records, which tend to have titles that are longer and more descriptive than book and journal titles. Closer investigation of the PubMed titles found 25% of the ambiguous titles to be generic type of publication, e.g., Editorial, and many appeared to be recurring column titles or series titles.

The Title (TI) field in PubMed contains both English language titles and translations of foreign language titles. To capture the actual title that appears on an article, and which would be cited, the Translated Title (TT) field was given preference. This revealed almost 29,000 titles that were not available in the vernacular. Omission of these cases lacking title and/or date elements netted the 850,000 PubMed titles studied, which is reasonably close to NLM's published figure—considering our exclusion of unavailable foreign language titles.

## *Normalization and other limitations*

Time constraints prevented normalization of data involving differences in punctuation, capitalization, spacing, initial articles, etc., for this initial study. A closer look at such titles revealed that differences, particularly in punctuation, raise the issue of accuracy of these results. Generally, ignoring such differences tends to skew the results toward somewhat less ambiguity than reported. One example in the Lane data illustrates the effect of trailing punctuation, ignored by library system indexing, but treated as part of the text string by Excel.

> Correspondence Consultation Department: [32 times]
> Correspondence Consultation Department / [52 times]

Taken together these 84 occurrences surpassed the otherwise most ambiguous Lane title, "[Portrait of William Harvey]", tallied at 57 occurrences. Some, but not all, punctuation issues could be easily resolved at this stage, but many were problematic and therefore were not systematically corrected. Clearly, normalization of the data prior to analysis is needed.

While the quantitative approach used revealed much about technical differences, it does not support delving into the substance of ambiguous titles, e.g., cases of two or more unrelated works with the same title. Similarly, while title length might be considered a predictor of ambiguity, it does not appear to correlate directly. The data studied included one-word titles in the high title counts, but also in the low title counts, e.g., Accutan, Adrenals, Bandaging, and the acronym ACLS. However, the overall number of words per title does appear to decrease as times found increases.

## Conclusion

Despite difficulties in comparing data from different sources, this study revealed that 13–19% of descriptive titles were not unique. Furthermore, non-unique titles could be reduced to 2–3% by appending enumerative and, especially, chronological data elements by automated means. Title/date combinations are a good starting point for eliminating title ambiguity. Appending chronology to the title reduces ambiguity to just 3% in the NLM Catalog data and to 2% in the Lane Catalog data. Enumeration, while important for identification, provides a measure of disambiguation, but its effect is minimal compared to chronology. The resulting residue of ambiguity seems manageable for catalogers, especially when considered on an annualized basis.

Beyond chronology and enumeration, there was not time to delve into the most effective means of further disambiguation. At this point, context becomes a determinant, and it is likely that form, author surnames, organization names, and language have merit. Serial title disambiguation practice may be generalizable. One area not pursued was correlation of the ambiguous results subset of this study with records that also include uniform titles, an implied indication of ambiguity. It would be interesting to analyze the subset of records containing fields 130/240 in contrast with the automated technical disambiguation described here. What percent of cases were missed versus those which were technically unambiguous, but likely substantively ambiguous?

Careful inspection of a large number of titles of scientific works revealed a range of problem areas related to title clarity, uniqueness, and stability. These aspects of titles influence the ability of users to both determine the relevance of works retrieved to their needs and to understand relationships to other potentially relevant works. Structured titles represent a promising method of succinctly presenting unambiguous bibliographic identities and relationships for user review.

## Acknowledgments

Olya Gary (graphics). Initial results of this study were presented at the Annual Meeting of the Medical Library Association in Toronto, Ontario in May 2016, as "Bibliographic Identities and Linked Data: An Investigation of Title Ambiguity in the Scientific Literature."

## Notes

1. Barbara B. Tillett, "Considerations for Authority Control in the Online Environment," *Cataloging & Classification Quarterly* 9, no. 3 (1989): 2.

2. Tom Delsey, "Authority Control in an International Context," *Cataloging & Classification Quarterly* 9, no. 3 (1989): 13.

3. Kuang-Hua Chen and Chi-Nan Hsieh, "Ambiguity Resolution for Author Names of Bibliographic Data," *Journal of Educational Media & Library Science* 49, no. 2 (2011): 215–240, http://joemls.dils.tku.edu.tw/fulltext/49/49-2/215-240.pdf.

4. Anderson A. Ferreira, Marcos André Gonçalves, and Alberto H. F. Laender, "Disambiguating Author Names Using Minimum Bibliographic Information," *World Digital Libraries* 7, no. 1 (2014): 71–84, doi: 10.3233/WDL-120115.

5. Yanan Qian et al., "Dynamic Author Name Disambiguation for Growing Digital Libraries," *Information Retrieval Journal* 18, no. 5 (2015):379–412, doi: 10.1007/s10791-015-9261-3.

6. Jane Sandberg and Qiang Jin, "How Should Catalogers Provide Authority Control for Journal Article Authors? Name Identifiers in the Linked Data World," *Cataloging & Classification Quarterly* 54, no. 8 (2016): 537–552, doi: 10.1080/01639374.2016.1238429.

7. Requiring ORCID in Publication Workflows: Open Letter, Accessed May 12, 2017, https://orcid.org/content/requiring-orcid-publication-workflows-open-letter

8. W. Patrick Leonard, "The Card Catalog Mentality or We Have Always Done It This Way," *The Journal of Academic Librarianship* 6, no. 1 (1980): 38.

9. R. Conrad Winke, "Discarding the Main Entry in an Online Cataloging Environment," *Cataloging & Classification Quarterly* 16, no. 1 (1993): 69.

10. Lynne C. Howarth and Jean Weihs, "Enigma Variations: Parsing the Riddle of Main Entry and the "Rule of Three" from AACR2 to RDA," *Cataloging & Classification Quarterly* 46, no. 2 (2008): 204–205, doi: 10.1080/01639370802177620.

11. Snunith Snoham and Susan S. Lazinger, "The Non-main-entry Principle and the Automated Catalog," *Cataloging & Classification Quarterly* 12, nos. 3/4 (1991): 64.

12. Allyson Carlyle, Sara Ranger, and Joel Summerlin, "Making the Pieces Fit: Little Women, Works, and the Pursuit of Quality," *Cataloging & Classification Quarterly* 46, no. 1 (2008): 35, doi: 10.1080/01639370802182992.

13. Sherry L. Vellucci, "Uniform Titles as Linking Devices," *Cataloging & Classification Quarterly* 12, no. 1 (1990): 57.

14. American Psychological Association, *Publication Manual of the American Psychological Association* (Washington, D.C.: American Psychological Association, 2009), 23.

15. Adrian Letchford, Helen Susannah Moat, and Tobias Pries, "The Advantage of Short Paper Titles," *Royal Society Open Science* 2 (2015): 1, doi: 10.1098/rsos.150266.

16. Robert M. Hallock and Kari M. Dillner, "Comment: Should Title Lengths Really Adhere to the American Psychological Association's Twelve Word Limit?" *American Psychologist* 71, no. 3 (2016): 241, doi: 10.1037/a0040226.

17. Dick R. Miller and Kevin S. Clarke, *Putting XML to Work in the Library: Tools for Improving Access and Management* (Chicago: American Library Association, 2004), 117–120.

18. Richard P. Smiraglia, "Authority Control of Works: Cataloging's Chimera?," *Cataloging & Classification Quarterly* 38, nos. 3/4 (2004): 293, doi: 10.1300/J104v38n03_22.

19. RDA Toolkit, Accessed March 1, 2017. http://access.rdatoolkit.org/

20. Jean Weihs and Lynne C. Howarth, "Uniform Titles from AACR to RDA," *Cataloging & Classification Quarterly* 46, no. 4 (2008): 380, doi: 10.1080/01639370802322853.

21. Document Type Definitions (DTDs) for NLM Databases, Accessed January 23, 2016. https://www.nlm.nih.gov/databases/dtd/

# Transforming the CIP Data Block: Assessing User Needs to Re-envision a Venerable Library Icon

Karl Debus-López, Marilyn McCroskey, Regina Romano Reynolds, Caroline Saccucci, Camilla Williams, and Michele Zwierski

**ABSTRACT**

Between 2013 and 2015, the Library of Congress and experts from school, public, and academic library communities revised the 42-year-old Cataloging in Publication (CIP) data block (back-of-title-page cataloging data). This article describes the assessments, including development and analysis of two surveys, used in this data-driven process. The revised data block replaces the catalog card layout with a labeled layout that identifies components within the block, merges print and electronic information, and provides additional descriptive and subject access points. A 2017 follow-up assessment confirmed the project's success in meeting the needs of its principal users, those in school and public libraries.

## Introduction

Changing the content and appearance of the iconic Library of Congress CIP data block, the text block of cataloging information that often appears on the back of book title pages, was not a project to be undertaken lightly. Headed by the legend, "Library of Congress Cataloging-in-Publication Data," this symbol of work done at the Library of Congress had appeared virtually unchanged on almost two million books since the inception of the CIP program in 1971. The project called for careful assessment of the status quo, thoughtful deliberation about potential changes, and follow-up assessment of results. This article takes an historical and chronological approach to the story of how the CIP Data Block Committee, a group of LC and external librarians charged with the revision project, assessed and revised this library icon.

The CIP Program provides pre-publication metadata to the nation's libraries for cataloging and other information purposes. The CIP cataloging process results in two products, both based on prepublication submissions by the publisher usually consisting of a galley of the forthcoming book and prepublication metadata. Catalogers first create the prepublication electronic bibliographic record from which the CIP data block is then programmatically derived and provided to the publisher for display in the published book. The data block revision project focused only on determining which data elements from the MARC record should be displayed in the data block and the best layout for display of these elements.

Between 1971 and 2012, the CIP data block underwent only minor changes. By 2013, in response to rapid developments in the bibliographic environment, Library of Congress management determined that it was necessary to conduct a thorough review of the data elements and the layout of the CIP data block to determine whether it should be changed, and if so, how. In 2014, the CIP Data Block Committee surveyed librarians and other data block stakeholders to learn about their use of the existing data block and sought their input about potential new elements and layouts. After an exhaustive analysis of the results of the survey, the committee and Library of Congress staff developed and implemented a completely redesigned data block. The new data block was crafted to better meet the needs of its users, especially school and public libraries, a sector that the 2014 survey had confirmed as continuing to rely on the data block. The new CIP data block includes additional descriptive elements and data from additional subject thesauri and classifications; combines information about both the print and electronic versions of a title; and uses a labeled layout that no longer resembles a catalog card. In 2017, a follow-up survey confirmed the success of the revised data block.

This article presents a detailed overview of the assessment process, including development and analysis of two surveys and a follow-up assessment of the data-driven changes made to the data block. The article also includes a literature review, and sections on the history of the CIP data block, problems encountered and lessons learned, how this research might be valuable to others, and suggestions for future research.

## Literature review

Robert R. Newlen provides a brief history of the CIP program in his 1991 article celebrating the twentieth anniversary of the program. After an initial year-long experiment in 1958 called Cataloging in Source, the CIP program officially began on July 1, 1971. Newlen states, "Twenty years later, and now part of LC's operating budget, the CIP program has processed more than half a million titles."[1] In 2000, the LC CIP Program launched the ECIP (Electronic Cataloging in Publication) program to create CIP data more efficiently. This program uses an electronic workflow to streamline the cataloging process and additional non-LC cataloging partners now contribute. In the article, "The Electronic Cataloging in Publication Program: A Model for Cooperative Cataloging for the Twenty-First Century," Karl E. Debus-López concludes that the ECIP program "represents a true partnership between publishers, libraries of all types, and the Library of Congress." He highlights the value of the program as "faster and better metadata processing to the benefit of the national and international library communities."[2]

The CIP data block itself has multiple uses and benefits. Joanna Fountain points out that "because the CIP data are printed in the book, anyone holding it can refer to them." She adds, "Students, bookstore browsers, or parents at home can look at the CIP data and find useful information…. It is not necessary to consult a library catalog…."[3] In a history of LC's Cataloging Distribution Service, Paul Edlund surmises that the convenient location of the CIP data block perhaps evolved from publishers printing the LCCN (Library of Congress Card Number) on the verso of title pages.[4]

Library science textbooks use examples of the CIP data block to introduce cataloging and classification concepts. In *Introduction to Cataloging and Classification,* authors Joudrey, Taylor, and Miller relate: "Some libraries use the CIP records for preliminary cataloging. Other libraries may use the brief CIP record instead of full cataloging."[5] Jean Weihs and Sheila Intner include instructions on using the CIP data block for copy cataloging in the textbook, *Beginning Cataloging.*[6] The literature also presents concerns about the incompleteness and inaccuracy of CIP data. In *Fundamentals of Technical Services,* John Sandstron and Liz Miller recommend checking the accuracy of CIP data against the resource and advise that "you will probably need to add some information … because typically this information wasn't available when the CIP record was created."[7] Jean Weihs cautions that "a cataloguer should not assume LC or LAC [Library and Archives Canada] knows best."[8] Author Mary Mortimer in *Learn Descriptive Cataloging* adds, "However it [the CIP data] is still valuable, especially if no other records are readily available."[9] In spite of these concerns, which are the inevitable result of working with pre-publication data, the CIP data block remains an authoritative source for descriptive cataloging, subject analysis and classification. Kevin Cretsos from the University of Dayton Libraries blogs, "As you can see, the CIP data block gives you a quick and condensed version of the catalog record and this can be useful for libraries with limited cataloging expertise."[10] By 2013, the time seemed right for what Debus-López called "a radical transformation" in the article, "Introducing the New CIP Data Block," which describes the new data block and summarizes its genesis and development.[11]

## Development of the CIP data block, 1971–2013

From the very beginning, the CIP Program created full-level pre-publication metadata, using the current descriptive cataloging code and subject analysis guidelines. Most of the bibliographic elements that appeared on a catalog card appeared in the CIP data block. CIP data blocks always included titles proper, other title information, statements of responsibility, edition statements, and series information. Library of Congress Subject Headings (LCSH) and/or LC juvenile subject headings,

Library of Congress Classification (LCC), and Dewey Decimal Classification (DDC) also appeared in each CIP data block, as did the International Standard Book Number (ISBN). CIP data blocks have also always included LCCN (Library of Congress Control Number, formerly the Library of Congress Card Number used for ordering card sets). However, the place and name of the publisher, the date of publication, and the price were all omitted. The "p. cm." found in the physical description area of the data block was a placeholder for the pagination and size that the Library of Congress would later add to the MARC record after receiving the published book.

Whenever the CIP Program considered changes to the CIP data block, it turned to its customers, primarily libraries but also publishers and vendors, to provide feedback by means of surveys and discussions at CIP Advisory Group (CAG) meetings at American Library Association (ALA) conferences. For instance, addition of the Dewey edition number, beginning with DDC 19, and notation that designated cataloging according to *Anglo-American Cataloguing Rules,* 2nd edition (AACR2) resulted from a CAG proposal at ALA Midwinter 1981.[12] At ALA Annual 1982, CAG proposed adding a qualifier to the ISBN for alkaline (acid-free) paper, based on concerns expressed by the Z39.Subcommittee S: Paper Audits for Library Books.[13] The CIP data block has included the qualifier "(alk. paper)" in CIP MARC records and the CIP data block ever since. At ALA Annual 1984, CAG members gave a lukewarm response to adding publisher-supplied summaries for adult books because the text would take up extra space on the data block and catalog cards.[14]

By 1985, LC's CIP data block was well established and the CIP Program helped to shape the final report of the International Federation of Library Associations and Institutions (IFLA) Working Group on a Standardized Format for the CIP Record in the Book. The list agreed upon by the IFLA Working Group (see Appendix A) included mandatory elements (title proper, added entries) and elements required if available/applicable (parallel title, series, ISBN, main entry, subject headings, and classification numbers). The IFLA recommendations created a flexible policy that allowed each CIP agency to establish local practice appropriate to the situation and in accordance with publisher needs.[15] CIP customers in the U.S. clearly agreed with the principles set out in the IFLA guidelines. The CIP data block included almost all of the optional elements, with the exception of the place and name of the publisher and/or distributor, the date of publication, the terms of availability and price, the key title of a series or subseries, and the government document number. The IFLA Working Group did not address the layout of the CIP data block.

From the earliest days of the CIP Program, LC believed the card image format was the appropriate way to provide the bibliographic data on the title page verso. This layout replicated the format of the catalog card originally printed for the Library of Congress card catalog, a *de facto* standard for all

Library of Congress Cataloging-in-Publication Data

Aretha, David.
    Foul ball frame-up at Wrigley Field / David Aretha.
       pages cm. -- (The Baseball Geeks adventures ; book 2)
    Summary: When eleven-year-old Omar is unfairly blamed by the media for a Chicago Cubs loss at home, his fellow Baseball
Geeks try to clear his name.
    ISBN 978-1-62285-123-2
    1. Wrigley Field (Chicago, Ill.)--Juvenile fiction. 2. Chicago Cubs (Baseball team)--Juvenile fiction. [1. Wrigley Field
(Chicago, Ill.)--Fiction. 2. Chicago Cubs (Baseball team)--Fiction. 3. Baseball--Fiction. 4. Blame--Fiction.] I. Title.
    PZ7.A6845Fo 2014
    [Fic]--dc23
                                      2012049039

**Figure 1.** The CIP data block 1971–2015.

card catalogs. See Figure 1 for an example of the original layout of the CIP data block.

The CIP Program provided very strict specifications for how publishers should print this information. Although these instructions were intended to ensure that the card image format was replicated,[16] nothing has prevented publishers from altering this layout in their published books, because this information is sent via e-mail as pre-formatted text, not as an image. There are many examples of CIP data blocks with centered justification or displayed, for instance, as swirling images, depending on the design of the copyright page. Results of a 2006 survey by the CIP Review Group (CRG) indicated that although the card image format seemed outdated in the era of online catalogs, the card layout and International Standard Bibliographic Description (ISBD) punctuation identified cataloging information and helped users correctly interpret the CIP data without the addition of "cumbersome labels." Unable to identify a more "efficient" format, the CRG recommended that the card layout be reviewed in the future.[17]

Requests for enhancements to the CIP data block in the ensuing years included some interest in broad genre headings (e.g., science fiction, western, detective/ mystery) for works of American fiction, accurate display of diacritics,[18] and a suggestion in 2003 to explore using ONIX data in the CIP process.[19] Although BISAC headings, which were one of the added value elements in the ONIX data, could not be displayed at that time in the CIP data block,[20] in 2009 the Library began using an "ONIX to MARC converter" to maximize use of descriptive metadata included within ONIX.

In 2012, the CIP E-books Program began to create metadata for e-books that are simultaneously published with print books. The program issued separate CIP data blocks for the print and e-book versions. The CIP data block for e-books had a few elements specific to the e-version: a "general materials designation" (GMD) [electronic resource], the note, "Description based on print version record and CIP data provided by publisher; resource not viewed," and the physical description, "1 online resource."[21] When the Library of Congress decided to stop using the GMD in MARC records, this element was removed from the CIP data block.

By 2013, this venerable icon was showing signs of age, most notably in its use of a catalog card layout when generations of students had never even seen a catalog card; its inability to completely accommodate changes brought about by RDA; and the challenge of adapting to the simultaneous publication of books in print and e-formats. The stage was set for some potential rejuvenation.

## 2013–2015 CIP data block assessment

### Formation and charge of the CIP Data Block Committee

The development of the new CIP data block had its roots in changes to the data block to accommodate the new cataloging standard, *Resource Description and Access* (RDA), that were proposed at the CAG meeting at ALA Annual 2013. The primary recommendations presented at CAG were to (1) add relationship designators to all name access points, (2) add the copyright date from the galley in brackets instead of including a separate copyright date, and (3) record all ISBNs available in the galley. CAG also proposed a change not related to the implementation of RDA: removal of the physical description field, (p. cm.) which occupied one full line of the data block. CAG members also suggested addition of a Quick Response Code (QR code) to allow for scanning and direct input of the MARC version of the data block into library systems.[22] Based on the CAG discussion, LC CIP managers agreed that it was time to conduct a review of the data elements and layout of the CIP data block.

In August 2013, CIP program management sought volunteers to form a committee to review the CIP data block. The newly formed CIP Data Block Committee represented school, public, and academic library communities, and began meeting in September 2013. LC members included the division chief with managerial oversight of the CIP Program who served as the chair, the CIP Program Manager, the CIP Program Specialist, a computer automation specialist, and the head of the U.S. ISSN Center, which resides in the same division as the CIP Program.[23] Since the committee believed that the assessment should focus on the needs and concerns of librarians, publishers were not represented. The committee developed its own charge: "… to possibly redesign the CIP data block. The committee will be looking at the CIP data block line by line to determine if lines should be added or removed, or the addition of other elements such as QR codes. At the end of this process, the committee will have two to three mock-ups of the CIP data block to share with various constituents."[24]

### Assessment methodology

The committee first determined the scope of their assessment. A reasonable question, given the online availability of the LC online catalog where full MARC records for all CIP titles would be found, was whether the data block currently had enough value to warrant its continued presence in books. Leaders of the school library community, the principal user community for the data block, affirmed unanimously that school librarians were still heavily reliant on the data block as a source of cataloging. The committee therefore agreed that the assessment would not be a referendum on the data block's continued existence. Instead, the outcome would determine how to modify the data block to best serve its existing users.

Also out of the scope for further consideration, despite the committee charge of "line by line review," were certain elements deemed "core" to the data block. Without the following elements, the data block would not include enough information to create a basic bibliographic record: Library of Congress Control Number (LCCN), International Standard Book Number (ISBN), Library of Congress Call Number, Dewey Decimal Classification Number, Authorized Access Point (formerly called Main Entry), Title Statement, Edition Statement, and Library of Congress Subject Headings. A summary (for juvenile and young adult literature) was also included to support the work of the Children's and Young Adults' Cataloging (CYAC) Program at the Library of Congress.

The committee took multiple approaches to obtaining input. They obtained informal information from experts in the field and daily users of the CIP data block. The CIP Data Block Committee representative from the school library community sought input from time to time from a small subset of school library leaders. The ISSN Network was queried to learn how other national libraries presented CIP data. The committee asked Library of Congress catalogers in the foreign acquiring divisions to share examples of CIP data they used for cataloging non-U.S. books. Other expert groups such as the Library of Congress Acquisitions and Bibliographic Access Management Team, the Library's Policy and Standards Division, and The Joint Steering Committee for the Development of RDA (now the RDA Steering Committee) provided input. The CIP Data Block Committee also wanted input from front-line librarians, technicians, volunteers, and others who use the data block on a daily basis to create bibliographic records. Since the CIP Program had successfully used surveys in the past to assess the impact of services provided to libraries and publishers, the committee agreed that the principal tool for the assessment would be an online survey.

### Development of the 2014 CIP data block survey

Since it was available at the Library of Congress, widely known, and had the ability to perform cross-sectional analyses, SurveyMonkey was chosen as the tool to create the survey. The survey was designed to provide data that could be analyzed from both quantitative and qualitative perspectives. For most questions asked, participants could add comments. The committee anticipated that comments would be just as important as the quantitative data. The main topics for revision of the data block on which the survey sought input were: elements beyond the core that could be added, deleted, or changed, including author affiliations within the title statement; the addition of selective new classifications, genre/form terms, and subject thesauri; the catalog card layout vs. a labeled layout; and combining information about print and e-book versions into one data block.

The resulting survey included 11 questions on the type of library and systems environment in which the respondent worked; 11 questions on use of the data block for cataloging purposes; 21 questions on the removal or addition of data block elements; and 6 questions on the data block layout. The committee released an initial draft survey to a select group of testers at the Library of Congress and the ECIP cataloging partners. Once the committee believed that the survey instrument was sound, on May 1, 2014, it was sent to 13 electronic mailing lists that would reach the broadest range of libraries that use the data block for cataloging purposes.[25] The participants were asked to complete the survey by June 1, 2014.

### Survey results

A total of 420 individuals answered the survey. This constitutes a convenience sample, as the e-mail lists receiving the survey had a high percentage of catalogers and technicians who were likely to use the data block. While the response was not a true representative sample, the committee felt that the large number of responses could be considered indicative of the opinions about the data block held by the library community. Respondents could choose more than one type of library, resulting in 523 responses concerning the type of library represented. While most responses constituted the sole answer from a particular institution, in some cases several individuals answered from larger institutions. Accordingly, this summary of the survey results refers to "respondents" from a type of library as opposed to the library type itself, since there is not a one-to-one correspondence between a response and a library type.

As expected, the largest number of respondents, 235 (45%), came from school libraries, key users of CIP data. Along with public library respondents, 53 (10%), a group that was also identified as reliant on CIP data, the two groups represented 55% of all respondents. There were 117 (22%) college/university respondents. The rest of the responses came from the following groups: hospital/medical libraries, 27 (5%); corporate/military/prison/church/law libraries, 26 (5%); government libraries, 22 (4%); national libraries, 17 (3%); non-U.S. libraries, 15 (3%); and vendors, 11 (2%). Fifty-one percent of the participants came from libraries with collections of fewer than 25,000 volumes. Seventy percent worked in libraries with fewer than 100,000 volumes. Forty-three percent indicated that they cataloged fewer than 500 titles per year. Fifty-two percent of the survey participants worked in libraries where they were the only cataloger. Eighty-two percent worked in libraries with five or fewer cataloging staff. The survey also addressed the use of print vs. online catalogs: 91% of the respondents said that they used an integrated library system. Only six said that they continued to use a print card catalog and only one said that they did not have access to the Internet. The survey results indicated that the library participants represented users of most interest to this assessment: librarians or other individuals who performed cataloging in smaller library settings, most likely with more limited resources than a larger research library and most likely heavily reliant on the CIP data block. A majority were from school or public libraries.

### *CIP data block usage*

Fifty-six percent of CIP survey participants indicated that they do not use the CIP data block as a primary source of cataloging, and 54% said that they do not transcribe the complete CIP data block to create their bibliographic records. However, when asked whether they "referred" to the CIP data block, 96% of the respondents said that they did—either frequently (53%) or sometimes (43%). Similarly, when asked if they transcribe parts of the CIP data block, 81% said that they did. The most commonly transcribed parts of the CIP data block were: ISBN (61%); series statement (56%); Dewey classification number (56%); title and statements of responsibility (52%); Library of Congress Subject Headings (51%); and name headings (50%).

Responses from school library survey participants clearly demonstrate their continued strong reliance on the CIP data block. The majority indicated that they used the CIP data block as a primary source of cataloging (63%) and that they transcribed the complete CIP data block to create their bibliographic records (72%). Participants who worked in public libraries also clearly relied on the CIP data block; 58% used it as a primary cataloging source, and 55% "sometimes" manually transcribed the CIP data block. In contrast, college and university libraries overwhelmingly reported they did not use the CIP data block as a primary source of cataloging (83%) and that they did not manually transcribe the complete data block when creating bibliographic records (73%).

The responses to this section of the survey validated that the CIP data block remains an essential tool for most school librarians as they perform their cataloging, a fact which strongly influenced the changes in the CIP data block that the committee ultimately made. Other user groups indicated that they still valued and used the CIP data block, but were more likely to use it to verify cataloging data and as a source for additional information to include within bibliographic records, rather than as their primary cataloging source.

### *CIP data block: Survey results and recommendations*

The bulk of the survey asked questions about potential changes to the data block in order to provide the CIP Data Block Committee with a broad sense of how changes under consideration would be viewed across the range of data block stakeholders. The committee subjected the survey results to in-depth analysis, including assessing results by community, by element, and by topic. All free-text comments were taken into account. Additionally, over the course of the almost two years following the survey, the committee sought further input from various experts and communities, deliberated extensively about data block elements, investigated options for layouts, and experimented with various versions of a new data block. After careful consideration of the survey results and the comments from the various library communities, the committee recommended changes to the CIP data block that best met user needs and provided the greatest practicable enhancements.

## Data block elements

In order to learn of additional data elements that could be included in the revised data block, the survey asked which "Non-CIP data block elements" respondents added to their bibliographic records. Results indicated: publishing information (53%); pagination and size (53%); summary (44%); form/genre terms (33%); additional LC subject headings (30%); local subject headings (29%); Sears subject headings (27%); audience level (25%); table of contents (18%); and BISAC headings (2%).

Based on the committee's assessment of the survey data, plus the committee's additional input and deliberations, the committee added the following elements to the data block: publication data; genre/form terms; all but one relationship designator; and BISAC headings. Eighty-eight percent of the respondents endorsed addition of publisher name and place, and 61% endorsed addition of the projected publication date. These elements assist catalogers by providing a nearly complete bibliographic record for their use. Participants supported the inclusion of genre/form terms by a solid 78%. As LC and other U.S. libraries are developing more genre/form terminology sets, inclusion of these terms complements the subject access already present in the data block. Seventy-six percent of the respondents indicated that they wanted relationship designators included within the CIP data block, with a preference for the following: editor (82%); illustrator (81%); author (79%); translator (73%); photographer (62%); compiler (52%); sponsoring body (37%); issuing body (36%); cartographer (33%); abridger (32%); enacting jurisdiction (14%); and honoree (14%). The committee approved including relationship designators, with the exception of "sponsoring body" because its use is generally limited to records for serials.

There was less agreement from respondents as to whether BISAC access points should be included, with 54% of school librarians indicating that the headings should be included but broad rejection (73% against) of including BISAC codes. After considerable discussion, the committee decided to include BISAC headings but not the codes, realizing that some school and public libraries organize their collections by BISAC headings, and because these headings are generally included with ONIX data supplied by some publishers. After the Government Publishing Office (GPO) joined the ECIP Cataloging Partnership Program in 2014, the committee agreed to add the Superintendent of Documents (SUDOC) number to the data block.

Respondents endorsed the following existing elements for continued inclusion: series information (94%); language note (89%); audience note (84%); preferred (uniform) title–primary access point (80%); preferred (uniform) title–foreign title (80%); preferred (uniform) title–commonly known title (79%); bibliographical references note (76%); general note –"includes index" (75%); general note (67%); and preferred (uniform) title–collective title (67%). Following additional input and discussions, the data block committee agreed to keep all but one of these elements: preferred (uniform) title—collective title, and to remove the two elements that participants generally did not feel were helpful: the physical description field (p. cm.) which 77% did not feel was needed, and author affiliations which 61% wanted removed even though they had been included in accordance with RDA. These affiliations added little useful information, took up space, and interrupted the flow of author names.

The decision to not include the "preferred (uniform) title – collective title" is one of the cases where the committee decided to go against the preferences of the survey participants. Sixty-nine percent of the respondents wanted the "preferred (uniform) title—collective title" to remain in the data block. This came as a surprise, as committee members had heard complaints from librarians about this data element. Such titles are common, particularly for literary works (e.g. "Poems. Selections"), but do not provide much additional information, so the committee removed them from the data block.

The committee took survey results into account as they reviewed all note elements. Survey respondents preferred retaining the note, "Includes index," but the committee decided to omit it to ensure a compact data block. However, they decided to retain notes indicating the presence of bibliographical references as important to researchers. The committee also decided that contents notes would be included only for multi-part sets and re-affirmed that summaries would be included only for juvenile and young adult literature. Moreover, the committee agreed that audience notes by age and grade would be included if provided by the publisher. These notes would include a legend indicating that the information came from the publisher.

### CIP data block layout

Early in the assessment process, the committee agreed to explore possible new data block layouts. Responses from national libraries queried by their ISSN center generally indicated that CIP data was presented either in a catalog card layout or via a statement that bibliographic data was available in the national library catalog. Such statements sometimes included a unique identifier by which data could be found. The committee was intrigued by the labeled layout used by the National Library of Iran but wondered whether such a departure from the traditional catalog card layout would be confusing for those libraries keying data into their local input system.[26] Accordingly, the CIP Data Block Committee queried a small set of school librarians and the results indicated that input systems used most by school librarians had labeled input screens which could be at least somewhat aligned with a labeled data block layout. The committee therefore decided to include in the survey a proposed layout that used labels for broad areas further subdivided by vertical bars (the "pipe" character) to distinguish information contained within each area. The initial labels proposed were "Names," "Description," "Identifiers," "Subjects," and "Classification."

To further determine whether a catalog card or labeled layout would be more suitable for users of the data block, several questions in the "Demographics" section of the survey asked about library systems used for cataloging. Fifty-eight percent of respondents worked with input systems that used both MARC and labeled input screens; 39% used MARC screens; and 10% percent used only labels. These answers indicated that the cataloging environment in most libraries would support a labeled layout. The survey presented two draft layout examples for the same title: one using the traditional layout and the other using a labeled layout. The survey participants were asked: "Considering how cataloging data may be created in the future with new cataloging rules and new data display and transmission formats, please provide comments about each of the 2 examples above." A subsequent question asked "Do you have any other ideas for possible changes to the CIP data block layout?"

Of the 316 comments received, 54% preferred the labeled layout, 27% preferred the print card catalog layout, and 19% indicated no preference. Many of the positive comments indicated a need to move away from the card catalog layout and implement a new look. Others said the labeled layout was clearer and easier to read: "I like the labeled layout better because it looks more visually pleasing and easier to discern the information"; "Easier to read with the additional spaces"; "Has a modern look and the style may adapt to changing technology overall"; and "The labeled layout is more concise and organized thereby making it easier to locate the information I need faster." Some comments were less positive, "Too spread out: readability studies will show that less will be read in this case. Too many labels and labels are too technical." Others did not like the label "Description." One person wrote, "Description is not going to mean 'title' to the general public. That's confusing. Otherwise, okay." Several of the participants who preferred the catalog card layout mentioned that they learned cataloging before online systems were in use and they considered themselves "old school." One person noted: "I am old (ish) I started when I was actually typing up catalog cards so it makes sense to me. I can see how newer catalogers who have never had the privilege would not understand the reason for the old format. Do what is best for YOU! We can adapt."

Since there was a preference for a labeled layout and since most input systems used by schools generally include a labeled input screen, the committee adopted a labeled layout for the new CIP data block. Based on the comments from the survey participants, the number of labels was increased from five to seven, with "Titles" and "Other Titles" being separated from "Description." Data elements would be categorized into seven over-arching areas in the data block: Names, Titles, Other Titles, Description, Identifiers, Subjects, and Classification.

Not as many survey participants responded to the question asking for additional ideas for the data block, although several answers were quite useful. For example: "Perhaps using the labeled layout, but instead of using the label 'Description,' use the label 'Title' for the title, and have a separate section for 'Description' which would include notes, etc."; "Add a barcode for access to the data, instead of (or in addition to) a camera-readable graphic. Librarians should not have to invest in new technology in order to see and/or download the data; most already have bar-code readers."; "For classification labels, use 'Library of Congress' and 'Dewey.'"; "A publishing section that clearly states the publisher, place of publication, date of publication and copyright date."; and, "If the labels (Names, Description, etc.) were bolded it certainly helps the cataloging content and information about the book to be easily discernable."

Where possible, the committee made revisions to the layout based on survey comments. To address concerns that classifications and thesaurus terms were differentiated only by use of the vertical pipe bar, the committee agreed that the appropriate acronym and colon would appear before the classification number or subject heading. To further identify the inclusion of series information and summaries within the Description area, the committee included additional labels, "Series," and "Summary," to precede this critical information.

### Combined data block for print and online, QR codes

A business need of the CIP Program was to eliminate the confusion and errors made by publishers who received separate data blocks for print and e-book versions. An example of a CIP data block that displayed information on both versions was included in the survey, and the participants were asked, "Do you think this is an acceptable method for providing CIP data for a title to the publisher in one block that can be printed in the book as well as included in the e-book?" Eighty-five percent of the responses were positive, with one writing, "Only one CIP data block should be acceptable for both formats. Combined CIP data blocks could emphasize/advertise the fact that there are two formats available for that title." Another wrote, "Yes, one CIP with both forms of info is enough. We can figure it out." An additional comment in support of the merger was: "I don't see a reason to have separate records when most of the data is the same." Others were not as supportive of the combined data block; "We are still figuring out how to display our e-book records, so not sure on this." Nonetheless the committee became convinced that librarians and other users of the CIP data block would benefit from having complete information on all formats of the title in one data block that included the LCCNs and the LC Classifications for both the print and electronic titles. Accordingly, after extensive experimentation with how to present all needed information, the committee adopted a combined layout.

To reduce the time data block users might spend manually keying CIP data into their catalogs, respondents were asked whether they were interested in a QR code that could access encoded CIP data or link to the Library of Congress bibliographic record. Sixty-seven percent preferred encoded CIP data. Seventy percent preferred a link to the LC record. The committee wanted to incorporate a QR code linked to the LC record and spent several months working to make this succeed. Unfortunately, technical difficulties prevented the addition of a QR code. Coded data is still a goal as discussed below under "Areas for Future Research." However, the committee decided to include an LCCN Permalink for each title to allow users to retrieve a complete bibliographic record in electronic format from the LC Permalink database. The database record can also be downloaded to a local library catalog, reducing keying and errors.

### Options not incorporated within the final CIP data block

There were a number of suggestions that were not approved by the data block committee, mainly for practical reasons. Several survey participants and Gordon Dunsire on behalf of the Joint Steering Committee (JSC) on the Development of RDA noted that the information in the new data block was "dense." They recommended highlighting the labels while others recommended making the vertical pipe bar thicker. Neither was possible because of technical limitations in the program used to output information to the publisher. In addition to participant comments about the label, "Description," the JSC thought that publication information should have its own heading.[27] The committee decided that adding another section would increase the length of the data block unacceptably.

The Committee agreed in principle with the chair of the ALA Subject Access Committee Subcommittee on Genre/Form Implementation and the LC Policy and Standards Division that genre/form terms are not subject data. However, the committee felt that it could not justify including a separate label and line for these terms which are closely related to subject data. Many of the school librarians expressed an interest in adding Sears Subject Headings to the data block. The committee agreed that this was desirable but could not provide a programmatic way to generate Sears headings at this time. Currently, Sears Subject Headings are owned by EBSCO. OCLC Research is investigating a potential correlation tool that would map LC Subject Headings to Sears Subject Headings and make this addition potentially more feasible in the future. A member of the CIP Advisory Group requested adding the controlled vocabulary of the Book Industry Study Group (BISG) Educational Taxonomy Working Group. It was determined that the terms were too specific and not used extensively enough by librarians to warrant addition to the data block.

### *Release of the new CIP data block*

The CIP Data Block Committee agreed on final changes to the data elements and layout by July 2015. Between July and September, the CIP home page was updated with a detailed "Frequently Asked Questions" page on the new features of the CIP data block. The home page included several examples to emphasize different aspects of the new layout, and detailed diagrams that demonstrated how the various MARC fields for data elements mapped to the new labeled sections. The September 29, 2015 *LCCN* newsletter presented the reasons for the change and the process undertaken to create the new data block.[28] The Library of Congress CIP Program developed a plan to educate catalogers on how to use the new data block for cataloging through webinars and presentations at conferences.[29] Finally, at the end of fiscal year 2015, the CIP Program implemented a single "print + e" CIP data block, suitable for inclusion in both formats.[30]

On October 1, 2015, the Library of Congress formally implemented the new CIP data block. Publishers began receiving the CIP data in the new format. By early 2016, libraries, vendors, and bookstores were receiving newly published books with the new data block. While the CIP Data Block Committee did not have a predetermined vision of what the new layout would look like when they began the assessment process, the end result was a much richer display than initially anticipated. Additional descriptive information appears in the new layout. The layout has more subject, classification, and genre/form access than the previous data block. Complete information on the existence of both print and electronic versions of a title is available. Through the addition of clear labels and acronyms, catalogers

```
Library of Congress Cataloging-in-Publication Data

Names: Terrell, Brandon, 1978- author. | Epelbaum, Mariano, 1975-
    illustrator. | Terrell, Brandon, 1978- Snoops, Inc.
Title: Phantom of the library / by Brandon Terrell ; illustrated by Mariano
    Epelbaum.
Description: North Mankato, Minnesota : Stone Arch Books, a Capstone imprint,
    [2018] | Series: Snoops, inc. | Summary: The Ghost Grabbers (an internet
    program, and Jaden's heroes) are filming a seance at the Pendleton Public
    Library, where the recently discovered unpublished manuscripts of the late
    horror author and library founder Alistair Pendleton are on display--so
    when the lights go out, and the manuscripts disappear, Jaden (who thinks a
    ghost took them), his twin sister Hayden, and the other members of Snoops
    Inc. swing into action to solve the mystery.
Identifiers: LCCN 2017002465 (print) | LCCN 2017005200 (ebook) | ISBN
    9781496550606 (library binding) | ISBN 9781496550620 (pbk.) | ISBN
    9781496550644 (eBook PDF)
Subjects: LCSH: Public libraries--Juvenile fiction. | Theft--Juvenile
    fiction. | Video recording--Juvenile fiction. | Twins--Juvenile fiction. |
    Brothers and sisters--Juvenile fiction. | Friendship--Juvenile fiction. |
    Detective and mystery stories. | CYAC: Mystery and detective stories. |
    Libraries--Fiction. | Stealing--Fiction. | Internet television--Fiction. |
    Twins--Fiction. | Brothers and sisters--Fiction. | Friendship--Fiction. |
    GSAFD: Mystery fiction. | LCGFT: Detective and mystery fiction.
Classification: LCC PZ7.T273 Ph 2018 (print) | LCC PZ7.T273 (ebook) | DDC
    813.6 [Fic] --dc23
LC record available at https://lccn.loc.gov/2017002465
```

Figure 2. The new CIP data block. Implemented October 1, 2015.

who use the data block as they perform their work can easily determine where information should be entered on their input screens. The members of the CIP Data Block Committee believed that the new layout was a significant improvement from the previous version. Appendix B lists all of the decisions made by the Committee as to the MARC fields included or excluded within the new data block, relationship designators added, and layout changes. An example of the new CIP data block appears in Figure 2.

## Assessing the success of the new CIP data block

In January 2017, in order to assess the new CIP data block, the CIP Data Block Committee again used SurveyMonkey to distribute a new short (15-question) survey to see whether the user communities did, indeed, support the changes that had been made in the data block, and whether they found the new version valuable to their work. For this second survey, the committee invited publishers and vendors to participate, since they were now providing the new LC CIP data in their books. The new survey was posted to the same electronic mailing lists as the 2014 survey. Two hundred and sixty responses were received, including 72 (28%) from academic libraries; 65 (25%) from school libraries; 48 (18%) from public libraries; 20 (8%) from publishers; and 9 (3%) from vendors. The remainder came from other types of libraries. To ensure that those answering the survey had some knowledge of the new data block before being asked to provide more specific input, the survey asked "Are you aware that the Cataloging in Publication Data Block was changed in October 2015 to the following labeled layout?" and included an image of the new data block. Somewhat surprisingly, between 30% and 36% of respondents in each of the major groups surveyed (school libraries, public libraries, academic libraries, publishers and vendors) were not aware that the data block had changed. Reasons given were more or less evenly divided among "do not use the data block," "cataloging is done elsewhere," and "no new books yet received" that included the new data block. The survey did not ask these respondents further questions.

Questions for the remaining respondents assessed whether the changes made to the data block were successful, and where there might be a need for further improvement. Overall, the survey results were quite positive: around 85% of respondents found the new layout "useful" (34%), "rather useful" (30%), or "very useful" (21%). Even more positive were the responses from school libraries, primary users of the data block. Ninety-nine percent of school library respondents found the new layout useful (31%), rather useful (34%), or very useful (34%).

The most obvious change from the former data block consisted of replacing the catalog card layout with a labeled layout that identified groups of elements. Other key changes included providing the previously-omitted publisher name, place of publication, and publication date; including additional types of subject data such as BISAC headings, SUDOC classifications, and genre/form headings; and combining information about the print version and e-book version into a single data block. While respondents generally regarded the changes as positive, responses were also somewhat dependent on the group to which the respondent belonged and the purpose(s) for which the respondent used the data block.

One of the challenges of the data block is that it is used by different communities, and for different purposes even within the same community. For example: 91% of school libraries use the data block for cataloging, subject headings (77%) or classification (68%) whereas only 77% of academic libraries use the data block for cataloging, 25% for subject headings and 35% for classification.

### Preference for the new data block

A key question asked whether the respondent preferred the new layout over the old layout. Overall, 59% preferred the new layout, 15% preferred the old layout, and 26% did not have a preference. This result correlates with the 2014 survey where 54% of the overall comments about the proposed labeled layout were positive. In 2017, school librarians were the most positive about the new layout, with 74% preferring it, none preferring the old layout, and 26% having no preference. Even among academic librarians where 22% preferred the old layout, the majority (52%) still preferred the new layout, and 26% had no preference. The majority of public librarians as well as publishers and vendors all preferred the new layout. Some positive comments included: "I really like the new format, works great for cataloging"; "About time"; "Easier to find specific parts"; "Very easy to read: very clean organization to find useful information about the book."

However, there were holdouts regarding the card format, such that overall, in a list of elements that respondents liked and did not like, 39 mentioned liking that the new data block was no longer the card format while 30 mentioned that they did not like the fact that it was no longer the card format. Negative comments included: "Quite ugly compared to the previous one"; "I do not like the way things are scrunched together"; "Sorry, old school librarian"; "Quit tinkering with things that work well and have worked well for decades!" Some of the concerns were: "small print"; "text in the block is much harder to read—it seems jumbled"; "seems more compact, harder to read (especially the ISBNs)." Multiple comments indicated that the ISBN was more difficult to locate (it was previously one of the first few elements). These comments were surprising, given how readily the ISBN can be found on most books.

Since academic libraries mainly base their cataloging on existing MARC records, it is not surprising that some comments from that community present a different perspective on the CIP data block. "All I care about is accessing a good MARC record. So, to me, the only worthwhile piece of data in the new CIP data block is the LC link," or "Giving us a MARC record on the t.p. verso would be more helpful." Several comments specifically mentioned liking the

"LCCN Permalink," a feature of the new data block that was added subsequent to the original survey.

## Labels

A key characteristic of the new data block layout is its use of labels. Responses indicated that 34% liked the labels; 7% disliked the labels; and 3% did not understand the labels. Respondents did not have to provide input on each of the items, resulting in responses that do not add up to 100%. Not surprisingly, some labels were more problematic than others. As with the 2014 survey, several of the concerned respondents indicated they expected the label "Description" to contain a summary of the book rather than elements such as publisher, place, date, catalogers' notes, and other information considered "descriptive" in cataloging terms. Because the sample of the new data block did not include a summary, various comments mentioned summaries as missing and desired elements. Currently, LC catalogers include summaries for juvenile fiction titles only. Other comments objected to the label "Names": "Names is an unhelpful label for the 1XXs and 7XXs, which are confusingly lumped together as if equals. The uniform title is also lumped in with 'Names,' which also becomes confusing." The data block committee struggled to come up with labels that would be understood by both catalogers and non-catalogers. Similar comments had surfaced in the 2014 survey, but the committee felt they represented only minority opinions, which seemed to be the case in the 2017 survey as well. Nonetheless, the labels provoked some of the most critical comments and should be considered as an area for future improvement.

## Combined data block for print and e-book

A significant innovation was combining information about both print and electronic versions of books available in both formats into one data block that would be displayed in both formats. Respondents to the 2014 survey did not foresee this combined data block as a problem. The combined data block was a very positive feature for school library respondents who answered the 2017 survey. In the lists of elements that respondents liked and did not like, 57% of school library respondents vs. 36% of respondents overall liked the combined data block. None of the school library respondents disliked the combined data block, while 22% of all other respondents disliked it. Twenty-six percent of public library respondents liked the combined data block, while 39% disliked it. One public librarian asked if the print information could be left out of the information for the electronic version, but only two respondents included the combination as an element they did not understand. Academic library respondents liked this change the least: only 18% liked the combined data block vs. 28% that disliked it. One possible reason might be that the RDA cataloging rules and Program for Cooperative Cataloging (PCC) practice is to create separate records for print and e-book versions. However, publisher and vendor respondents were quite positive about the combined data block, with 61% liking it and only 6% disliking it. One likely reason is that they would not have to display different data blocks in publications that were basically the same.

### Addition of place, publisher, and date

Although the addition of this information seemed a possible risk to the data block committee because it can change before the book is published, its addition seems to have been well accepted. While 80 (53%) of the 151 respondents indicated this on a list of elements they liked, only three noted that they disliked this addition. Only one respondent expressed a concern: "The place and date of publication often change with publication."

### Additional subject terms and classifications

The new data block also included a variety of additional subject headings and classifications such as BISAC headings, SUDOC numbers, and genre terms. Overall, 60% liked the additional headings while only 1% disliked them. Among school librarians, 89% liked them and none disliked them. There were a few comments indicating that libraries do not use BISAC subject headings, and others were concerned that genre terms are being phased out. Somewhat surprisingly, only 45% of academic librarians indicated that they liked additional subject headings and classifications even though some specialized information, such as headings by the American Mathematical Society, National Library of Medicine, and others are included.

### What's missing?

One question asked if there were any data elements or features the respondent would like added to the data block. Several requested book summaries, and others asked for series information. Unfortunately, the sample data block presented in the survey did not include a series or a summary (provided only for juvenile fiction). Both kinds of information are still included. Some respondents requested Sears subject headings, data that was not possible to provide, as discussed above. Other respondents requested information about the book's size, pagination, and illustrations—information deemed not stable enough or available enough to provide until after publication. It seemed as if not all survey respondents realized that CIP information is provided by the publisher before the book is published. This is an area that the CIP Program can focus on for future educational outreach, particularly to school librarians.

## Survey outcome

All in all, the 2017 survey indicated that the new data block succeeded in its goals of being more user-friendly, providing a more current layout, and containing more information, especially for its primary user group, school libraries. In addition to providing the most positive answers to specific questions in the survey, school librarians also made some of the most positive free-text comments: "I like the organization and format. It is much easier to find information I need to catalog books for my high school library"; "It would be awesome if all publishers were using the new data block"; "Thank you for listening to the needs of school librarians who lack the resources of larger libraries." Happily, the data block seems most successful for its primary users.

## Problems encountered and lessons learned

The CIP Program encountered a few problems when trying to implement the new CIP data block. Most of the new additional fields for the CIP data block were completed in time for the rollout; however, the element "target audience" had to be slated for a future rollout. Both the ECIP Traffic Manager, the database that manages the flow of CIP applications, and On-the-MARC, in-house software that translates publisher data into the draft MARC record, need programming changes that have not yet been possible. Manual keying of this data by catalogers was not deemed practicable.

Once the new CIP data block was implemented, the CIP Program received requests for explicit formatting instructions from a few publishers in the Preassigned Control Number (PCN) Program, which assigns the LCCNs to forthcoming titles. PCN publishers often rely on vendor-created CIP data, also known as "P-CIP," in lieu of official Library of Congress CIP data. In order for P-CIP data to appear "legitimate," P-CIP providers mimic the formatting of the LC CIP block data as much as possible. For example, the CIP Program received this very specific request for CIP data block formatting instructions:

> Could you send me the layout of one title? Since it has a writer, artist, colorist, and letterer, I'm not sure about the layout for the CIP to be printed in the book. Many of these types of Fiction books (741.5) just say Graphic novels for a subject heading. That seems to be inadequate. Do you have any suggestions for other subject headings?

The CIP Program also received questions about how to display bibliographic information for multi-parts, how to include a pseudonym, and how to treat a translation.

The 2015 CIP data block survey results showed that there was confusion about the relationship between the MARC record and the CIP data block for use in bibliographic data creation and enhancement. As a way to assist all users of the CIP data block on how to use it to create a MARC record, the CIP Program created color-coded mappings. These mappings showed a CIP data block and its associated MARC bibliographic record. A mapping from the CIP data block to a labeled view was also created to assist those users who work in a cataloging environment with a labeled display. These mappings and detailed information about the new CIP data block now appear on the CIP website.

An ongoing issue with the CIP data block is limitations in the mailer program used by LC staff to send the CIP data block to publishers. The mailer uses plain text format and often displays diacritics in the data block as a blank space or an inverted question mark. The new CIP data block has not resolved this problem.

## Areas for future research

Despite the time and energy that went into the 2014 assessment, revision, and 2017 assessment of the data block, exciting areas for future research remain. Some ideas that surfaced either through current and previous surveys, presentations at conferences, or through committee discussions include: providing CIP data as an image rather than as text; encoding CIP data or the LC permalink into a QR or other code as part of the data block; and providing a mobile device application that could upload a MARC record from the data block or LC catalog into the user's integrated library system.

Since the CIP data block is based on RDA catalog records as represented in MARC 21, another important area for future research will be the effect of the changing bibliographic environment on LC catalog records and therefore on the data block. As of this writing (March 2017), RDA is being re-cast to accommodate the new IFLA Library Reference Model (LRM), while LC and others are exploring BIBFRAME and additional possible approaches for formatting bibliographic data as linked data. How will the CIP data block have to be modified to accommodate these likely future changes to LC catalog records?

Of particular interest to the CIP Program is providing publishers with an image of the data block to insert into the book. An image could solve some of the issues that surfaced in committee discussions about designing the new data block and in survey comments. For example, the technology now used to produce the data block and send it to publishers cannot accommodate different fonts or formatting that could distinguish labels from content, or add helpful spacing to make the block easier to read and interpret. Also, as already noted, currently, publishers can all too easily change the text block by centering lines, changing the information, or embellishing the block in artistic ways they deem more compatible with the design of the book. One 2014 survey respondent noted, "The typography by the publishers make[s] it all the more difficult." An image would lock down the data block text and layout and also provide the ability to include CIP data encoded in a QR or other code, something the data block committee explored but was not able to develop for a variety of reasons, including the inability to provide an image.

The idea to include CIP data in encoded form in the data block surfaced in 1998 during a meeting of the CIP Advisory Group. The 1998 presentation was delivered by Symbol Technologies, developer of the PDF417 code, a symbology now used by organizations such as the USPS for encoding postage and by airlines on boarding passes. As noted above, 2014 discussions resurrected the idea of using QR codes.

Future research is needed to determine the optimum code, how to produce and send the code to publishers in the distributed production environment of the CIP program, and how the code should operate. One intriguing possibility that would provide a service to those libraries most interested in the MARC record would be an application available on mobile devices that could read the code and enter the bibliographic data straight into the library's catalog.

Before further changes are made to the data block, it would be useful to explore the methods, tools, and training of those who create records for school libraries by transcribing all or parts of the CIP data block. Although the 2014 survey provided some data that indicated manual transcription is a common way that school librarians use CIP data, a clearer understanding of the specifics of this process would provide information that could better inform the difficult decisions that LC might make about any changes. Further into the future, the CIP Program would benefit from an investigation into how much longer it might be necessary to provide bibliographic data within the book itself (whether in print or online) as opposed to simply providing a national bibliography number or permalink by which cataloging data can be accessed in the national library catalog. National libraries such as in Germany and other countries have moved away from providing CIP data in the book in favor of providing the national bibliography number for 100% of their titles.

## How the research is helpful to other libraries

The revisions, additions, and redesign incorporated in the new CIP data block expand traditional functionality to support the needs of a changing library world. With every new CIP block, catalogers can review a model of current cataloging practice either to transcribe directly, or to use as a learning tool. The act of reading, interpreting, and transcribing the information within the data block affirms the cataloger's understanding of RDA. This authoritative cataloging record available in a resource provides a perfect example of transcription of bibliographic description and application of RDA elements, including relator terms. The new labels added to the CIP data block define the content clearly and support consistent interpretation of these elements.

Librarians have always used the CIP data block for classification recommendations. The addition of BISAC headings in the new CIP data block supports the activities of libraries using these headings to organize their collections. The addition of genre terms provides classifiers an authoritative recommendation for fiction collections. The opportunities for paraprofessional library workers to confidently classify materials have been expanded with the addition of these CIP data block elements.

With the addition of a LCCN Permalink in the new CIP data block, libraries with limited resources now have direct access to an individual bibliographic record from the Library of Congress. After activating the link, a user is taken to the LC catalog, where they can view the record in the MARC format to further aid in transcription. Once in the LC catalog, a user can also download the MARC record for use in a local ILS.

The CIP data block continues to be the source of convenient, authoritative bibliographic data. Whether it is used to build better library catalogs or to simply know more about the book in hand, the new CIP data block supports a more robust and a more successful discovery experience.

## Conclusion

How do you update an icon? Carefully and deliberately, retaining the essence but taking well-considered risks with the appearance. The CIP data block on the title page verso had provided catalogers with an almost-complete catalog record in the form of a catalog card for more than 40 years. For libraries that could not afford to join OCLC or other bibliographic utility, the CIP data block was an essential source of cataloging data, its card layout unchanged over the years—perhaps unchangeable?

In Fall 2015, after gathering a variety of input from stakeholders and a two-year effort from the CIP Data Block Committee, LC successfully changed the iconic look of the data block, replacing the card layout with a more easily interpreted labeled layout. RDA elements as well as subject terms from additional thesauri and classifications were added; print and e-book information was included in a single data block. The results of a 2017 assessment survey strongly indicated that the new CIP data block was very well received, especially by its primary user group, school libraries. The new layout was deemed more user-friendly and contained additional useful cataloging data. The survey also provided suggestions to consider for the future, such as including QR codes in the data block that would lead to the MARC record, and sending publishers an image file that would preclude their making layout and text changes. The survey also indicated that some additional training in using the new CIP data block would be valuable, such as LC hosting online webinars and sessions presented at conferences.

The CIP user surveys and positive reception of the new data block have affirmed the value of the LC CIP data block in newly published books and have demonstrated that librarians are quite willing to provide input into decisions that affect their daily work.

## Notes

1. Robert R. Newlen, "Read the Fine Print: The Power of CIP." *Library Journal* (July 1991): 38–42.
2. Karl E. Debus-López, et al. "The Electronic Cataloging in Publication Cataloging Partnership Program: A Model for Cooperative Cataloging for the Twenty-First Century," *Cataloging & Classification Quarterly* 51, no. 1–3 (2012): 29.

3. Joanna F. Fountain and Michele Zwierski, "How the CIP Program Helps Children's Librarians" in *Cataloging Correctly for Kids*, 5th ed. (Chicago: American Library Association, 2011), 164.

4. Paul Edlund. "A Monster and a Miracle: The Cataloging Distribution Service of the Library of Congress, 1901–1976." *Quarterly Journal of the Library of Congress* (October 1976), 32.

5. Daniel N. Joudrey, Arlene G. Taylor, and David P. Miller. *Introduction to Cataloging and Classification*, 11th ed. (Santa Barbara, Calif.: Libraries Unlimited, 2015), 933.

6. Jean Weihs and Sheila S. Intner. *Beginning Cataloging.* (Santa Barbara, CA: Libraries Unlimited, 2009), 5–12.

7. John Sandstrom and Liz Miller. *Fundamentals of Technical Services* (Chicago: Neal-Schuman, 2015), 95.

8. Jean Weihs "An Investigation of Cataloging-In-Publication as an Important Tool," *Interfaces* 37, no. 1 (January/February 2017), 10–12.

9. Mary Mortimer. *Learn Descriptive Cataloging*, 2nd North American ed. (Friendswood, TX: Total Recall Publications, Inc., 2007), 198.

10. Kevin Crestsos. "What's in a Catalog Record?" *University of Dayton Libraries Blog*, University of Dayton Libraries, October 12, 2015, https://udayton.edu/blogs/libraries/2015-10-12-catalog.php/

11. Karl E. Debus-López, "Introducing the new CIP data block," *LCCN*, September 29, 2015.

12. CAG Minutes, February 2, 1981.

13. CAG Minutes, July 11, 1982.

14. CAG Minutes, January 8, 1984.

15. Susan H. Vita. *Final Report: IFLA Working Group on a Standardized Format for the CIP Record in the Book*, June 1985.

16. *Electronic CIP Publishers Manual.* Updated February 14, 2006.

17. *CIP Poised for Change: Survey Findings and Recommendations of the 2006 CIP Review Group*, 2007. 59–60.

18. CAG Minutes, January 25, 2003.

19. CAG Minutes, June 21, 2003.

20. CAG Minutes, June 26, 2010.

21. CAG Minutes, June 23, 2012.

22. CAG Minutes, June 30, 2013.

23. CIP Data Block Committee members: Karl Debus-Lopez, Chief, U.S. Programs, Law, and Literature Division; Lynnette Fields, ALCTS representative; Marilyn McCroskey, AASL representative; Rebecca Mugridge, ACRL representative; Regina Reynolds, Director, U.S. ISSN Center; Caroline Saccucci, CIP Program Manager; Camilla Williams, CIP Program Specialist; David Williamson, ABA Automation Specialist; and Michele Zwierski, PLA representative.

24. CIP Data Block Committee Meeting Summary, September 23, 2013.

25. The survey was sent to the following electronic mailing lists: AASL Forum, ALCTS Central, ASCLA-L, CAG, Community College Listserv, FAFLRT, FEDLIB, ISSN Directors, LM_NET, MEDLIB-L, OCLC-CAT, PCC, and PUBLIB.

26. Regina Reynolds, Overview of CIP responses from 12 ISSN centers.

27. Gordon Dunsire, *Comments from the Joint Steering Committee for the Development of RDA*, June 4, 2015.

28. Karl E. Debus-López, "Introducing the new CIP data block," *LCCN*, September 29, 2015.

29. Shortly after the release of the new data block, webinars were hosted by ALCTS, AASL, and the Western New York Library Resources Council. A presentation on the data block was also given at the New England Library Association/New Hampshire Library Association meeting in October 2015. Additional training was considered, but was not followed through on as it seemed that users of the data block easily adapted to the new format.

30. 2015 Annual Report of the CIP Section.

# Appendix A

**Table A1.** IFLA Working Group on a standardized format for the CIP record in the book: list of mandatory, required if available, and optional elements in a CIP record, 1985.

| | |
|---|---|
| Title proper | Mandatory |
| Parallel title | Required if available |
| Other title information | Optional |
| Statement of responsibility | Optional |
| Edition statement | Optional |
| Statements of responsibility relating to the edition | Optional |
| Place of publication and/or distribution | Optional |
| Name of publisher and/or distributor | Optional |
| Date of publication and/or distributor | Optional |
| Physical description | Optional |
| Title proper of series or subseries | Required if available |
| Parallel title of series or subseries | Optional |
| Key title of the series or subseries | Required if available |
| International Standard Serial Number of series or subseries | Required if available |
| Numbering within series or subseries | Required if available |
| Translation and dissertation notes | Required if available |
| Summary statement | Optional |
| International Standard Book Number | Required if available |
| Terms of availability and/or price | Optional |
| Main entry (author or title) | Required if applicable [in effect, mandatory] |
| Added entries | Mandatory |
| Government document number | Optional |
| National bibliography number | Optional |
| Subject headings | Required if available |
| Subject classification number | Required if available |
| Book number | Optional |

## Appendix B

**Table B1.** New CIP data block: data element and layout changes, implemented October 1, 2015.

| MARC field | MARC field name | Decision |
|---|---|---|
| 010 | Library of Congress Control Number | Include (print + electronic) |
| 020 | ISBN | Include all |
| 050 | Library of Congress Classification Number | Include (print + electronic) |
| 060 | National Library of Medicine Classification Number | Include |
| 082 | Dewey Decimal Classification Number | Include |
| 084 | BISAC Codes | Exclude |
| 1XX | Primary Authorized Access Point (Main Entry) | Include |
| 130 | Preferred (Uniform) Title – Primary Access Point | Include |
| 240 | Preferred (Uniform) Title – Foreign Title | Include |
| 240 | Preferred (Uniform) Title – Commonly Known Title | Include |
| 240 | Preferred (Uniform) Title – Collective Title | Exclude |
| 245 | Title Statement | Include |
| 245 | Author Affiliations | Exclude |
| 250 | Edition Statement | Include |
| 264 | Publisher Name, Place and Publication Date | Include |
| 300 | Physical description (pages cm) | Exclude |
| 490 | Series Statement | Include |
| 500 | General Note | Include, except when it only has "Includes Index" |
| 504 | Bibliographic Reference Note | Include |
| 505 | Contents | Exclude unless the record is a multi-part set |
| 520 | Summary | Include for juvenile and young adult literature |
| 521 | Audience Note | Include |
| 546 | Language Note | Include |
| 6XX | Library of Congress Subject Headings | Include |
| 6XX | Medical Subject Headings (MESH) | Include |
| 650_7 | American Mathematical Society subject headings | Include |
| 650_7 | BISAC Headings | Include |
| 655_7 | Genre/Form terms | Include |
| 7XX | Relationship Designators | Include* |
| 8XX | Authorized Access Point for Series | Include |

*Relationship Designators included within the CIP data block

Abridger

Author

Cartographer

Compiler

Editor

Enacting jurisdiction

Honoree

Illustrator

Issuing body

Photographer

Translator

**Layout changes**

<u>Labels Used</u>

Names
Title
Other titles
Description
Summary (included within Description)
Series (included within Description)
Identifiers
Subjects
Classification

<u>Acronyms Used</u>

*Classifications*

LCC     Library of Congress Classification
DDC    Dewey Decimal Classification
NLM    NLM Classification
SUDOC  Superintendent of Documents Classification

*Subject Headings*

| | |
|---|---|
| LCSH | Library of Congress Subject Headings |
| AMS | American Mathematical Society Subject Headings |
| BISAC | BISAC Subject Headings |
| CYAC | Children's and Young Adults' Cataloging Subject Headings |
| GSAFD | SGenre/Form terms |
| MESH | Medical Subject Headings |

| | |
|---|---|
| Library of Congress Control Number | Add – links to record in LC Catalog |
| Permalink | |
| Combined Layout | Use if title has both print and electronic |

114

# New Approaches to Subject Indexing at the British Library

Janet Ashton and Caroline Kent

**ABSTRACT**

The constantly changing metadata landscape means that libraries need to re-think their approach to standards and subject analysis, to enable the discovery of vast areas of both print and digital content. This article presents a case study from the British Library that assesses the feasibility of adopting FAST (Faceted Application of Subject Terminology) to selectively extend the scope of subject indexing of current and legacy content, or implement FAST as a replacement for all LCSH in current cataloging workflows.

This article presents a case study from the British Library assessing the feasibility of adopting FAST (Faceted Application of Subject Terminology) for different types of material. We will explain why FAST was selected, how we conducted our study, our conclusions, and the reactions of colleagues in the broader profession. We also briefly discuss future possibilities.

The British Library is the U.K.'s national library and also a legal deposit library. Since 2013, Legal Deposit has extended to include non-print resources, including electronic media. The British Library also holds very substantial purchased and donated collections. However, it is actually relatively new as an institution: it was established in 1973 by amalgamating several older institutions with widely different approaches to cataloging and subject standards. Differences in the bibliographic approaches taken by different collection areas persisted for many years.

Changes of approach within specific areas of the collections have taken place as the Library continually aims to make efficiencies and to keep abreast of evolving user needs. Some parts of the Library's collections have continued to adhere to basic cataloging standards without the use of any subject headings. Other collection areas used local schemes (such as the British Museum system) which are now deemed out of date. Some headings were not considered appropriate for adding to the on-line catalog when the bibliographic records were converted from card to digital, creating a significant gap in indexing. There were also schemes based on shelfmarks, which were understood historically by curators but are opaque to current users. Further, since 1974, the standard used to subject index legal deposit and other trade literature acquired by the library has been inconsistent, with LCSH (Library of Congress Subject Headings), local schemes such as PRECIS (Preserved Context Index System) and COMPASS (Computer Aided Subject System) all in use at various times. However, following a significant review and extensive staff training, in 1995 the British Library committed to working solely with LCSH as the preferred subject heading scheme applied across the majority of book and serial collections. However, despite improved consistency in recent years, users cannot discover everything the library holds on a given subject in a single search. Multiple searches and strategies are required. Substantial areas continue to have limited retrievability, and can currently only be found by users who know the exact title they are looking for. In current workflows, 78% of intake is subject indexed. This compares with just 8% of the retrospectively converted records now within the British Library catalog and 53% overall.

In addition to historical problems, the Library also faces contemporary funding issues. Since 2010, funding has gradually reduced resulting in a concomitant reduction in staff numbers. This has created a significant challenge to the Library's ability to keep abreast of intake, despite the use of innovative workflows such as contracting out of modern English-language cataloging and electronic upgrade of other records by automatically overlaying basic records with full-level records from the Library of Congress or OCLC.

These ongoing constraints coincided with the full implementation in 2013 of the 2003 Act of Parliament which widened the scope of Legal Deposit, and enabled the Library to collect electronic publications as well as print, subject to negotiation with publishers. The widening of content types has resulted in the deposit of large amounts of recently digitized back-catalogs, as well as new publications born-digital, leading to an increase in the quantity of material received and requiring a catalog record. A reduction in print material, which was predicted to follow the migration to emedia, has failed to materialize, and there are often multiple different versions of the electronic copies, all of which are duly deposited. By 2014, it had become clear that further efficiencies were needed in the cataloging workflows so that material handled by catalogers can be processed as efficiently as possible while meeting emerging requirements in the publishing landscape.

In addition to changes in the financial and publishing environments, metadata requirements have continued to evolve. Library catalogs are just one element in a complex information discovery landscape. This is coupled with a high level of end user expectations with regard to the ease of finding and using resources, as users can be time poor and unlikely to engage with complicated subject systems when seeking for library resources. This is especially the case if there is a requirement to learn library centric approaches to searching and understanding data. Subject schemes such as LCSH were designed for a library environment, where assistance and understanding of a librarian was readily available, and alternative search processes and materials were not. Such schemes were designed for the left-anchored indexes of card catalogs making them a challenge in current discovery systems that are not developed to make full use of them. Equally important is the fact that such approaches are not easily compatible with linked data, where unique terms, identifiers and clear relationships are necessary to build an environment that leads users from found resources to related resources in clear and precise steps.

These are the issues that led the British Library's Collection Management department to review levels and extent of subject coverage with an aim to improve coverage in areas that had previously had limited intervention, and maintain existing quality levels and coverage for those workflows that currently use LCSH. A pilot project was developed and run from late 2014, during which time catalogers used the FAST scheme in place of LCSH on selected materials.

Before committing to FAST, we undertook a basic review of literature evaluating the scheme and looking for evidence and comments relating to application in other institutions. As yet, there is no very substantive body of work on it. However, the American Library Association's "FAST for Cataloging and Discovery: e-Forum Summary," at http://www.ala.org/alctsnews/features/fast-cataloging was a good introduction, and OCLC's report: "FAST (Faceted Application of Subject Terminology) Users: Summary and Case Studies" by Jeffrey Mixter and Eric R. Childress was encouraging. We then obtained a copy of *FAST: Faceted Application of Subject Terminology Principles and Application* by Lois Mai Chan and Edward T. O'Neill (Libraries Unlimited: 2010). There has been growing interest in FAST throughout the period of our study, and while published studies remain scarce the scheme has been the subject of a number of conference sessions, workshops and presentations, some of which we will discuss below.

As the published literature outlines, the FAST standard has been developed as a scheme which is:
- simple and easy to apply and to comprehend;
- intuitive so that sophisticated training in subject indexing and classification, while highly desirable, is not required in order to implement;
- logical so that it requires the least effort to understand and implement; and
- scalable for implementation from the simplest to the most sophisticated.[1]

The stated intention to "retain the very rich vocabulary of LCSH while making the schema easier to understand, control, apply, and use" means that the terms it uses are mainly derived directly from LCSH or from the Library of Congress's name authority file. Only a few terms have been specifically created if there is no LCSH equivalent, and these are justified by the literary warrant of records in WorldCat. As with LCSH, a controlled vocabulary collates all records on the same topic in the same place, regardless of the term used by the searcher. FAST is a thesaural system: there are references from non-preferred to preferred terms, and common usage is preferred to formal terminology. FAST is an enumerative rather than synthetic scheme. In contrast to LCSH, FAST terms are divided into six facets and there is no need to combine terms, no string-building, or crossing of facets.

FAST is therefore more compatible with the expression of subject terminology as linked data than LCSH.

The six FAST facets are as follows.

**Topical:** simple nouns, more than one noun, or phrase headings with prepositions. They can represent a concept or also a physical object; fictitious or legendary characters; named animals.

**Geographic:** constructed according to the same principles as LCSH and NACO: some are jurisdictional; others non-jurisdictional; the latest name rule applies in the same way. English is the language of these terms, and FAST mirrors the LCSH concepts of "first order" and "second order" political divisions in its "first level" and "second level" divisions, with city sections designated as "third level." For example, England is a "first order/level" political division of Great Britain, while the city of London is second, and either can be used in LCSH for subdividing topical terms to indicate when events occur in certain places. This means that "East End" of London, a third-order division, is not available to be used this way. FAST preserves the concept if not the same usage in subdivision, since FAST headings cannot be reversed and added to topical terms as they can in LCSH.

**Chronological:** consisting of one date, or more than one in a term. These differ from LCSH in that they are only established when needed for a cross-reference; otherwise, the cataloger can assign any date range he or she feels appropriate. This facet contains dates expressed as numerals, not in words. For example, the names of centuries formulated as "Twentieth century," for example, are topical terms used for works which discuss those periods rather than take place in them.

**Events:** are distinct from topics, differing once more in this respect from LCSH. Events in FAST terms include meetings and conferences as well as specific historical occurrences.

**Personal and corporate names as subjects:** taken from the Library of Congress Name Authority File; family names from LCSH. These terms are all copied to the FAST file so the cataloger does not have to switch back and forth between a name authority file and the subject authorities, as is the case when using LCSH. This also conforms with the FRSAD (Functional Requirements of Subject Authority Data) concepts of "aboutness," which recommends that all possible subject terms be grouped together, or contained in one file: "the first broad objective of FRSAD is to ensure that the scope of the entities defined is sufficient to cover everything that a user of a library catalog might view as a 'subject.'"[2]

Name-titles authorities are also FAST terms, based on WorldCat warrant and are formulated slightly differently to the LC/NACO form.

**Form/genre:** are derived from LCSH subdivisions and from LCGFT (Library of Congress Genre and Form Terms).

Some of these FAST terms have subdivisions attached, but because these pairings don't "cross facets" (i.e., involve more than one facet), this is permissible in FAST terms.

This faceting fulfils the stated aims of the British Library project making FAST simpler to assign than LCSH, and helping users understand it more readily. FAST is fully thesaural in this regard; more so than LCSH, whose synthetic structure ensures that there is no comprehensive list of valid subject terms. LCSH's pre-coordinated strings were designed for, and best suited to, card catalogs, which tried to limit the number of terms used in order to limit how many multiple entries were needed. This renders it less amenable to linked data applications than FAST is, since not all possible terms have a unique identifier. Post-coordinate indexing is more suited to linked data search and discovery. The use of discrete facets, each term with its unique numerical identifier, means that FAST is far friendlier to linked data than LCSH can be—in fact, it might be said to be "born friendly" by design.

FAST uses the same coding schemes as LCSH, currently MARC in most libraries, but it can also be accommodated in other schemes such as Dublin Core.[3]

FAST terms can be loaded onto Library Management Systems as an authority file. This would be the most efficient method for implementing them in the British Library's main cataloging workflow, but for other workflows and for practice and assessment it can be accessed as a web tool through the OCLC applications Assign-Fast (http://experimental.worldcat.org/fast/assignfast) and SearchFast (http://fast.oclc.org/searchfast/).

SearchFAST is the version British Library catalogers have come to prefer as more user-friendly: it consists of a very simple keyword search with one box and a drop-down list to select indexes. From the results page catalogers can refine the search. Those who know LCSH can find the corresponding FAST term by selecting the "keyword-in-source-record" search. A WorldCat link enables them to see how each term is used and what it might mean. Catalogers can copy the MARC-coded heading directly from the search interface into the record they are working on using copy and paste.

Until 2014, FAST was in use in collections such as emedia and other specialist collections by institutions such as Harvard University and Cornell University, and was largely treated as a test (beta) system, albeit one to which LC and OCLC were committed. However, usage increased when FAST terms were added to OCLC's database, through conversion of existing LCSH terminology, so that many records now contain both approaches.

For all the reasons above, FAST seemed to offer a solution to several of the library's needs, and the project sought to investigate the achievability of three main aims: (1) to achieve 100% coverage of current intake of trade publications; (2) to assign subject terms to legacy data lacking any index terms; and (3) to extend indexing to workflows that do not currently apply any scheme.

A short training session was developed and delivered to a small group of catalogers from Boston Spa and St Pancras in early 2015 to familiarize them with

FAST. From that point on, the FAST-trained catalogers were asked to apply only FAST terms in their bibliographic records. One cataloger worked on electronic serial publications, while four cataloged European language monographs purchased for the reference collection. Specifically, FAST terms can now be found on academic material in Norwegian, Danish, Swedish, German, French, Spanish, regional Hispanic languages, Portuguese, Slovenian, Croatian, Serbian, Bosnian, and Bulgarian. All the catalogers involved had been working with LCSH for many years, and found the switch to FAST relatively easy.

A further group of collection staff with some cataloging background began to apply FAST to an electronic social science database of titles, working from a set list of terms which had been pre-agreed with the Collection Management staff leading the project. Shortly afterward, FAST was also adopted as the preferred subject scheme for interns and staff on short-term contracts, with limited time allocated for training. These staff are involved in projects that create records for older, backlogged material which had never been cataloged due to lack of resources. Records are created using spreadsheets and simple element sets rather than full MARC21 records. None of these staff were familiar with LCSH, but they found FAST to be intuitive and felt confident with its use quickly. A significant benefit for time limited projects and backlog reduction is that training for short-term staff can concentrate on the principles of subject analysis, without the need for extensive scheme training and complex strings and subject heading arrays.

Feedback from participants in the internal project covered both the practicalities such as the stability of the search interface, and questions about the possible use of headings and lack of others, notably those to cover more specialized topics and smaller languages. The project identified many potential benefits, with some areas of concern addressed later in the article. The project also sought feedback around the Library, and set up further trials to address some of the issues raised.

One aspect of the project designed to look at efficiencies consisted of time and motion studies. This involved different catalogers applying LCSH and FAST to the same record in sequence, in order to assess the potential efficiencies that could be gained. Surprisingly, the two approaches appear to take the same amount of time. However, analysis of resulting records suggests that this is due to technical limitations, including using FAST on the internet rather than as a local authority file, and to the fact that the project operated without set rules. FAST relies on cataloger judgement which resulted in catalogers erring towards over-indexing as they became confident in making decisions around level of indexing required and the scope of coverage without the guidance, for example, of a 20% rule. However, this flexibility in application of FAST is considered to be a core benefit, allowing the same standard to be utilized in different ways for different collection areas while maintaining compatibility. Further, initial retrievability studies with reading-room users in specific subject areas have suggested that books are found accurately, regardless of whether the system is LCSH or FAST. Key terms are as successful as strings, and possibly more so when form and genre are part of the search.

Following internal trials, the British Library conducted an external consultation, posted on the British Library's website and advertised through discussion lists and social media, as well as targeted invitation to specific partners. The majority of replies came from other libraries.

We asked stakeholders to comment on the following proposals.

1. The British Library proposes to adopt FAST selectively to extend the scope of subject indexing of current and legacy content.
2. The British Library proposes to implement FAST as a replacement for LCSH in all current cataloging, subject to mitigation of the risks identified above, in particular the question of sustainability.

The proposals were intended to be radical and initially included a proposal in relation to classification, a separate project, beyond the scope of this article. The response overall toward FAST was not encouraging, at least in relation to using FAST on current material. However, comments that were provided clarify concerns already raised internally and as such gave valuable evidence for how to take next steps. Concerns raised can be broadly categorized as professional, technical, and developmental.

Professional concerns arose regarding the perceived "dumbing down" of subject analysis, due to FAST's accessibility to paraprofessional staff. Further concerns were raised about the lack of precise terminology. For example, one comment identified a book on World War Two that had been indexed as "War", and found this unacceptably imprecise. However, there are appropriate FAST terms available for World War Two, and the use of the broader term in this case could be either a choice about level of granularity at a particular institution, or for a particular project, or possibly an error in application of the scheme. Precision is not an issue with the FAST per se, but of a chosen application profile.

Such concerns might be addressed through awareness and training of potential users. Staff involved in the project were reassured that the focus of their work became accurate analytical assessment of resources, and not a reliance on one specific vocabulary. Other suggestions for improving awareness suggested by staff involved in the application process include delivering talks and seminars, as well as providing guidance such as FAQs, that could be published for external audiences by institutions such as the British Library if implementing FAST. Cornell University has produced its own local guidance, which could act as a starting point, though this is not currently publicly available. There were also concerns that institutions which currently use British Library records would be obliged to add LCSH themselves if the records began to come through with FAST instead, as LCSH would still be wanted by readers. This, again, may be addressed by improving awareness of and familiarity with FAST, and explain how it may better suit end-users in a modern resource discovery environment. A full summary of the consultation and stakeholder responses is available here: http://www.bl.uk/bibliographic/nbsnews.html.

Some comments also reflected technical concerns, including the usability of the FAST web interface, noting that catalogers sometimes struggled to register key strokes and that there were problems with the retrieval of certain headings when diacritics were present. There was also a concern that loading FAST headings to local systems could prove impossible without conflicting with existing LCSH authorities, and that even if this were achieved there could still be additional problems in synchronizing updates on authority and bibliographic files.

Throughout internal trials and internal and external consultation, a significant concern emerged regarding the governance and sustainability of FAST as a fully supported OCLC product. This has led to various consultations with OCLC and interested parties in other libraries. The British Library is also engaging with wider audiences through participation in subject indexing forums and discussions. Suggestions for a future product have included the necessity for libraries and other bibliographic agencies to contribute to the development of FAST terminology, for example through proposals for new/changed terminology, and, the ability to review or contribute to the scheme developments and principles.

There is growing support within the Library community for a shift away from pre-coordination, towards a faceted approach to subject indexing. A number of conferences have included discussions about the future of subject indexing. Thurstan Young, Metadata Analyst, British Library, gave a presentation at the American Library Association conference in 2016, introducing the British Library's work. Janet Ashton, Cataloguing Team Manager, presented a paper at a dedicated subject conference at the National Library of Germany later in the year.[4] Both presentations were well received, with German librarians proving particularly enthusiastic about a move to a faceted scheme which mirrors their own in many ways.

Further, a number of organizations are already experimenting with new approaches. Columbia University, for example, has begun to deconstruct its LCSH headings into facets to fit a new resource discovery system. This has been welcomed by users, overall.[5] The Getty Research Institute has done similar things and supports FAST as an alternative to attempting to deal with incorrectly constructed LCSH strings. New York Public Library finds faceted terms to be more user-friendly than LCSH, and New York University shares the British Library's view that a persistent identifier best supports linked data applications.[6] The bibliographic agency Casalini and numerous Italian university libraries are working on a project to convert their data, including subjects, to linked open data and publish it on a single portal.[7]

Discussions at ALA Midwinter conference in early 2017, suggested that a task group be convened with British Library and OCLC representation to consider the future governance of the system, taking into account possible future users, vocabulary and relationship to LCSH, as well as methods of adding or contributing to the scheme.

As a result of the British Library project and subsequent external consultations, the recommendation was made to the strategic decision-making group responsible for metadata at the British Library, that the Library work with external partners to facilitate the adoption of FAST. This would be subject to mitigation of some of the outstanding concerns relating to sustainability. However, overall, the Project group cited a number of benefits in support of their recommendation.

The first, relating to efficiency gains are threefold. FAST is quicker to manually apply in cataloging workflows and is also quicker to search. And even more significantly it is quicker to train people in FAST. Further, the widespread application of FAST in WorldCat means that derivable metadata already contains headings, aiding an efficient cataloging through the possibility of automated record enhancement. OCLC also provide tools to convert LCSH headings, thus allowing for some degree of retrospective enhancement of existing data. Further studies will look at the application of some LCSH guidance, such as the rule of three and the 20% rule, in the application of FAST, in order to see how this improves output in full level cataloging.

The second category in which FAST impressed us concerns the potential for future improvements in resource discovery related to linked-data. Many current catalogs do not offer a left-anchored browse option, which limits the use of LCSH strings. FAST overcomes this design issue, since it uses terms and not strings, which are suitable for keyword searching, and facet browsing, familiar from many current library and wider search environments. Further, some catalogs index LCSH as key words regardless of the intellectual time and effort in creating the complex strings. The data is presented as key terms, thus rendering the value of the string moot. In addition, the FAST form/genre terms have proven particularly useful to end users. Feedback from colleagues managing requests and queries suggest that readers really appreciate these. The easy and rapid extension of subject terminology to unindexed collections would be invaluable in improving satisfaction with British Library catalogs overall. While it is recognized that some terminology in FAST needs to be revised to remove remaining inconsistencies such as inverted headings, this was considered to be an acceptable short-term problem. It is no worse than similar issues with LCSH, and there is the potential to resolve this in a new and evolving standard such as FAST.

The third benefit identified was of economy, related to overheads in terms of training. Evidence from the project suggests a move to FAST would be relatively simple, whereas adopting new standards or systems can often be costly and time consuming. FAST appears to require only minimal training for experienced staff and as shown with staff on short-term contracts initial basic training is also reduced in terms of time required to become proficient in using FAST. For the British Library, moving experienced staff from LCSH to a scheme which uses similar principles and vocabulary, as well as the NACO authority file, is relatively simple, though it is recognized that the level of impact will vary across institutions with differing levels of experience and initial approach. We also could transfer easily to FAST in terms of system compatibility as the scheme can be used in MARC bibliographic records.

The British Library sees many potential advantages in adopting FAST, including improved efficiencies and resource discovery, as well as future-proofing subject data. We are already applying FAST to open up uncataloged and indexed collections to researchers and other stakeholders.

We are committed to providing good quality, consistent subject access to our collections. We believe that FAST will enable us to do this more cost effectively than LCSH. We acknowledge the concerns of stakeholders regarding the wider application of FAST and are working with OCLC to address the issue of sustainability.

The British Library's experiences with FAST can potentially be of use to other libraries currently re-considering subject indexing as part of ongoing efficiency drives in the creation of robust and comprehensive bibliographic data. Such data supports both user needs and automated processes such as management information and linked data services. The Library has created documentation that can be shared, and can assist others with training, or offer advice on the levels of training required for different levels of experience. Discussion of FAST will form part of a one-day course on subject access which the Library is currently developing for paying customers. Our experiments with using FAST on various types of material and employing different methods of data entry place us in a good position to offer advice on the scheme's advantages and disadvantages in a variety of situations.

Potential future directions for the Library include working with OCLC to develop FAST as a robust product, as well as potentially participating in documentation and training on an international level. Other directions could also include multilingual mapping of the scheme, which would certainly be a simpler process than similar attempts to map LCSH. Given the interest shown by libraries using faceted schemes in other languages (e.g., German), this would be an exciting and feasible development.

## Acknowledgments

Special thanks to Andrew MacEwan, Head of Content & Metadata Processing, British Library and Alan Danskin, Collection Metadata Standards Manager, British Library, for input, ideas, and revision, and to colleagues from across Collection Management for their involvement in the testing and projects described.

## Notes

1. Rebecca J. Dean, "FAST: Development of Simplified Headings for Metadata," *Cataloging & Classification Quarterly* 39, nos. 1–2 (2004–5): 331–352.
2. "Functional Requirements for Subject Authority Data (FRSAD) A Conceptual Model," (2010), http://www.ifla.org/files/assets/classification-and-indexing/functional-requirements-for-sub ject-authority-data/frsad-model.pdf (accessed May 14, 2017).
3. See also "FAST linked data: FAST authority file", http://experimental.worldcat.org/fast (accessed July 1, 2017).
4. See http://connect.ala.org/node/255461 Thurstan Young, "FAST at the British Library," (paper delivered at ALA Annual Conference, June 2016), and Janet Ashton, "Strings or terms? Experiments with FAST indexing at the British Library", (paper delivered at "Subject Cataloguing: Quo Vadis?" a satellite conference associated with the annual meeting of

the RDA Steering Committee RSC, 4 November 2016 at the German National Library in Frankfurt; http://www.dnb.de/EN/Standardisierung/International/rscSatelliteMeetingProgramm.html)

5. OCLC. "Research Library partners metadata managers focus group Round Robin 1: Faceted Vocabularies," by email to participants.

6. OCLC. "Research Library partners metadata managers focus group Round Robin 1: Faceted Vocabularies," by email to participants.

7. See "Share catalogue online", http://www.atcult.it/en/news-en/2016/05/share-catalogue-online/ (accessed July 7, 2017) and Tiziana Possemato, "The central role of URIs in Subject Cataloguing." (paper delivered at "Subject cataloguing: Quo Vadis?" a satellite conference associated with the annual meeting of the RDA Steering Committee RSC, 4 November 2016 at the German National Library in Frankfurt (http://www.dnb.de/EN/Standardisierung/International/rscSatelliteMeetingProgramm.html)

# Managing Bibliographic Data Quality for Electronic Resources

David Van Kleeck ⓘ, Hikaru Nakano ⓘ, Gerald Langford ⓘ, Trey Shelton ⓘ, Jimmie Lundgren ⓘ, and Allison Jai O'Dell ⓘ

**ABSTRACT**

This article presents a case study of quality management issues for electronic resource metadata to assess the support of user tasks (find, select, and obtain library resources) and potential for increased efficiencies in acquisitions and cataloging workflows. The authors evaluated the quality of existing bibliographic records (mostly vendor supplied) for e-resource collections as compared with records for the same collections in OCLC's WorldShare Collection Manager (WCM). Findings are that WCM records better support user tasks by containing more summaries and tables of contents; other checkpoints are largely comparable between the two source record groups. The transition to WCM records is discussed.

## Introduction

In the literature, the term "quality management" refers to an array of measures, including "quality assurance" and "quality control." Quality assurance focuses on incoming data and on correcting errors prior to the creation and ingest of records into the catalog, while quality control deals with post-ingest issues. For the most part, manually cataloged resources naturally undergo metadata quality control as the cataloger works her or his way through the bibliographic record, while batch-loaded records for electronic resources (e-resources) often miss this detailed examination. Since poor-quality metadata hampers discovery, it is prudent to select e-resource metadata of the highest quality available. Thus, to understand the relative quality of metadata for various e-resource collections, the research discussed in this article compared the quality of existing bibliographic records (mostly vendor-supplied) for e-resource collections with records for the same collections in Online Computer Library Center's (OCLC) WorldShare Collection Manager (WCM) service. This comparison was designed to determine the best source for quality e-resource metadata. Findings from this comparison were used to inform decisions regarding record sources, staffing, and workflow for quality control activities.

## Background

The George A. Smathers Libraries of the University of Florida (UF) have cataloged e-resources since the early 1990s. Initially, UF catalogers in the Cataloging Services department (CatS) included a link to the electronic version of a resource in the catalog record for the print version. Since UF is a Regional Federal Depository Library, many of the earliest e-resources cataloged were government documents. Electronic journals (e-journals) were listed alphabetically with links to separate websites for patron access. As national best practices changed, as reflected in OCLC's *Bibliographic Formats and Standards*[1] and *Cataloging Electronic Resources: OCLC-MARC Coding Guidelines*,[2] to endorse separate records for print and electronic versions, so did UF's. UF catalogers adopted this practice in 2004.

In addition, UF is part of an 11-member consortium of the state's public university libraries. In 2012, the library catalogs of the various consortium members merged into one union catalog. By agreement, the consortium has a set of shared bibliographic guidelines that govern how and what bibliographic data is entered into the consortial catalog. As a result of the merger and changes to national best practices and state guidelines, multiple cleanup issues were identified, some of which are still being addressed.

As the number of quality concerns for electronic resource (e-resource) metadata grew, cross-departmental groups such as an "856 Working Group" and "Links Monitoring and Maintenance Task Group" were charged to seek solutions. Link-checkers were successfully used by these groups to reduce the number of incorrect Uniform Resource Locators (URLs). By 2004, the number of e-journals had sky-rocketed and the Links Monitoring and Maintenance Task Group recommended that UF contract with Serials Solutions, now ProQuest, to provide bibliographic records for e-journals using the 360 MARC Updates service. Eventually, this service was extended to include some of the Libraries' electronic book (e-book) collections. However, due to a dramatic increase in e-book holdings (UF Libraries held approximately 1.3 million e-books at the end of the 2016 fiscal year), concerns regarding the quality of Serials Solutions records, and variances in availability of quality MAchine-Readable Cataloging (MARC) record sources for a given collection, a mixture of vendor-supplied and OCLC WorldCat records have been used to supplement the 360 MARC Update subscription over the years.

More often than not, MARC records for new e-book acquisitions could be obtained from multiple sources and, in increasingly rare cases, could be negotiated as part of the purchase agreement. For example, records for individual e-books ordered via Yankee Book Peddler (YBP) or Coutts could be obtained from the seller, the publisher/aggregator, Serials Solutions, or OCLC. Similarly, records for e-book collections might come from the publisher/aggregator, Serials Solutions, or OCLC. However, not all sources offer the same quality of records for all platforms and for certain collections, some sources have proven to be easier to manage than others.

Sources for record sets were selected through an informal process of assessing the acquisition stream of the resource (firm orders, patron driven acquisitions (PDA)/demand driven acquisitions (DDA)/evidence based acquisitions (EBA), packages, subscriptions), availability and quality of records, and ease of maintenance for updating record sets. Due to a variety of staffing and workflow issues, much of the batch loading of both print and electronic resource MARC records was transferred to the Electronic Resource Unit and the Print & Media Unit in the Acquisitions & Collections Services Department (AcqCS). These units now shoulder much of the responsibility for the maintenance of the Libraries' vast e-resource collection and for ensuring that a significant portion of newly acquired print materials are represented in the catalog in a timely manner by utilizing shelf-ready services.

Advantages to batch loading include reduction in staff hours devoted to cataloging and the ability to keep holdings updated as licensed e-resource packages change. Disadvantages include the loss of a built-in opportunity for quality control exercised through manual cataloging. Thus, in order to streamline workflows and prepare for an impending migration to a next-generation Integrated Library System (ILS), a need was identified to find the best source or sources for e-book metadata.

Quality control (QC) is addressed in several ways in the Cataloging Services and Acquisitions & Collections Services departments. Due to the sheer volume of e-resource records, the complexity and diversity of the records and their sources, and staffing-related budgetary restraints, pre-ingest quality control measures are very limited. Rarely are records evaluated prior to purchase or checked before they are loaded into the catalog. As a result, UF has had to rely more heavily on end-user problem reporting as a way to expose problems with these records. One way users can report problems or concerns with the information in the records is through the Libraries' online public access catalog (OPAC). At the bottom of the screen for every record in the OPAC, there is a "report a problem with this record" link. By clicking the link, users can report issues via email to the CatS department's "Catalog Problems" mailbox. Members of the department monitor the mailbox daily and try to address the issue within 24 business hours. Students, staff, and faculty all report issues via these links. Users may also report issues through "Ask A Librarian" transactions. This is a statewide virtual reference service available via email, chat, or text messaging. Faculty, staff, and students can also report problems through the Libraries' IT service request system known as "Grover." This service allows users to report problems or questions dealing with areas such as: access to e-journals, e-books, and databases; licensing issues; e-journal holdings; cost and usage reports, etc. Faculty and staff can also request the purchase of a new e-resource or the cancellation of a currently subscribed e-resource. Finally, problems are also reported directly to members of the two departments by other faculty or staff via email. Due to the size of the Libraries' e-resource collections, these methods are often the only ways that issues in records from e-resource packages are brought to the attention of CatS or AcqCS.

## Literature review

Ravit H. David and Dana Thomas detailed a study of metadata quality in e-book records found in the Ontario Council of University Libraries' Scholars Portal Platform.[3] The study "looked for accuracy and consistency as the main characters of metadata quality for books in digital format."[4] Noting that end-users generally aim their search strategies toward metadata in certain MARC fields and therefore, quality control measures could be more tightly focused, the authors determined that the three most important fields on which to focus QC efforts were subject, title, and author.[5] David and Thomas attempted to quantify the costs associated with the QC work done during their study and finding it expensive, concluded that "by understanding which fields were most important to end-users, we could prioritize, or even limit, error correction to these fields."[6]

Roman S. Panchyshyn discussed a tool developed at the Kent State University Libraries (KSUL), referred to as an "E-Book Checklist," which documents workflow decisions for each batch-loaded MARC record set.[7] The checklist asks a series of questions, many of which are aimed at identifying and potentially correcting quality issues with the MARC records.[8] The author noted several advantages to utilizing the checklist. It allowed for the creation of valuable documentation for batch cataloging projects; the capturing of information on the quality of vendor records used by KSUL, facilitating cooperation between acquisitions, cataloging, systems, and public services staff; and finally, helping to identify and address local workflow issues.[9]

Amalia Beisler and Lisa Kurt's 2012 article documented the University of Nevada, Reno (UNR) Library's history of e-book acquisitions and access workflows, discussed efforts aimed at addressing inefficiencies in those workflows, and outlined changes to organizational structure and workflows intended to improve processes.[10] Beisler and Kurt provided background on difficulties that have historically affected e-book workflows.[11] Many of the issues the UNR library dealt with in 2012 could be challenges for libraries struggling to understand and perfect their e-book workflows today. The authors addressed quality management by focusing on the role of communication between the departments involved. To a large extent, this communication involves quality assurance issues in the acquisitions and batch-load phases, but also encompasses quality control measures in the reporting of problems related to specific records that had been loaded previously.

UNR's history of e-book acquisitions is likely very similar to that of other academic libraries. As the number of methods for purchasing e-books rose, so too did the complications surrounding processes, eventually leading UNR to establish a task force to review all aspects of e-book workflows and to propose solutions to the many issues surrounding those workflows. One of the first considerations the UNR task force thought should be included in the assessment phase of any new purchase was the availability and quality of MARC records for that purchase.[12] Additionally, the task force implemented changes that address communication between the various units with responsibilities in the e-book lifecycle. They utilized a SharePoint form to apprise Cataloging & Metadata department staff as to how and where records could be retrieved and to provide a tracking mechanism for the staff to record the review of a record set.[13]

Kristen E. Martin and Kavita Mundle outlined their experiences at the University of Illinois at Chicago (UIC) with purchased vendor-supplied MARC records for Springer e-book materials.[14] The focus of their quality management efforts was centered on aspects of quality assurance prior to and soon after the purchase and loading of the records. As part of a consortium with a shared union catalog, UIC has additional considerations with purchased record sets. The consortium's administrative office batch loads records that the individual libraries have purchased into the union catalog for display in that library's catalog. Noting the advantages of having the weight of a consortium behind negotiations with vendors, the authors worked with the MarcEdit utility to evaluate sample records and shared their findings with the vendor in order to improve the quality of the records prior to ingest. They determined that there were three types of problems with the records. These were access issues, load issues, and record-quality issues.[15] Based on their experience, the authors recommended that libraries: (1) formulate requirements for the records to be purchased and use the requirements in negotiations with the vendors; (2) obtain a large sample set of records beforehand to be used in an evaluation; (3) determine a timeline for record improvements with the vendor; and (4) work together with other consortium libraries to improve records for mutual use.[16]

Annie Wu and Anne M. Mitchell at the University of Houston Libraries (UHL) discussed the growth of their e-book collections and the attendant issues of managing those collections.[17] Focused on large-scale batches of e-book records supplied by their vendors, the authors addressed quality management in the policies and procedures developed as a response to UHL's increased acquisition of electronic materials. Centering their efforts on the use of the MarcEdit tool and the adoption of provider-neutral cataloging guidelines, UHL incorporates both quality assurance and quality control measures at various stages. Wu and Mitchell noted that UHL catalogers examine each e-book package to determine a workflow. Records are edited in batch with MarcEdit prior to ingesting into the catalog. MarcEdit's "field count," "record deduplication," and "validate" functions are key in the overall process, as is the addition of a defined prefix in the 001 field to differentiate UHL's records from those of their partners in a shared catalog. Post-ingest quality control is addressed, in part, by periodic updates to the sets of vendor records. This is done by loading new record sets either annually or monthly, depending on the nature of a given e-book package. UHL's cataloging department maintains a table in its "intranet space detailing the package name and provider, syntax for the unique identifier, date of last update, and review frequency."[18] The authors observed that skills for managing these types of records and the skills typically used in print monograph cataloging are quite different. They acknowledged that UHL has begun to employ a "third party resource management (MARC) service to reconcile titles across packages and supply provider-neutral records" as a partial solution for handling the exponential growth and variety of their e-book collections.[19]

Richard Sapon-White outlined the development of various workflows required by the cataloging department at the Oregon State University Libraries (OSUL) for electronic books purchased for their collections.[20] He described the procedures implemented for each of three vendors, E-Book Library (EBL), Springer Verlag, and Morgan & Claypool. Essentially, their workflows are guided by "whether bibliographic records are ordered and downloaded in bulk or individually; the method for downloading bibliographic records; the quality of the bibliographic records, including description, subject analysis and the presence or absence of OCLC control numbers; and training personnel."[21] Because of this, each vendor generally requires a unique workflow. Also noting the common belief that vendor records can be of poor quality, he highlighted the issues of bringing these records up to national standards and their typical need for authority work. His discussion of quality management was largely folded into the description of the overall workflow for each vendor and was chiefly concerned with quality assurance on the front end of the process. For OSUL, the primary key in evaluating vendor records is whether the records contain OCLC control numbers and this, in turn, governs much of the subsequent workflow.[22]

Li Zhang at the Mississippi State Universities Libraries documented a 2013 presentation on e-book cataloging given by Miao Jin from Hinds Community College in Jackson, MS.[23] Jin provided her recommendations based on practices at Hinds and highlighted the importance of effective communication with vendors. Echoing Martin and Mundle at UIC, one recommendation of note was to request a large sample set of MARC records for evaluation before the library's e-book purchase is completed. The library can assess the quality of the records and then work with the vendors to make changes to the records before they are sent to the library. This, she maintained, will save cataloging time in the long run.[24]

Bénaud and Bordeianu outlined their experience at the University of New Mexico when its Library transitioned from a traditional ILS to OCLC's World-Share Management Services platform (WMS).[25] The article provides an overview of "cataloging" work in WMS and draws attention to a number of strengths and weaknesses in the platform. Noting that "in WMS, the OCLC master record is the de facto local record,"[26] the authors discussed several workflow changes that had to be adopted in order to accommodate the work traditionally done by their acquisitions staff and cataloging staff, especially around local data and local practices. The authors did not specifically address quality management, but indirectly raised a number of issues in their discussion of various features and procedures in

WMS. For instance, they noted that the WMS "interface is ... less nimble than its Connexion client counterpart because it does not support macros and shortcuts"[27] and "WMS terminology is ... puzzling because it is not consistent with established vocabulary in Connexion."[28] Additionally, authority record creation and updating must be done in Connexion, rather than in WMS. All of which invites disparity and potential for more cataloging errors due to increased reliance on manual data entry, interpretation of varying naming conventions, and more movement between the two interfaces. The potential for error is also amplified by WMS' lack of functionality for "list creation, global updates, and rapid updates,"[29] the need for libraries to develop workarounds for displaying holdings information for serials,[30] and the fact that local information for special collections materials "is not prominently displayed in the record and therefore harder for patrons to distinguish."[31] It is important to note that while there are a number of advantages to community-wide iterative updates to master records in the OCLC database, Bénaud and Bordeianu's article highlights the need for quality management scrutiny, no matter the source of the record.

Very little has been published regarding the quality control of streaming media records. McDonald and Johnston[32] provide a discussion on cataloging streaming video records in a consortium environment and outline steps taken to copy catalog titles using OCLC provider-neutral records with several local modifications. Additional research in the area of cataloging streaming media is needed in order to better understand the unique challenges these formats pose to catalogers.

This review of relevant literature indicates that an emphasis on assessing workflows is critical to developing QC best practices. Many of the articles addressed the need for QC and highlighted the development of policies and procedures based on local needs. The present article adds to the literature by examining data in specific MARC fields in order to provide a comparison between vendor-supplied records and records from WorldShare Collection Manager (WCM). This comparison can be used to inform decisions regarding the selection of e-book records.

## Methodology

The authors focused their attention on the question: Which source provides higher quality records—the standard vendors or WCM? The authors also wanted to know what implications there were for how libraries allocate their funding for e-resources and how they allocate their resources for quality management efforts. To that end, the authors selected several vendor-supplied and a few OCLC-supplied record sets for e-resources from the library catalog to analyze. These included vendor records from Serials Solutions and ProQuest's ebrary, and OCLC records for IEEE Xplore and Springer Publishing collections. These were compared with the corresponding record sets in WCM. Collections were chosen because they impacted workflows in both CatS and AcqCS, they offered a variety of format types, and because they represented different record sources.

## Observations and comparisons

The authors identified a number of checkpoints found in quality bibliographic records and looked to see whether the identified elements were appropriately described in the groups of sample records. Some of the checkpoints included were whether or not accurate titles were included, whether the listed author in the 100 field was controlled by a Library of Congress NACO Authority File (LCNAF) heading, and whether subject access points were present. Also considered were whether appropriate International Standard Book Numbers (ISBNs) were present, whether call numbers with cutters were included, whether summaries and contents were available, and whether the links in the records worked correctly. These check-points are equally important to the quality control involved in manual cataloging activity and are integral to the user's ability to find, select, and obtain library resources.

Ten purchased MARC records from each of 15 different e-book and streaming video collections were chosen from UF's Aleph ILS catalog as sample sets and were reviewed by the authors to see how the quality of the records would impact patron access (Table 1). E-books were chosen because they represent one of the most commonly accessed e-resource types used at the Libraries and streaming videos were chosen to broaden the scope of the review so that another e-resource format could be assessed. For ten of the fifteen collections, the e-resource vendor supplied the records for the collection (Books24×7 (B24×7), Digitalia, Ebrary E-Libro (Ebrary E-L), Ebrary SciTech (Ebrary ST), Education in Video (EIV), Henry Stewart Talks (HST), Humanities E-Book (HEB), Loeb Classical Library (LCL), PsycBooks (PB), and SUSPDA UF Purchase (PDA)). Records from OCLC WorldCat were loaded for four of the vendor collections (IEEE Xplore (IEEE), Knovel, Referex, Springer E-Book (Springer). One "collection" was comprised of e-books from a variety of sources (both purchased from vendors and open-access) for which Serials Solutions supplied the records (SerSolUFEbook (SerSol)). The authors then compared these records with records found in WCM for the same collections to get an idea of the differences between the two. All but one of the collections (Digitalia) were in WCM. To follow are more detailed descriptions of the comparisons and a chart that summarizes our observations (Figure 1).

Title matches: Although there were anecdotal reports of titles on records not matching the titles on the actual resource, this was not typical in the sample catalog records. Of the collections, eleven (B24×7, Digitalia, HEB, HST, IEEE, Knovel, LCL, PB, PDA, Referex, Springer) had perfect matches on 100% of their records; two (Ebrary E-L, SerSol) had matches on 90%; one (Ebrary ST) had matches on 80%; and one (EIV) had matches on 70%. The WCM records were not quite as good in this regard. Of the collections,

**Table 1.** Data elements in e-resource records by collection.

| Collection name | Title matches | Controlled author | Subject | ISBN (print and / or electronic) | Classification numbers | Summary | Table of contents | Link correct |
|---|---|---|---|---|---|---|---|---|
| Books 24×7 (B24×7) (Aleph, vendor) | 100% | 90% | 100% | 100% | 100% | 0% | 0% | 100% |
| Books 24×7 (B24×7) (WorldShare) | 100% | 64% | 100% | 100% | 100% | 83% | 100% | 100% |
| Digitalia (Aleph, vendor) | 100% | 60% | 100% | 100% | 100% | 0% | 20% | 100% |
| Digitalia (no WorldShare records) | N/A | N/A | N/A | N/A | N/A | N/A | N/A | N/A |
| Ebrary E-Libro (Ebrary E-L) (Aleph, vendor) | 90% | 20% | 100% | 60% | 100% | 0% | 0% | 100% |
| Ebrary E-Libro (Ebrary E-L) (WorldShare) | 50% | 50% | 33% | 83% | 100% | 0% | 0% | N/A |
| Ebrary SciTech (Ebrary ST) (Aleph, vendor) | 80% | 80% | 100% | 100% | 100% | 0% | 0% | 100% |
| Ebrary SciTech (Ebrary ST) (WorldShare) | 100% | 67% | 100% | 100% | 100% | 50% | 17% | N/A |
| Education in Video (EIV) (Aleph, vendor) | 70% | 90% | 100% | N/A | 0% | 100% | 0% | 100% |
| Education in Video (EIV) (WorldShare) | 100% | 57% | 100% | N/A | 0% | 83% | 0% | 83% |
| Henry Stewart Talks (HST) (Aleph, vendor) | 100% | 0% | 100% | N/A | 0% | 0% | 100% | 100% |
| Henry Stewart Talks (HST) (WorldShare) | 100% | 33% | 100% | N/A | 0% | 0% | 100% | 100% |
| Humanities E-Book (HEB) (Aleph, vendor) | 100% | 100% | 100% | 60% | 100% | 0% | 10% | 100% |
| Humanities E-Book (HEB) (WorldShare) | 100% | 100% | 100% | 100% | 100% | 17% | 0% | 100% |
| IEEE XPLORE (IEEE) (Aleph, OCLC) | 100% | 100% | 100% | 100% | 100% | 90% | 70% | 100% |
| IEEE XPLORE (IEEE) (WorldShare) | 100% | 91% | 100% | 100% | 100% | 100% | 83% | 100% |
| Knovel (Aleph, OCLC) | 100% | 100% | 100% | 100% | 100% | 0% | 10% | 90% |
| Knovel (WorldShare) | 100% | 92% | 100% | 100% | 100% | 50% | 50% | 100% |
| Loeb Classical Library (LCL) (Aleph, vendor) | 100% | 70% | 100% | 100% | 100% | 100% | 0% | 100% |
| Loeb Classical Library (LCL) (WorldShare) | 100% | 71% | 100% | 83% | 100% | 33% | 100% | 100% |
| PsycBooks (PB) (Aleph, vendor) | 100% | 90% | 100% | 70% | 100% | 100% | 60% | 100% |
| PsycBooks (PB) (WorldShare) | 100% | 100% | 100% | 0% | 100% | 100% | 0% | 100% |
| Referex (Aleph, OCLC) | 100% | 100% | 100% | 100% | 100% | 90% | 100% | 100% |
| Referex (WorldShare) | 100% | 100% | 100% | 100% | 100% | 100% | 100% | 100% |
| SerSolUFEbook (SerSol) (Aleph, vendor) | 90% | 0% | 10% | 10% | 10% | 0% | 0% | 80% |
| SerSolUFEbook (SerSol) (WorldShare) | 100% | 100% | 100% | 100% | 100% | 67% | 67% | 100% |
| Springer E-Book (Springer) (Aleph, OCLC) | 100% | 70% | 100% | 100% | 100% | 60% | 30% | 100% |
| Springer E-Book (Springer) (WorldShare) | 100% | 87% | 100% | 100% | 100% | 100% | 83% | 100% |
| SUSPDA UF Purchase (PDA) (Aleph, Coutts) | 100% | 100% | 100% | 100% | 100% | 0% | 0% | 100% |
| SUSPDA UF Purchase (PDA) (WorldShare) | 67% | 75% | 100% | 100% | 100% | 100% | 67% | 100% |
| **Total** | | | | | | | | |
| Catalog records (Vendor & OCLC) | 95% | 71% | 94% | 85% | 81% | 36% | 27% | 98% |
| WorldShare | 94% | 78% | 95% | 89% | 86% | 63% | 55% | 99% |

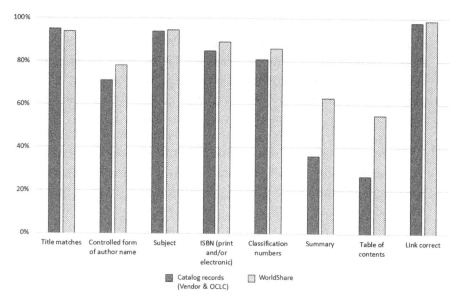

**Figure 1.** Data elements in e-resource records.

twelve (B24×7, Ebrary ST, EIV, HEB, HST, IEEE, Knovel, LCL, PB, Referex, SerSol, Springer) had perfect matches on 100% of their records, one (PDA) had matches on 67%, and one (Ebrary E-L) had matches on 50%.

**Author and controlled form of author**: The name of the author is among the most important access points for most works, and having all works by the same entity presented with the same form of the name is both valuable and expensive. Almost all the catalog records included authors when appropriate. Of the sample collections, six (EIV, HEB, IEEE, Knovel, PDA, Referex) always had consistent, controlled forms of names in the records, two (B24×7, PB) had them 90% of the time, four (Digitalia, Ebrary ST, LCL, Springer) had them 60–80% of the time, and three (Ebrary E-L, HST, SerSol) had them 20% of the time or less. The WCM records were slightly better; every collection but one had at least 50% of the forms of name controlled in the records. Of the collections, four (HEB, PB, Referex, SerSol) always used consistent, controlled forms of names, three (IEEE, Knovel, Springer) used them 87–92% of the time, four (B24×7, Ebrary ST, LCL, PDA) used them 64–75% of the time, and two (Ebrary E-L, EIV) used them 50–57% of the time. HST used them only 33% of the time.

**Subjects**: The subject of a nonfiction work is an important access point for users, even those who confine their search strategy to simple keywords. It offers what is possibly the most effective means of identifying desired works, other than searching for known titles. Of course, not all subject headings are of the same quality. For the purposes of this article, the authors only looked for the presence of subject headings and did not review them for currency of terminology or try to judge their relative merit. In the sample of catalog records, fourteen collections (all but SerSol) had subjects in all of the records. SerSol had them in only 10% of the records. The WCM records were similar. Of these collections, thirteen (all but Ebrary E-Libro) had subjects in all of the records; Ebrary E-Libro had them in only 33% of its records.

**ISBNs (print and/or electronic)**: ISBNs are vital to efficient access for staff working in any catalog, but even more so in a consortium. Two collections (EIV, HST) consist of streaming videos and therefore properly did not have ISBNs. Of the collections, three (Ebrary ST, IEEE, PDA) had print and electronic version ISBNs on all of the catalog records, three (Digitalia, Knovel, Springer) had both on 80–90% of the records, one (B24×7) had both on 60%, and one (PB) had both on 30%. Electronic version-only ISBNs were in the records for only one collection (Knovel), and were on only 20% of those records. Print version-only ISBNs were more common, being provided on 100% of the records in one collection (LCL), on 90% in one collection (Referex), on 60% in one collection (HEB), and on 10–40% in six collections (B24×7, Digitalia, Ebrary E-L, PB, SerSol, Springer). WCM records were similar to catalog records for most collections, but in a few cases were better sources for ISBNs.

**Classification and cutter numbers**: Classification can serve to bring like resources together, not only in the print environment, but also in the electronic. Virtual shelf-lists rely on the presence of at least a classification number in the record and can extend and enhance the presentation of both print and electronic resources for the user. One virtual shelf-list example at UF was prepared in order to search U.S. Federal Documents (housed off campus) by their Superintendent of Documents Classification (SuDoc) number. It can be seen at http://guides.uflib.ufl.edu/c.php?g=220611. In the catalog sample sets, seven collections (B24×7, Ebrary E-L, Ebrary ST, LCL, PB, PDA, Referex) had both class and cutter numbers for all the records, four (HEB, IEEE, Knovel, Springer) had either the class and cutter or just the class number for their records, one (Digitalia) had only class numbers for all the records, and two (EIV, HST) had no class numbers. One (SerSol) had both class and cutter, but on only 10% of the records. WCM records were again similar: twelve (B24×7, Ebrary E-L, Ebrary ST, HEB, IEEE, Knovel, LCL, PDA, PsycBooks, Referex, SerSol, Springer) provided at least a class number in all their records, only two (EIV, HST) provided no class numbers.

**Summaries**: The summary can serve to describe the coverage of a work and to facilitate access via uncontrolled keyword searching. This enhances discovery and supports selection and identification of useful resources. Summaries were included in 100% of the catalog records for three collections (EIV, LCL, PB), in 90% of the records for two (IEEE, Referex), in 60% of the records for one (Springer), and in none of the records for nine collections (B24×7, Digitalia, Ebrary E-L, Ebrary ST, HEB, HST, Knovel, PDA, SerSol). The WCM records were definitely better in this regard. Summaries were included in 100% of the records for five collections (IEEE, PB, PDA, Referex, Springer), in 83% of the records for two (B24×7, EIV), in 67% for one (SerSol), in 50% for two (Ebrary ST, Knovel), in 33% for one (LCL), in 17% for one (HEB), and in none of the records for only two collections (Ebrary E-L, HST).

**Tables of contents**: Like summaries, tables of contents can serve both descriptive and access purposes to connect users to resources and to enable them to more easily select and identify the resources they need. Some resources lend themselves better to useful tables of contents than others. Conference proceedings are a good example of when tables of contents can provide a rich source of data. In the sample catalog records there were two collections (HST, Referex) that had tables of contents in 100% of their records, one (IEEE) that had them in 70% of the records, one (PB) that had them in 60% of the records, one (Springer) that had them in 30%, one (Digitalia) that had them in 20%, two (HEB, Knovel) that had them in 10%, and seven (B24×7, Ebrary E-L, Ebrary ST, EIV, LCL, PDA, SerSol) that had them in none of the records. The WCM records were also markedly better in this regard. In the sample set there were four collections that had tables of contents in 100% of the records (B24×7, HST, LCL, Referex), two collections (IEEE, Springer) had one in 83% of the records, two (PDA, SerSol) in 67%, one (Knovel) in 50%, one (Ebrary ST) in 17%, and four collections (Ebrary E-L, EIV, HEB, PB) had no table of contents in any of the records.

**Correct links**: While the correct link is not generally helpful for description or indexing, the absence of a correct link is a deal-breaker for the user. Of the collections sampled from the catalog, thirteen (B24×7, Digitalia, Ebrary E-L, Ebrary ST, EIV, HEB, HST, IEEE, LCL, PB, PDA, Referex, Springer) had correct links on 100% of the records, one (Knovel) on 90%, and one (SerSol) on 80%. WCM seemed to have correct links in similar proportions. Eleven of those collections (B24×7, HEB, HST, IEEE, Knovel, LCL, PB, PDA, Referex, SerSol, Springer) had correct links on 100% of the records and one (EIV) had correct links on 83% of the records. The links in WCM for the two Ebrary collections that were sampled were generic links. These generic links do not allow UF users access to the e-books. If UF tagged the Ebrary collections in the knowledge base and requested WCM records, UF would also provide a library-specific identifier from Ebrary. OCLC would then include UF-specific links in the WCM records sent to us. Obviously, it is crucial for good customer service to be able to quickly identify and correct broken links to e-resources, no matter the source of the records.

A discussion follows of two other measures of quality that were not included in the "Data elements in e-resource records by collection" table, in each case for different reasons.

**Duplicate records**: Duplicate catalog records for the same e-resource supplied by different vendors often make the loading of revised records more difficult.

Since the UF catalog database is part of the consortial bibliographic file for all of Florida's public university libraries, the addition of an institution-specific URL to an existing record can be problematic. Duplicate records for the same resource may sometimes be confusing to patrons. If an institution has access to a resource through more than one vendor and one of the links is temporarily broken, the patron may not easily be able to go to another catalog record and click on the link there. In the sample catalog records, two collections (IEEE, PB) had records with 90% duplication, one (Referex) with 70%, one (Knovel) with 60%, two (SerSol, Springer) with 40%, two (Digitalia, PDA) with 30%, one (B24×7) with 20%, three (Ebrary E-L, Ebrary ST, HEB) with 10%, and only three collections (EIV, HST, LCL) had no duplication. OCLC aims to have only one provider-neutral record for the same electronic resource in the WorldCat database. There may be cases where a single WCM record could substitute for two or more catalog records representing different vendor sources for the same e-resource. The authors did not investigate this possibility in the case study, although certainly the reduction of record duplication would benefit both patrons and staff.

**Presence of OCLC numbers**: The OCLC number can be very useful for staff access and for managing duplication of records in the catalog. As mentioned, record duplication can have an impact on patron access. For each e-resource collection drawn from the catalog, it was noted whether the records were OCLC records or vendor records. Only four of the fifteen collections (27%) had OCLC records. For vendor records, the authors also noted whether or not there was an OCLC number in the record. The OCLC number was often, but not always, found to be for the corresponding OCLC record. For example, in some cases the OCLC number was for the print version, not the e-resource. Of the collections with vendor records, four (B24×7, Digitalia, HST, SerSol) had no OCLC numbers on the records, five (Ebrary E-L, Ebrary ST, EIV, HEB, PB) had them in 50–90% of the records, and two (LCL, PDA) had them in 100% of the records. All but one of the collections (Digitalia) were in WCM. Of the collections in WCM, ten (B24×7, Ebrary E-L, Ebrary ST, EIV, HEB, IEEE, Knovel, LCL, PDA, Springer) had OCLC records for all the sample titles, one (Referex) had OCLC records for 83% of the titles, and three (HST, PB, SerSol) had OCLC records for 50% of the titles.

While observed characteristics differed among the sets of vendor-supplied records, it was clear that OCLC WCM records were reliably of good quality and provided good support for discovery and access for users. As reflected in Table 1 and Figure 1, the sample data supported this conclusion. The WCM records were much more likely to include summaries and tables of contents. These records were slightly more likely to include classification numbers and the controlled forms of the author's names as well.

As can be seen in Table 1, there were several instances where vendor records either equaled or scored higher in measures of quality than WCM records. For example, PsycBooks vendor records mostly equaled or outscored WCM. They only scored slightly lower for controlled form of author names. Education in Video vendor records mostly equaled or outscored WCM (but scored lower for title matches). Likewise, Loeb Classical Library vendor records only scored lower for tables of contents. Henry Stewart Talks vendor records mostly equaled WCM (but scored lower for controlled form of author names). Humanities E-Book vendor records mostly equaled or nearly equaled WCM (but scored lower for ISBN). Nevertheless, the overall comparison demonstrated that the quality of the WCM records improved discoverability of and access to e-resources enough to justify the shift to WCM as the preferred record source.

## Discussion and outcomes

This analysis of record quality led the leadership of the Cataloging Services (CatS) and Acquisitions & Collections Services (AcqCS) departments to implement an initiative to utilize WorldShare Collection Manager (WCM) as a record source for as many e-book collection sets and streaming video sets as feasible in order to receive consistently high-quality records and to reduce the number of record sources for e-resources. This was a natural extension of an ongoing pilot/exploration project previously initiated by the two departments. Both had existing working groups that tackled workflow issues of this nature. Ad hoc subgroups from each department's working group were formed to focus specifically on the WCM migration and several joint meetings were held for planning purposes. The goal was to ensure selection of the best quality records and make what was once a complicated, if not convoluted, workflow simpler. However, it became apparent that, even if using a data-driven approach to establish preferred sources of MARC records, implementing this type of change is not always easy.

The shift to WCM was paralleled with a transfer of responsibility for batch record loading entirely to the AcqCS department. Previously, the technical expertise for batch record loading and maintenance was held in both departments. While AcqCS staff often devised record loading parameters, profiles, and workflows, a key staff member in CatS with the expertise to review record loading setup, profiles, technical workflows, load records, and make global changes was frequently consulted on complicated loading parameters and complex workflows. During the initial stages of the migration to WCM, staff from both AcqCS and CatS loaded and reviewed sets of WCM records for select e-resource collections. In January 2017, the CatS staff member primarily responsible for batch record loading was assigned to the E-Resources Unit of the AcqCS department. In turn, AcqCS assumed responsibility for all batch record loading activities, including the WCM migration. This led to a number of workflow changes.

Prior to identifying WCM as the preferred source of e-book and streaming media MARC records the Libraries would either load vendor-provided MARC records or Serials Solutions 360 MARC service records for most of these materials.

The AcqCS department is now in the process of identifying perpetually owned and subscription e-book and streaming media currently represented in the catalog by vendor or Serials Solutions records and replacing those with WCM records. A core team of expert record loaders formed of staff from both the Print & Media Unit and the E-Resource Unit of AcqCS is coordinating the WCM migration, but all staff from both units are participating in migration efforts. Future plans include utilizing WCM for firm ordered e-books and creating custom collections in WCM for resources that are not represented in the knowledge base. Serials Solutions will continue to be utilized for collections and databases containing journals or a mixture of formats for now, with plans to migrate to the EBSCO MARC Update service when the Libraries migrate to EBSCO's EDS discovery index.

There have been definite advantages for UF in using WCM as a source of e-resource records. When UF requests MARC records for an e-resource collection in WCM, UF's holdings are automatically updated in WorldCat, and WCM offers the ability to set OCLC holdings for collections tagged in the knowledge base and to set interlibrary loan (ILL) restrictions for collections where the library did not license those rights. UF shares bibliographic records with the other state universities in a consortial catalog and the intent is to have a single bibliographic record in the catalog for each unique resource. A significant number of e-resource records in the catalog are OCLC records. Duplicate records in the catalog for the same e-resource can cause problems for both patrons and library staff. OCLC's policy to have only one provider-neutral record for an e-resource results in a single record with links to various platforms. Therefore, for example, an incoming UF WCM record with links to the Springer and Books24×7 platforms can match on an existing catalog record with links to different platforms for other consortial libraries. This can result in a significant reduction in numbers of duplicate records in the catalog.

Nevertheless, several challenges have surfaced as a result of loading available WCM records. Since UF shares bibliographic records with the other state university libraries, staff in the consortium libraries try to avoid overlaying fields added to a catalog record by another institution. These can include, for example, MeSH headings added by a health sciences cataloger or a note that an e-book was purchased with funds from a particular endowment. Therefore, the profiles for loading records are configured so that when the record loader finds a "matching" record in the catalog, only the 856 field with a specific link for UF is added to the existing record. Currently, no other fields from the incoming record are added to the existing record, but there are plans to revise loading profiles to update fields in the existing record with incoming fields key to discoverability, like title, author, subject headings, and call numbers.

There are also issues which have slowed the changeover from vendor records to WCM records. It can be difficult to identify which WCM collection or collections match a collection for which UF has vendor records. In some cases, staff need to identify the individual titles within a WCM collection to which UF has access. The changeover has required collection-by-collection analysis since once WCM records are loaded for a collection, the corresponding vendor records need to be deleted from the catalog. Therefore, staff must request separate record files for each WCM collection. This has resulted in a large number of small, individual files to load. Eventually, staff will be able to request that records from all the collections come in larger, combined files.

The record loader is now set to look for a catalog record or records with a matching OCLC number. One of the problems resulting from the merge of the universities' bibliographic records in the shared catalog is that records from the same university with the same OCLC number were not merged. In addition, there are a significant number of vendor records that contain OCLC numbers as well as a vendor record number. Whenever the record loader encounters more than one catalog record with the same OCLC number, the incoming record is not loaded. Staff have to spend a great deal of time determining if duplicate catalog records can be merged or not, then adding UF's link and holdings to an existing catalog record.

Since WCM records will largely replace vendor records in this shift, staff will have many vendor records to delete as WCM records are added. As of December 2016, UF had 636,590 records coming from the Libraries' major supplier of e-book records. UF has tens of thousands of e-book records from other vendors as well.

There are additional challenges yet to be tackled. Several of the e-resource collections for which the Libraries have vendor records are not currently represented in WCM. Hopefully, some of these collections will become available before the migration to the next-generation ILS. It is possible to identify relevant WorldCat records and create new e-resource collections in WCM. However, this can be a time-consuming process for departments with limited staffing. By the time of the migration to the new ILS, UF will no longer have the e-book records from its largest supplier and there will be a need to find record sources other than WCM for some e-resource collections.

As outlined above, there are difficulties with replacing vendor records with WCM records. Nevertheless, the better quality overall of the WCM records and the reduction in duplicate records in the catalog for the same resource should result in improved e-resource retrievability for the Libraries' users and more effective use of library staff time.

## Conclusions

Because of the complexity and volume of e-resource records and the method of ingest into the catalog, managing their bibliographic data quality is best served by selecting the highest quality records available. A comparison of bibliographic records for vendor-supplied e-resource collections with records for the same resources in OCLC's WCM service found that many metadata values were comparable, but that WCM records had many more summaries and tables of contents and slightly more classification numbers and controlled forms of authors' names. Since summaries and tables of contents bolster keyword searching and selection of resources, classification numbers aid with online browsing, and controlled forms of authors' names aid with retrievability of all relevant records, the research presented here shows that WCM records better support user ability to find, select, and obtain e-resources than vendor-supplied records. Libraries can use this information to make decisions regarding record sources, to negotiate with vendors, and to develop quality management efforts in cataloging workflows. At the University of Florida, this information informed a decision to select e-book and streaming video record sets from WCM when possible.

## ORCID

David Van Kleeck (iD) http://orcid.org/0000-0001-5649-321X
Hikaru Nakano (iD) http://orcid.org/0000-0003-0928-9800
Gerald Langford (iD) http://orcid.org/0000-0001-8567-7202
Trey Shelton (iD) http://orcid.org/0000-0002-5531-1549
Jimmie Lundgren (iD) http://orcid.org/0000-0002-5537-3133
Allison Jai O'Dell (iD) http://orcid.org/0000-0002-1261-0987

## Notes

1. OCLC, "Bibliographic Formats and Standards." Accessed January 18, 2017, https://www.oclc.org/bibformats/en.html
2. OCLC, "Cataloging Electronic Resources: OCLC-MARC Coding Guidelines." Accessed January 18, 2017, https://www.oclc.org/support/services/worldcat/documentation/cataloging/electronicresources.en.html
3. Ravit H. David and Dana Thomas, "Assessing Metadata and Controlling Quality in Scholarly Ebooks," *Cataloging & Classification Quarterly* 53, no. 7 (2015): 801–824, https://doi.org/10.1080/01639374.2015.1018397
4. Ibid., 807.
5. Ibid., 810.
6. Ibid., 818.
7. Roman S. Panchyshyn, "Asking the Right Questions: An E-Resource Checklist for Documenting Cataloging Decisions for Batch Cataloging Projects." *Technical Services Quarterly* 30, no. 1 (2012): 15–37, DOI: 10.1080/07317131.2013.735951
8. Ibid., 24–32.
9. Ibid., 24–25.
10. Amalia Beisler and Lisa Kurt, "E-book Workflow from Inquiry to Access: Facing the Challenges to Implementing E-book Access at the University of Nevada, Reno," *Collaborative Librarianship* 4, no. 3 (2012): 96–116.
11. Ibid., 101–102.
12. Ibid., 104.
13. Ibid., 112.
14. Kristin E. Martin and Kavita Mundle, "Cataloging e-books and vendor records: a case study at the University of Illinois at Chicago." *Library Resources & Technical Services* 54, no. 4 (2010): 227–237.
15. Ibid., 232.
16. Ibid., 235.
17. Anne M. Mitchell and Annie Wu. "Mass management of e-book catalog records: approaches, challenges, and solutions." *Library Resources & Technical Services* 54, no. 3 (2010): 164–174.

18. Ibid., 172.
19. Ibid., 173.
20. Richard Sapon-White, "E-book cataloging workflows at Oregon State University." *Library Resources & Technical Services* 58, no. 2 (2014): 127–136.
21. Ibid., 133.
22. Ibid., 134.
23. Li Zhang and Miao Jin, "Cataloging E-Books: Dealing with Vendors and Various Other Problems." *The Serials Librarian* 67, no. 1 (2014): 76–80, https://doi.org/10.1080/0361526X.2014.899295
24. Ibid., 79.
25. Claire-Lise Bénaud and Sever Bordeianu, "OCLC's WorldShare Management Services: A Brave New World for Catalogers," *Cataloging & Classification Quarterly* 53, no. 7 (2015): 738–752, https://doi.org/10.1080/01639374.2014.1003668
26. Ibid., 742.
27. Ibid., 745
28. Ibid., 751.
29. Ibid., 748.
30. Ibid., 749.
31. Ibid., 750.
32. Elizabeth McDonald. "Showtime! Cataloging and Providing Access to Streaming Video Records in the Online Catalog," *Tennessee Libraries* 58, no. 2 (2008): 1–5.

# Planning, Implementing, and Assessing a CD Reclassification Project

Robert B. Freeborn

**ABSTRACT**

In 2015, plans were put in place to relocate the entire compact disc collection of the Music and Media Center in the Arts and Humanities Library at Penn State's University Park campus, and to reclassify them from an accession number system to a more user-browsable one based on the Library of Congress Classification scheme. This article looks at the path that has being taken to reach this goal, and provides an initial assessment of the project at the halfway point.

## Introduction

In 2015, the music public services librarian at The Pennsylvania State University approached her music cataloging colleague about the possibility of reclassifying the entire musical compact disc (CD) collection housed in the Music and Media Center (MMC) of the University Park campus' Arts and Humanities (AH) Library. The collection of some 17,000 titles had been originally classified according to a local accession scheme and shelved in a closed-stack location, but now the music librarian proposed giving them Library of Congress Classification (LCC) numbers and creating a browsable open-shelving environment in which to house them. After a couple of test runs with specific genres, it was decided in 2016 to move ahead with the reclassification of all classical music titles; these discs represent the majority of MMC's CD holdings. While not complete, over a third of the collection has been reclassified at the time of writing. Based on this premise, the author will attempt to provide a history of the collection in question, review the literature, and examine similar library collections for insight and direction, detail the planning and implementation that was undertaken, and finally assess the work that has been completed.

## Background

The MMC began life in the Penn State School of Music as part of their Arts and Music Library. The collection of long playing vinyl records (LPs) was housed in a small caged area along with a selection of rare art books and music scores; all of which saw limited circulation. In 1978, the majority of the LPs and scores were moved from the School of Music to the University Libraries, and housed together in the Music Listening Room (later rechristened the Music and Media Center). The LPs were stored in a closed-stack environment located behind the reference desk, and classified using a home-grown accession system. The structure of this system is illustrated below:

Disc M83 Disc18 = Type of format

M = Musical

83 = Received in 1983

18 = This was the 18th disc received in 1983

When the library began accepting audiocassettes and compact discs, the system was adapted to work with these newer formats:

Cassette = Cass MC88 − 14 ("MC" standing for "Musical Cassette")

Compact disc = Disc MCD16 − 123 ("MCD" standing for "Musical Compact Disc")

Even when the University Libraries' Cataloging Department began processing these items, the accession classification system was retained for consistency's sake, mainly because the collection was not browsable. It should be noted that this system was only applied to musical recordings at the main University Park campus. Those few recordings located at one of Penn State's other 24 campuses are classified according to LCC, but their numbers are very small when compared to the MMC's acquisition rates.

After her arrival in 1994, the current music public services librarian inquired about the possibility of reclassifying the collection. While there was no opposition to this idea from either the library administration or the cataloging department, it would cost money in terms of staff time to reclassify them all, and there was no funding available for such an expense. It was not until the late 2010s when moving the collection to public browsing shelves was approved and special funding was acquired that the idea of reclassification became reality.

## Literature review and examination of other libraries

In her historical overview of music cataloging and classification in American libraries, Carol June Bradley noted that "although there has been a consistent effort to make [sound recordings] accessible to their users in such a way that their full potential will be realized, there has been little agreement about how best to accomplish this.[1] For her 1991 article, Linda Crow surveyed 123 academic libraries with collections of 5,000 or more sound recordings. Her results show that, while 78% of those contacted utilized Library of Congress Classification for their books and 74% for their scores, only 12% used it for their sound recordings. In fact, 66% stated that they classified their sound recordings using local accession numbers.[2] A quick examination of the online catalogs from our fellow Big 10 Academic Alliance Libraries appeared to bear out her findings. Using the terms "author = Beethoven" and "subject = symphonies," and by limiting the results to sound recordings, the author discovered that only 3 libraries out of the 13 searched utilized LCC for any of their CD collections. Expanding the search to include other large U.S. libraries (e.g., Harvard University, Library of Congress, University of North Carolina, University of Texas, UCLA, Yale University) show that they too utilize some form of locally created accession system.

So how did sound recordings often end up being classified differently from their print/score siblings? Daniel W. Kinney related in his article on classifying music moving image materials that there are several possible reasons for this separation. First, audiovisual formats were often housed in special locations for security reasons. Second, they needed special equipment to use them, and special shelving to accommodate their various sizes and shapes. Finally, Kinney noted: "a commonly held view was that audiovisual materials would eventually become worn and discarded; therefore, there was no real need for a classified arrangement, even if they were shelved in a public area."[3]

The author hypothesizes another reason for the use of accession numbers is the increased complexity of classifying sound recordings when compared to scores. Most printed musical titles consist of single or multiple works by a single composer, whereas sound recordings often feature various types of works by different composers. In addition, the emphasis of a recording might be focused on the performer rather than the composer (e.g., "Herbert von Karajan: The Great Recordings" published by EMI). When staff had to personally create catalog records for every title that came across their desk, simplifying sound recording classification made sense. In this age of cooperative cataloging, where numerous libraries share the collective cataloging and classification burden, this simplification is not as important as it used to be. Finally, there has been a recent push for academic libraries to adopt a more student-centered approach to their services, and moving the compact discs to open shelves fits perfectly with this approach. In her article on access to circulating videos in academic libraries, Rachel P. King advocated for open-stack browsing as being both more user-friendly and providing students with exposure to information-organization concepts that help hone their ability to understand and question the taxonomies being used "to bring order to libraries."[4] I believe that a similar approach to sound recordings would increase the collection's use and demonstrate the libraries' increased commitment to their users.

## Planning and implementation

Initial discussions began in March of 2015 with estimates on how many CDs the Cataloging Department's Music and Audiovisual Team could reclassify in an hour. The Team itself consists of 4 full time personnel, 1 faculty-level cataloger and 3 staff members, who handle the cataloging of all music and AV materials for Penn State's 24 campuses. In addition to musical scores, sound recordings, and video recordings, this includes non-musical sound and video recordings, kits, games, posters, activity cards, models, and assorted realia. After analyzing yearly statistics, it was estimated that with the Team's current workload they could probably reclassify 30–50 titles an hour. At that rate it would take the Team roughly 17 years to completely finish the entire collection. Based on these numbers, it was decided to try a couple of test reclassifications to gauge the public's interest while looking at additional assistance for the Team in order to complete this project in a shorter timeframe. In June 2015, the initial test began with the reclassification of complete opera recordings. They were chosen since the recordings consisted of a single work, making classification easier. Another reason was the perceived interest from the Music Department's voice faculty in the project's potential benefits to them and their students. Any titles that contained multiple operas or opera excerpts were removed from the test. The base call number for all titles was M1500 (Music–Vocal Music–Dramatic Music), followed by the first cutter for the composer listed in the MARC 100 field (Main Entry–Personal Name), the second cutter for the title as it appears in the MARC 240 field (Uniform Title), and finally the date stated in MARC 008/07–10 field (Date 1). If a 240 field isn't present, take the second cutter from the MARC 245 field (Title Statement). So the call number for a CD of Mozart's "Cosi fan tutte" from 2014 would look like this:

M1500.M69C6 2014

One staff member was made the point person on this test, receiving batches of 30–50 titles to reclassify at a time. These reclassified discs were then transferred in the online catalog from the "MUSIC-CTR" item location to "CD-AH" which reflected their new home status. Finally, they were put out for display on the new publicly-accessible shelves. This initial test took almost a year with only one person working regularly on it, but ultimately over 800 titles were now available for users to browse.

In late May of 2016, the jazz CD collection was chosen as the next test group. Although it numbered almost half the size of the opera test at just over 450 titles, it added new challenges that needed to be faced. Sometimes the name listed in the MARC 100 field was the performer and not necessarily the composer. Sometimes a MARC 110 field (Main Entry–Corporate Name) was present instead of a 100. Sometimes there wasn't either a 100 or a 110 field present at all. The music public services librarian created a cuttering tree with input from the music cataloging librarian to help guide the staff. This tree spelled out the multiple scenarios that one could face in reclassifying, and included examples from the online catalog (see Appendix A). With the help of an additional staff member from the Team assisting the point person, and thanks to the dramatic decline in new receipts due to the Summer break, the two of them were able to complete this test in just about two months.

At roughly the same time as the second test was undertaken, the two music librarians began discussing the possibility of hiring a temporary staff member to focus solely on the reclassification project. Thanks to one-time funding procured by the music public services librarian, they were able to advertise and hire a part-time staff assistant (a graduate student in orchestral conducting at the School of Music) by September of 2016. Capitalizing on the staff assistant's expertise, they started with the CDs containing symphonies. They created a cuttering tree similar to the one for jazz to help guide them in their decision making (see Appendix B). The base call number selected for symphonies and all large orchestral works was M1000, followed by cutters for composer, title, and date. If the title was a generic term (e.g., symphony), then the tree instructed the student to use the cutter for symphony (S9), and then add a qualifier in terms of symphony number, opus number, or specific catalog number for that composer (e.g., Mozart = Köchel). A complete example of this process would be:

Mozart symphony no. 38 = M1000.M8S9 K.504

Astute readers will notice that the cutter for Mozart in the opera example differed from the cutter in the symphony example. This was because we copied the composer cutters for the CDs from the ones that appeared on our scores in the effort to create a sense of uniformity in the online catalog.

After completing the large orchestral works, the staff assistant moved to the remainder of the instrumental CDs following cuttering decisions similar to those for the former. Having made great strides since their employment, they reclassified all of the instrumental CDs and have now moved on to vocal CDs (other than the complete operas that were done first). To date, the combined efforts of the music staff and the temporary staff assistant have resulted in almost 7,000 titles being reclassified; that is just under half of the collection completed in less than two years. The funding for the staff assistant will likely run out by this summer, so we're preparing for their absence by gathering their feedback on the cuttering trees as to what needs to be revised, and by working with the staff to incorporate this project into their daily work. While the rest of the collection will likely take longer than two years to complete without further temporary assistance, we're working hard now to make sure that it will be completed more quickly.

## Assessment

In her article on technical services assessment in Pennsylvania academic libraries, Rebecca Mugridge noted that one of the most-used methods for assessment is gathering usage data.[5] Utilizing this method for our project, we ran a report in our online catalog using the system's software. We chose their "Checkouts by Call Number Range" report, and applied the following filters:

$$\text{Item Library Description} = \text{Arts \& Humanities Library (UP)}$$
$$\text{Item Location} = \text{CD} - \text{AH}$$

$$\text{Item Type} = \text{Audio}$$

The results of this search were initially confusing, but thankfully local software experts were able to explain them. Many of the titles implied that they were being increasingly used, but others stated that "January 1, 1900" was the last time they had circulated. It turns out that the "1900-01-01" date is what the system displays when an item hasn't circulated. Based on this new information, we could determine that over 8,400 titles out of 9,513 had circulated since being reclassified. This seems to bear out the anecdotal evidence from the music public services librarian who noted in an email that use of the opera CDs in particular had increased. This bodes well for the reclassification of the popular music sound recordings which is planned to begin during the second half of 2017.

## Conclusion

This article has documented one library's attempt to reclassify their music CD collection from a local accession model to one based on Library of Congress Classification while the discs were relocated to shelving that was more publicly accessible. Initial results are promising, and hold great hope for the future use of the collection. We have two basic recommendations if another library was to undertake a similar project. The first is to make sure to get buy-in from all involved parties, and that those involved stay in regular communication. The other is to document decisions every step of the way. This cuts down on confusion mid-project, and makes sure that future staff can follow the correct procedures during ongoing maintenance at a later date, especially when those who were responsible for the decisions have eventually left the libraries.

## Acknowledgments

The author would like to acknowledge the tremendous help supplied by Amanda Maple, Music Librarian, Penn State University Libraries, and Walter Wells, Staff Supervisor (Ret.), Music and Media Center, Penn State University Libraries.

## Notes

1. Carol June Bradley, "Classifying and Cataloging Music in American Libraries: A Historical Overview," *Cataloging & Classification Quarterly* 35, nos. 3–4 (2003): 467–481.
2. Linda Crow, "Shelf Arrangement Systems for Sound Recordings: Survey of American Academic Music Libraries," *Technical Services Quarterly* 8, no. 4 (1991): 1–24.
3. Daniel W. Kinney, "The Classification of Music Moving Image Materials: Historical Perspectives, Problems, and Practical Solutions," *Cataloging & Classification Quarterly* 47, no. 1 (2009): 2–22.
4. Rachel P. King, "Access to Circulating Videos in Academic Libraries: From Policy Review to Action Plan," *Collection Management* 41, no. 4 (2016): 209–220.
5. Rebecca L. Mugridge, "Technical Services Assessment: A Survey of Pennsylvania Academic Libraries," *Library Resources & Technical Services* 58, no. 2 (2014): 103.

## Appendix A:  Jazz CD cuttering decision tree

Jazz = base call number M1366 (both instrumental & vocal)

First cutter

    1XX field: 100 – personal author/performer or personal author/composer

             110 – corporate author/performer

    Examples

        Personal author/composer:

            Title control number ocn262630449

            100 Moncur, Grachan, III, 1937-

        Personal author/performer:

            Title control number ocn287427820

            100 Davis, Miles

        Corporate author/performer

            Title control number ocn318542509

            110 Paul Chambers Quintet

            Title control number ocm85846841

            110 Miles Davis Quintet

[note: Miles Davis as performer will shelve under D for Davis, separately from the Miles Davis Quintet which will shelve under M for Miles. This is OK.]

When 1XX field is a name other than composer or performer (such as "compiler,"), use 245 as first cutter instead of 100

    Example

        Title control number i9781439083345

        100 is name of compiler Henry Martin

        245 Jazz: the first hundred years

When there is no 1XX field, use 245 title as first cutter (do not use names in 700 for cuttering)

Example

Title control number a487951

245 Jazz piano: a Smithsonian collection

Second cutter

245 field: title transcribed from item

When 245 is used as first cutter and a second cutter is needed, use publisher (label)

Third cutter if needed

Publisher (label)

Jazz with vocals (singer or singers), M1366 is still the base call number

First cutter

1XX field: 100 – personal author/performer or personal author/composer

110 – corporate author/performer

Second cutter

245 field: title transcribed from item

When 245 is used as first cutter and a second cutter is needed, use publisher (label)

Examples

Title control number ocm63601449

100 Ellington, Duke, 1899–1974

245 Ella Fitzgerald sings the Duke Ellington song book

Title control number LIAS2220739

100 Holiday, Billie, 1915–1959

245 Lady in Satin

Boxed Sets or Multi-Disc Collections

If cataloged on one MARC record as a set, with call numbers such as "disc.1" "disc.2" etc. to distinguish the discs on the shelf, use the "first cutter / second cutter" procedure above and keep the "disc.1" "disc.2" designations. No need to use a third cutter to bring out individual disc titles.

## Appendix B:  Orchestral music CDs cuttering decision tree

Base call number M1000

A. If the bibliographic record has a 100 field and 240 field:

1) First cutter = 100 field (personal author/composer)

2) Second cutter = 240 field (uniform title)

a. <u>Distinctive</u> uniform titles

Examples

Richard Strauss Also sprach Zarathustra

Title control number a2284562

M1000.S8A4

Philip Glass Itaipu
Title control number LIAS1721574
M1000.G5I7

In the case of "Selections," use a third cutter for the first-listed work, that is, the work on the first track. Here's how this instruction plays out in practice:

title control number ocm32414720
Disc contains selected symphonies for string orchestra by Mendelssohn (not the complete symphonies for string orchestra)
first work listed is Symphony No. 1, so the call number is:
M1000.M53S9 no.1

title control number ocm32414811
Same deal: disc contains selected symphonies for string orchestra by Mendelssohn (not the complete symphonies for string orchestra)
first work listed is Symphony No. 7, so the call number is:
M1000.M53S9 no.7

title control number ocm32414858
ditto above but first work listed (as far as I can tell) is Symphony No. 11, so the call number is:
M1000.M53S9 no.11

  b. Generic (form/genre) uniform titles
    Orchestra music = O7
      Example: Berwald overtures, concertos and symphonies
      Title control number ocn188870199
      M1000.B48O7
    Symphonic poems = S8
      Example: Richard Strauss tone poems
      Title control number ocm45440410
      M1000.S8S8
    Symphonies = S9
      Examples
      Beethoven symphony no. 4
      Title control numbers ocm38030232 and LIAS579301
      M1000.B4S9 no.4

      Mozart symphony no. 38
      Title control numbers ocn123191231 and ocm53129214
      M1000.M8S9 K.504
    Concertos = C6
  Third cutter: bring out the solo instrument as the third cutter (in the case of double or triple concertos, use the first solo instrument listed)
    Example: Beethoven piano concertos nos. 3 and 4
    Title control numbers: a2317837 and ocm43644953

M1000.B4C6P5 no.3
Beethoven violin concerto
Title control number: a2694031
M1000.B4C6V5

3) Date of publication
4) If further disambiguation is needed (in case of exact duplication of a call number), distinguish with lower-case alphabet suffix to DATE.

B. If the bibliographic record has a 100 field and is without a 240 field:
  1) First cutter = 100 field (personal author/ composer or conductor)
  2) Second cutter = 245 field (title as transcribed from the disc)
     Examples:
     title control number a2722875 [100 field personal author is for the conductor]
     title control number a2284563 [100 field is for the composer]
     title control number ocn668203507 [100 field is for the composer]
     title control number a12136978 [100 field is for the composer]
     Note: if the personal author is other than a composer or conductor, such as a "compiler," use the 245 field as the first cutter, rather than the 100 field.
     Example: title control number a2604930
  3) Date of publication
  4) If further disambiguation is needed (in case of exact duplication of a call number), distinguish with lower-case alphabet suffix to DATE.

C. If the bibliographic record has a 110 field and 245 field:
  1) First cutter = 110 field (corporate author/performer)
  2) Second cutter = 245 field (title as transcribed from the disc)
     Example: title control number ocm43724011
     110 Boston Pops Orchestra
  3) Date of publication
  4) If further disambiguation is needed (in case of exact duplication of a call number), distinguish with lower-case alphabet suffix to DATE.

D. If the bibliographic record is without a 100 or 110 field, use the 245 field as the first cutter. (Do not use names in 700 fields for cuttering).
     Example:
     title control number ocm60629702
     245 Signatures

Boxed Sets or Multi-Disc Collections
  If cataloged on one MARC record as a set, with call numbers such as "disc.1" "disc.2" etc. to distinguish the discs on the shelf, use the "first cutter / second cutter" procedure above and keep the "disc.1" "disc.2" designations. No need to use a third cutter to bring out individual disc titles.

# Assessing the ISSN Register: Defining, Evaluating, and Improving the Quality of a Shared International Bibliographic Database

Clément Oury (ID)

**ABSTRACT**

ISSN identifiers reliably identify serials and other ongoing resources worldwide. The ISSN Register, maintained by the ISSN International Centre, is an authoritative database providing access to 1.9 million ISSN records, and fed by a network of 89 National Centres. This article presents the "Data Quality Plan" currently implemented by the ISSN International Centre: its objectives, its assumptions and the methodology it follows. It focuses on several projects, ran in collaboration with stakeholders of the serials supply chain or members of the ISSN Network, intended to improve quality in three domains: bibliographic data, coverage of the ISSN Register, processes and workflows.

## The ISSN: An Identifier, a System, an International Centre, and a Network

The International Standard Serial Number (ISSN) is a number that unambiguously identifies continuing resources worldwide. The concept of continuing resources is broad: it does not only cover periodicals, newspapers, or monographic series; but also ongoing integrating resources such as databases or websites.[1] The ISSN is a unique and persistent identifier: an ISSN identifies only one resource on one medium; even when a publication ceases to exist, its ISSN is never re-assigned. Finally, it plays the role of a reference identifier as it has been established, since 1975, as the ISO standard for continuing resources (ISO 3297).

Uniqueness and persistence need to be ensured by a dedicated organization. Therefore, the term "ISSN" not only designates the number itself, but also a whole system: the ISSN system is made of the different rules and procedures which guarantee that these critical criteria (uniqueness and persistence) are met. Making that system work is the duty of ISSN National Centres which assign ISSNs to the continuing resources of their respective countries and produce the related bibliographic records. They are coordinated, from the bibliographic and organizational points of view, by the ISSN International Centre, an intergovernmental organiza-tion located in Paris.[2] The other duties of the ISSN International Centre are to maintain the ISSN Register—the database where all ISSN records are stored—and to provide access tools and services to potential users of ISSN information. Fur-thermore, the ISSN International Centre is in charge of the assignment of ISSN to resources published by international organizations or published in countries with-out a National Centre. Together, the ISSN International Centre and the National Centres form the ISSN Network.

The ISSN Network is one of the widest and most diverse networks in the biblio-graphic domain: eighty-nine countries are represented, on every continent.[3] It is also very active: the ISSN Register currently contains more than 1.9 million ISSN records, with an average increase of 65,000 new records per year. This figure does not take into account the numerous modifications of the records, either because the resource described has changed, or because the bibliographic standards have evolved. Around 10% of the total number of records in the Register was modified in 2016. Members of the ISSN Network have been able to face the challenge of new forms of publishing: more than 40% of the records created in 2016 to describe online resources.

But the ISSN Network is not fully homogeneous. First, in terms of institutions: National Centres may be hosted by national libraries, academic libraries, research centers or book chambers. The procedures followed by publishers to obtain an ISSN vary: ISSNs are generally assigned either upon direct request from publishers, or as part of legal deposit duties. But many institutions also allow for requests by third parties (e.g., libraries, digitization agencies). A common document, the ISSN Manual, explains how to implement the general rules stated by the ISSN standard. It is maintained by a dedicated body, the ISSN Review Group. The ISSN Manual is also aligned with the instructions stated by the International Standard Biblio-graphic Description (ISBD). However, the Manual allows for a certain level of flex-ibility, and differences may be seen in catalogue records produced by institutions following ISBD, AACR2, or RDA traditions. More importantly, the organizational context (e.g., scientific objectives of the institution, dedicated resources, assignment procedures) may have an impact on the scope of ISSN identification. Some National Centres extensively identify continuing resources, even including collec-tions of DVDs or serial publications dedicated to puzzles and games. Conversely, other institutions focus on scholarly journals or on publications intended for an international distribution.

Finally, the delivery system and how the records are ingested into the Register differ from one institution to another. More than a third of the Network members directly use the cataloging application provided by the ISSN International Centre.[4] Other centers prefer cataloging in their own system and transfer the records as MARC files, either by FTP or through OAI-PMH. Centres lacking cataloging facili-ties can also send bibliographic information in Excel spreadsheets.

The ISSN Register ingests these various records and stores them in a unique for-mat: MARC21. The information is then made available through the services provided by the ISSN International Centre: individual searches on the ISSN portal, batch download of the whole database, delivery of Register updates thanks to Z39.50 or OAI-PMH protocols, etc., in both MARC21 and UNIMARC. Some tailored exports are also possible. Access to these services is restricted to ISSN customers (e.g., publishers, discovery services, libraries) and members of the ISSN Network.

As the ISSN has been, for more than 40 years, the reference identifier for continuing resources, and as the ISSN Register is the only authoritative source for ISSN information, the quality of the Register has always been considered as an important issue. However, recent trends and evolutions have made it even more critical. First, the ISSN standard itself is currently under revision. As every ISO standard, the ISO 3297 is regularly assessed in order to ensure it still fits the needs of actual and potential users. In September 2016, the ISSN International Centre and its network decided to launch a revision process: a dedicated working group was set up in 2017.

Second, the emergence of the web, and particularly of the web of data, has emphasized the importance of identifiers. Unique, unambiguous, and persistent identifiers are the milestones of any endeavor to publish datasets as linked data. For this reason, the ISSN International Centre has recently initiated a project in order to release under an open license a subpart of its data: this subpart corresponds, for each record, to the essential elements which allow for the precise identification of the resource.[5] The new Portal, intended to distribute the freely available information as well as the content restricted to ISSN subscribers, will be launched by the end of 2017.

Openly exposing (a subpart of) its data elements means that they can be accessed, assessed, and potentially reviewed by everyone. Tools providing ISSN information, especially for ISSN customers, will also be more efficient. The ISSN International Centre will for example provide APIs to let users automatically retrieve ISSN metadata, in order to encourage external stakeholders to use ISSN URIs—hence, assuring to its users the reliability of its bibliographic information and of its services. With great usage comes great responsibility: the semantic web is built on trust—the upper layer of the famous "Semantic Web Layer Cake"[6]— and the ISSN International Centre wishes to ensure that ISSN numbering is a trusted brand. To that end, it is critical to control, validate, and enhance data quality.

This article intends to present the "Data Quality Plan" devised by the ISSN International Centre: its objectives, its assumptions, the methodology it follows, and its first outcomes. It will start with a review of the recent discussions about quality of bibliographic records and services, and then will explain how the ISSN International Centre seeks to define quality in its own context. It will show that the ISSN International Centre has divided the general concept of quality into three domains of application: for each domain, it has identified quality criteria, which are themselves assessed by indicators that may evolve over time. This article will finally present some of the experiments and projects the ISSN International Centre has recently achieved or launched in that field.

This article will not only investigate the methods used to deal with quality issues within a framework where information is received in a multiplicity of languages, scripts, cataloging rules and formats, but it will also address the issues that arise when metadata are delivered by stakeholders outside of the library world, such as publishers. In a sense, it tries to understand how the traditional concept of quality is questioned by the need to free bibliographic information from silos and to maximize its use by a growing number of stakeholders.

## Literature review

Quality is a concept that has been adapted to numerous domains of human activity. The most overarching documents to define quality are the reference standard ISO 9000:2015 (Quality management systems — Fundamentals and vocabulary), which describes the fundamental concepts and principles of quality management, and the other standards of the ISO 9000 family.[7] There is also a standard (published in multiple parts) specifically dedicated to data quality: ISO 8000, which arose from the manufacturing engineering community.[8] Within the ISO Technical Committee 46, the committee in charge of all standards related to the Information and Documentation domains, the standards pertaining to quality assessment are elaborated within the Sub-Committee 8, dedicated to "Quality – Statistics and performance evaluation." This Sub-Committee has notably issued two documents specifically dealing with library issues: ISO 2789:2013 (International library statistics)[9] and ISO 11620:2014 (Library performance indicators).[10]

These two standards cover all main branches of librarianship, from acquisition to reference services. Only a few statistics and indicators relate to cataloging quality: out of 45 performance indicators listed in ISO 11620:2014, only one, the "Subject Catalogue Search Success Rate" is directly related to cataloging.[11] However, the scientific and professional literature offers numerous papers or reports dedicated to the quality of cataloging or to the quality of bibliographic records—the discussions addressing these topics started to appear in the 1970s and 1980s, coinciding with the rise of cataloging networks and the increasing need to share bibliographic data between libraries.[12] Yet there is still no agreed upon definition of "quality" in this field.

However, the scholarly literature presents some attempts to provide lists of quality criteria. In 1990, Peter S. Graham identified two characteristics: extent ("how much information is provided in the record") and accuracy ("the correctness of what is provided").[13] Thomas R. Bruce and Diane I. Hillmann, in their article "The continuum of metadata quality," provide a more detailed categorization with seven quality measures for bibliographic metadata: completeness, accuracy, provenance, conformance to expectations, logical consistency and coherence, timeliness, and accessibility.[14] The latter author pursues in "Metadata quality: from evaluation to augmentation" her examination of the methods to define, evaluate, and improve metadata quality.[15] These two articles stress the importance of taking into account the "context" and "the economic, political and technical constraints [that] are part of every decision affecting quality and perception of quality."[16] The need to consider the "context", in order to define priorities in terms of quality, is also emphasized by David Bade in his article dedicated to the examination of the controversial concept of the "perfect bibliographic record."[17]

It is actually easier to find papers or professional reports focusing on specific cases, at the level of a single institution, or of a cataloging network or consortium. Stina Degerstedt and Joakim Philipson provide for example an insight into the issues pertaining to the bibliographic description of content received through e-legal deposit; they especially address issues arising when the National Library of Sweden retrieves metadata from publishers.[18] Collaborative cataloging raises other sets of problems, especially related to the existence of duplicate records, as shown by the reports provided by Libraries Australia or by OCLC. These two reports insist on the importance of maintaining a network of links (between different bibliographic records, between bibliographic and authority records).

These issues are also recognized by David Van Kleeck et al. in their examination of the problems and solutions encountered by the Cataloging and Discovery Services Department in the George A. Smathers Libraries at the University of Florida.[19] As a conclusion, their article emphasizes the new needs emerging with the shift toward linked data.

## Defining quality for an identifier system

Quality is officially defined, in ISO 9000:2015, as "the degree to which a set of inherent characteristics fulfils requirements"—that is, in most common terms, the "fitness for the purpose" of specific data, tools or services. The first difficulty when it comes to defining quality is then... to identify what the purpose is. The ISSN Register is a bibliographic database: it is therefore relevant to look at the analysis of the objectives of bibliographic records performed by the working group on the Functional Requirements for Bibliographic Records. Its final report, published in 1998,[20] lists four main purposes ("find, identify, select, obtain"). Furthermore, the document intended to replace the FRBR report, called the "Library Reference Model," adds a fifth one to the original list ("Explore").[21] We can refer to that list in order to figure out what are the main objectives of ISSN records.

- Find: to search on any relevant criteria in order to bring together information about one or more resources of interest.
- Identify: to clearly understand the nature of the resources found and to distinguish between similar resources.
- Select: to determine the suitability of the resources found and to choose (by accepting or by rejecting) specific resources.
- Obtain: to access the content of the resource.

- Explore: to use the relationships between one resource and another to place them in a context.

Obviously, the most important purpose of the records used by an identifier database is the "Identify" task: any user of the ISSN Registry should be able to unambiguously find the ISSN of a specific resource—or, starting from a given ISSN, identify the corresponding publication. The fifth purpose, "Explore," is almost as critical as the first one. Due to the characteristics of continuing publications, which are dynamic resources, ISSN records are highly interlinked: relationships are established between different language editions or between a main edition and local editions; between a predecessor title and a successor title; not to mention the complex networks that may be created between publications when splits or merges occur.

However, ISSN records are often produced by National Centres not only for the sole purposes of the ISSN system, but also as part of their mandate to describe the continuing resources published in their country—notably when they are in charge of a National Bibliography. Besides, many institutions (ISSN customers or members of the ISSN Network) download ISSN records to serve the users of their own catalogs. From that point of view, the other tasks (Find, Select, Obtain) should not be forgotten. Finally, contrary to the former ISSN Portal which was mostly dedicated to professional users (publishers or librarians), the future Portal intends to reach a greater audience, whose types of use are not known yet: ISSN records should then be conceptualized as being used for a wider range of purposes.

But what are the entities that the ISSN Register is intended to describe? Again, it is possible to refer to the Library Reference Model. The traditional and "monolithic" view of the bibliographic record has been replaced, since 1998, and the first publication of the FRBR final report, by a more granular approach, which distinguishes between Work, Expression, Manifestation, and Item. But this new model does not perfectly fit with the characteristics of continuing resources. The FRBR final report itself acknowledges that "certain aspects of the model merit more detailed examination ... In particular, the notion of "seriality" and the dynamic nature of entities recorded in digital formats merit further analysis."[22] The IFLA-LRM goes even further. It recognizes that: "The description of serials is particularly difficult to model, because it does not limit itself to a description of the past, but is also intended to allow end-users to make assumptions about what the behavior of a serial will be in at least the near future."[23] This is why it recognizes that, strictly speaking, collocation is not possible for continuing resources: "It ensues that any serial work can be said to have only one expression and only one manifestation."[24]

Finally, the IFLA-LRM refers on one hand to PRESSoo, a specialized bibliographic model for continuing resources, for a detailed examination of these issues,[25] on the other hand, it refers to the ISSN system to provide for the practical establishment of a linking mechanism between continuing resources. As stated above, ISSN records describe a title on a specific medium (e.g., print, online). In order to create a bridge between the different medium versions of the same title, the 2007 revision of the ISSN standard designed the Linking ISSN or ISSN-L, which identifies a title whatever its medium.[26] Besides, the ISSN standard revision that is currently under way may create new entities. The title "families" could group together, for example, the main edition of a serial and all the local editions; or the different ISSN assigned to a resource, whatever its title changes.[27] These new types of entities are not considered by the IFLA-LRM.

Many factors should be taken into account when trying to define the quality of an ISSN record and of the ISSN Register: the difficulty to provide a data model for continuing resources, the heterogeneity of data providers, the variety of workflows, and the evolving roles of ISSN records: support for precise and reliable identification of resources; support for linked data applications; and support for new research and discovery services within the ISSN Portal. This is why it was deemed important to re-evaluate the notion of quality so as to improve the current working processes of the ISSN International Centre. It was critical as well to be able to communicate on our quality policy, with the producers of the data (the institutions within the ISSN Network) as well as with users. To that end, it was decided to set up a "quality plan," as a tool to evaluate our records; improve our internal and external processes; and to publicize our goals and issues.

The first step of the design of this quality plan was an internal workshop within the ISSN International Centre, held in September 2016. In that framework the objectives of the Quality Plan were discussed, as well as the issues to be solved and the projects related to quality issues. Quality is traditionally associated with the respect of standards and best practices; it was therefore decided to list the relevant rules and documents:

- first and foremost, ISO identification and description standards, under the responsibility of TC46/SC9,[28] particularly the ISSN standard itself;[29]
- bibliographic models and codes produced by IFLA (FRBR, LRM, ISBD) or other organizations (RDA Steering Committee);
- technical standards, especially those produced by the World Wide Web Consortium (W3C); and
- standards related to quality, statistics and usage, notably the ISO 9000 family (Quality management) and the documents produced by ISO TC46/SC8 (Quality - Statistics and performance evaluation).

Rather than trying to find a concise definition of quality, there was an attempt to explore the different fields where quality could be reached, evaluated and improved. Three main domains were identified:

- the quality of the bibliographic data, i.e., the quality of the ISSN records themselves;
- the quality of the ISSN coverage, i.e., the quality of the Register as a whole;
- the quality of the processes and workflows.

For each field, several quality criteria were identified.

### *Quality criteria of the bibliographic data*

Quality criteria related to bibliographic data are listed by order of importance. It is not a strict order; for example, there may be minor issues related to validity that will be deemed less important than major problems of reliability.

(a) **Uniqueness**: absence of duplicate records in the Register. Each ISSN should unambiguously identify one title, and each title should be identified by only one ISSN. This is theoretically ensured by the automated controls of the bibliographic database. However, in very rare cases, it may happen that a title is described twice: for example, a cataloger might describe a resource already cataloged because he or she was unable to find out the resource was already in the Register as there was a typo in the title of the first record.

(b) **Validity**: structural quality of the record, related to the respect of standards: cataloging rules (ISSN Manual), format (MARC21). Many structural problems are identified and solved when the records are ingested into the Register—or, in the case of direct cataloging, when the cataloger validates the record. However, minor structural problems may remain because they are not blocking the ingestion or the final validation of the record.

(c) **Consistency**: quality of the record within a network of links. Many links between records should indeed be bi-directional, such as the "another medium version" link.

(d) **Reliability**: conformity of what is described in the record with the "reality" of the resource.

(e) **Timeliness**: the fact that the records are up-to-date. This criterion is distinguished from the previous one in the sense that a record may be reliable (it rightly describes the state of the resource at the time it is cataloged) but not up-to-date. This kind of timeliness is named "currency" in Hillmann and Bruce's article.[30]

(f) **Richness**: number of data elements available in a record, beyond the mandatory fields. Accuracy of information, i.e., the ability to finely describe a resource, is part of richness. Within richness, some aspects may be further prioritized: for example, in the framework of ISSN-linked data policy, all information providing additional internal or external links is deemed of major importance.

This relative order of importance also corresponds to practical constraints: criteria (d), (e), and (f) can hardly be automatically assessed by the ISSN International Centre, as they require a verification of the original resource. However, some clues may help identify quality issues: for example, records which are not regularly modified are more likely to be outdated. Besides, the ISSN International Centre can rely on the feedback of users of ISSN data to identify quality issues.

Finally, it should be noted that the cataloging principles and rules have constantly evolved since 1975. Some optional information may have become mandatory, and some mandatory information may have become optional. The Register should be understood as a heritage of the past, with different layers of records following different quality standards.

### Quality criteria of the ISSN coverage

The quality of the ISSN coverage corresponds to the ability of the ISSN Register to reflect the current state of the worldwide publishing industry of continuing resources. While the first set of criteria is mainly related to cataloging codes and formats, quality criteria for ISSN coverage correspond to the respect of the specific principles, rules and procedures stated by the ISSN standard and the ISSN Manual. For example: the ISSN assignment scope, the granularity of identification, and the reporting of records in the ISSN Register.

(a) **Comprehensiveness** of the Register: its capacity to reference all assigned ISSNs. Assignment of ISSNs is a decentralized process: first, a "range" of ISSNs is given to a particular National Centre for its own use. All ISSNs belonging to that range are successively assigned to newly identified publications; bibliographic description is performed in parallel. The National Centres regularly send back the records to the International Centre, in order to ensure the Register comprises all ISSNs from already opened ranges. It may happen that some records are not reported or that there are delays in reporting: in that case, the ISSN Register is not able to provide identification elements. This issue may be related to the question of "lag" identified by Hillmann and Bruce.[31]

(b) **"Systematicity" of assignment.** As stated in the standards, each different medium version of a same title should be identified by a different ISSN. This principle may sometimes not be well understood by publishers: it may happen that they use the ISSN of the print version for the digital one, or conversely, which prevents the precise identification of their resources.

(c) **Respect of assignment scope.** The ISSN Manual states that "All continuing resources, whether past, present, or to be produced in the foreseeable future, whatever the medium of production, are eligible for ISSN assignment."[32] Practically, however, the assignment scope of National Centres may be sometimes narrower: due to local policies (e.g., alignment with legal deposit regulations) or to staffing issues, National Centres may exclude some types of continuing resources. The fact that blogs, websites or databases belonging to the scholarly domain should get an ISSN may also be interpreted diversely.

Again, this list shows an order of importance: unreported ISSNs are an issue for "identification", the main purpose of the Register; while local exclusions in assignment scope are not threatening the ISSN system itself and only restrict the usefulness of the Register for the "find" or "select" tasks.

## Quality criteria of the processes and workflows

The ISSN International Centre is in charge of monitoring two main kinds of workflows:

- on one hand, there is the ingest into the Register of data sent by National Centres;
- on the other hand, the handling of requests sent by international organizations; or publishers in countries without a national center.

However, common criteria may be defined.

(a) The **efficiency** of the processes, i.e., the ratio of effectiveness vs. cost, has to be sought. Exchanges between publishers and the ISSN International Centre should be fast; as well as ingest processes from National Centres to the ISSN Register. This issue is also related to the timeliness of the ISSN records.

(b) **Clarity of communication** is essential to that end. Publishers should identify what the ISSN International Centre is requesting from them; instructions from the ISSN International Centre should be well understood. In general, the role and the usefulness of the ISSN numbering and the ISSN Register should be recognized by the different parties.

(c) The **security** of the processes, especially in terms of data. This means not only ensuring security of bibliographic records, whose availability must not be affected by technical issues, but also archiving the "documentary evidence" used as the basis for the assignment of an ISSN.

## Assessing, monitoring, and reporting on quality

Listing the quality criteria in these different domains has laid the theoretical foundations for more practical decisions: first, figure out how these criteria could be assessed; second, improve the quality; and, finally, regularly check there is no regression.

To that end, each criterion needs to be related to indicators. Statistics and indicators should be distinguished: statistics are objective data which provide the basis for further analysis and interpretation. Indicators, on the other hand, are "expressions (which may be numeric, symbolic or verbal) used to characterize activities ... both in quantitative and qualitative terms in order to assess the value of the activities characterized."[33] In other terms, an indicator is a statistic assessed against a goal. Statistics last for a long time, while indicators may be used to reflect a progress expected in a specific area.

The definition of a list of indicators depends therefore on a specific context; and its elaboration is still a work in progress at the ISSN International Centre. Below is a small sample of already existing indicators:

- Domain: Quality of bibliographic data
  - **For "Validity"**: number of "error" or "warning" reports at ingest in the ISSN Register

- ○ **For "Richness"**: number of records lacking classification (Dewey and/or UDC)
- • Domain: ISSN coverage:
  - ○ **For "Comprehensiveness"**: total number of unreported ("free") records
  - ○ **For "Respect of assignment scope"**: percentage of National Centres assigning ISSN to blogs, databases, etc.
- • Domain: processes and workflow:
  - ○ **For "Efficiency of processes"** between publishers and ISSN International Centres: average delay of treatment of ISSN requests issued by publishers.
  - ○ **For "Efficiency of processes"** between National Centres and the ISSN International Centres: percentage of National Centres directly using the Register cataloging software; or reporting on a weekly or a monthly basis.

Many indicators may be calculated at the level of the whole Register but also for a specific year; as a total number or as a percentage; to identify a state of the Register or a current trend. A global reporting document has to be designed for the purpose of monitoring the quality plan.

This list of indicators needs also to be further discussed within the ISSN Network: indeed, reporting on quality indicators is not only intended to help assessing the quality of the ISSN Register, but also to improve the ISSN system. This objective cannot be achieved without the support of the National Centres.

## Current achievements

### *ISSN coverage: Improving our knowledge on National Centre practices*

Several projects have been launched that could improve these indicators: some of them were specifically designed in the framework of this quality plan; but others, already existing, were retrospectively acknowledged to be part of this objective. The list of projects presented below is not comprehensive: they are only examples intended to illustrate the variety of operations performed by the ISSN International Centre to that end.

As stated above, the ISSN system is based on a network of institutions which are supposed to follow two sets of rules: on the one hand, their national instructions, and on the other hand the standards of the ISSN system (ISSN standard and ISSN Manual). This situation sometimes implies differences of practices between National Centres. Yet these differences are not an issue, provided the main principles of the ISSN system are followed and provided these differences are known, understood and acknowledged.

The scope of ISSN assignment is one of the fields where variations are often noticed. As the only internationally recognized identifier for continuing resources, the ISSN is used in all countries by publishers—especially scholarly publishers—wishing to reach a worldwide audience. However, ISSN assignment may not be requested for publications limited to a strictly national distribution —as for every ISO standard, the ISSN standard is used on a voluntary basis.

Generally, ISSN are requested for local publications in countries where the ISSN is used in the barcode – and thus mandatory for the logistics of serials. Moreover, in many countries, ISSNs are systematically assigned to publications submitted to legal deposit, when the legal deposit and ISSN numbering workflows are merged. Finally, even though ISSN records are generally produced for print as well as for digital serials, some types of scholarly content may be less often described, such as blogs and websites: again, it depends on the approach of the institution toward digital documentation; on the vitality of online scholarly publishing in the country, etc.

As far as users—the different stakeholders of the supply chain—are satisfied, these differences of scope are accepted; but it is essential to be aware of them as they can cause some bias in the interpretation of the Register data. For example, a user of the ISSN Register should be able to know, for a specific country, whether some publications are rarely described because they just do not exist, or because they are excluded from ISSN assignment due to local policies. In order to be better informed on that issue of ISSN scope, the ISSN International Centre performed a survey in October–November 2016. The results of the survey show for example an excellent rate of ISSN assignment to online journals or monographic series (100% and 87.5% of the respondents, respectively), or a shared sensibility to the issues related to the description of ceased publications (96.4% of the respondents assign ISSN to ceased resources, especially in the framework of digitization projects).

### ISSN coverage: A collaboration with ProQuest to foster retrospective identification of continuing resources

The survey demonstrated that scholarly journals, either print or online, are a type of resources that are systematically identified by an ISSN. However, some journals may not have been identified: either because they were already published when the ISSN system was designed, or because they were for any reason missed by the National Centre in charge of their description. Retrospective identification of continuing resources is therefore necessary, in these cases, in order to improve the coverage of the ISSN Register.

To that end, a joint project has been initiated by the ISSN International Centre and ProQuest. Its goal is to identify serial titles in Ulrich's Periodicals Directory and in Ulrichsweb, which are deprived of any ISSN. The lists of publications without ISSN are sent, under the supervision of the International Centre, to the relevant National Centres, in order to proceed to assignment.[34] It started in 2015 with a first set of 200 ISSN assigned by the National Centre of Netherlands—a total of 900 ISSN is expected for that country. This project was extended to Sweden and the UK in 2016 while Germany and Ireland are about to join.

### Processes and workflows: Improving the ingest frequency through OAI-PMH

Timeliness of data is an essential quality criterion for continuing resources, as they are often subject to unexpected changes, e.g., in titles, frequencies, or ownerships.

To ensure the ISSN Register is always up to date, it is necessary to ensure that new ISSN assignments and record modifications are frequently and efficiently ingested. To that end, the ISSN International Centre is supporting the use of the OAI-PMH protocol. OAI-PMH stands for Open Archives Initiative-Protocol for Metadata Harvesting: it is a web-based protocol allowing for the continuous synchronization of large amounts of data.[35]

Use of OAI-PMH to retrieve records produced by a National Centre has been tested first with the German Centre in 2015.[36] Thanks to weekly requests to the OAI-PMH repository of the Deutsche Nationalbibliothek, the ISSN Register is able to harvest new or modified records without soliciting any human resources within the German National Centre. This successful experiment should be extended to other Centres: in March 2017, the Norwegian Centre also adopted a similar process.

### Processes and workflows: Centralizing ISSN assignment for international publishers—An experiment with Springer Nature

A further step in the improvement of the timeliness of ISSN information is to centralize assignment for certain types of publishers: in that case, the ISSN Register becomes the original source of information which is then retrieved by the local systems of the National Centres. Multinational publishers may be particularly interested by centralization, as it is generally cumbersome for them to request ISSNs from numerous organizations, depending on the country in which they are publishing. A first experiment to set up a centralized and automated assignment workflow has been performed in 2016 by the ISSN International Centre and Springer Nature, with the support of the German National Centre.

The goal of this project was to automate the assignment of ISSNs to pre-publications thanks to an automated ingest of Springer Nature metadata, in order:

- for the publisher, to obtain its ISSN as fast as possible;
- for the ISSN Network, to quickly include information related to pre-publications in the Register; and
- while lowering the costs in terms of human resources.

The new workflow was launched on January 1, 2017.

- Springer Nature regularly sends to the ISSN International Centre Excel files containing mandatory metadata.
- The ISSN International Centre automatically generates a "pre-publication record" containing an ISSN, a key-title, and the information delivered by the publisher.
- The ISSN International Centre sends back the files enriched with ISSN and key-title.
- The German National Centre retrieves the pre-publication record from the Register and creates a "register" (i.e., fully valid) record when the resource is acquired through legal deposit.

The process is now run in production mode; and the ISSN International Centre is seeking to extend this successful experiment to other multinational publishers.

### *Richness of data: Improving the links with other identifiers and other resources*

As part of its linked data strategy, the ISSN International Centre intends to enrich its Register with as many relevant identifiers as possible, in order to build bridges between ISSN records and information provided by other organizations: not only libraries, but also cultural or scientific organizations, publishers, and service providers.

This is why the ISSN International Centre has shown a particular interest in the development of the ISNI (ISO 27729:2012), the International Standard Name Identifier. The ISNI is an identifier for public parties (either physical persons or organizations): the ISNI database, run by OCLC, is governed by the ISNI International Authority, where right agencies, service providers or libraries are represented. In bibliographic databases, ISNIs are generally assigned to authors of resources, but also to issuing bodies—and maybe in the future to publishers.

ISSN records may therefore contain ISNI numbers in the "issuing body" fields (710 and 720 in MARC21). Some National Centres (such as France or Italy) have already started to provide records containing ISNI to the ISSN Register. On the other hand, the ISSN International Centre is a member of the ISNI system. Therefore, it is able to:

- either retrieve ISNI from the ISNI database; or
- ask for ISNI assignment to issuing bodies that are not yet referenced in that database.

In order to check the relevance and the modalities of the assignment of ISNI to the resources under the direct responsibility of the ISSN International Centre, a first experiment was performed on the records of South African publications containing issuing body fields.[37] Through a semi-automated process (using the API of the ISNI database), it was possible to identify issuing bodies which were already associated to an ISNI. In that case, the ISNI was added to the ISSN record.

The study performed on this sample showed that 42% of records with 710 or 720 fields have been enriched with an ISNI (1,103 records out of a total of 2,637). A total of 1,765 ISNI were added (several ISNI may be recorded in a same record, when the "issuing body" field is repeated). The ISSN Register currently contains around 14,000 ISNI, thanks to that project and to the inputs of the National Centres.

The next steps of this experiment, not launched yet, would be to ask for the assignment of new ISNIs for issuing bodies lacking an ISNI; and to improve the retrieval of ISNIs provided by National Centres.

The inclusion of the ISNI is one of the several data enrichment projects performed by the ISSN International Centre in the perspective of the launch of its new Portal. This tool is intended to provide, notably through the use of linked data technologies, additional metadata that were not initially available in the records originally sent by National Centres.

For example, every record has a publication place: this information can be linked to the Geonames database, in order to get their geo-coordinates and to be able to precisely show them on a map.[38] Moreover, the ISSN number itself may be used as a matching key to align Register information with external database. This was the original goal of ROAD, the Directory of Open Access scholarly Resources, a service launched by the ISSN International Centre with the support of UNESCO.[39] In ROAD, information related to Open Access publications, coming from the ISSN Register, is crossed with data provided by partners, such as the Directory of Open Access Journal;[40] Latindex, the database of Latin-American periodicals;[41] or the Keepers Registry, which monitors which digital publications are kept safe by heritage institutions—and which are not.[42]

With the new ISSN Portal, thanks to the development of a dedicated enrichment module, the ROAD model is being extended to the whole Register. ISSN customers will be informed, for each resource, if it is preserved by a public organization, if it is under an open access license and which one, or what are its impact factors according to Scopus.

## Future work

These examples show that quality is a never-ending process, and that its criteria evolve following the changing needs of users.

The ISSN Quality Plan is still in a maturation phase: the list of criteria is likely to be amended; several indicators are still missing, and new projects will arise. These issues need to be further investigated with the National Centres, with the partners of the ISSN Network, and more generally with users or potential users of the ISSN Register. This is necessary to let the ISSN International Centre decide what domains, what criteria, and what improvements operations should be given priority.

In any case, the discussion held in order to define the Quality Plan helped bringing out the deep coherence of the different projects and operations already launched, or envisaged by the ISSN International Centre. It will hopefully allow for a consistent and synthetic reporting of its activities in that domain. It will finally contribute to a better understanding, by the different stakeholders of the serials supply chain, of the issues, problems and opportunities facing a Register dedicated to the description of continuing resources.

## Acknowledgment

The author wishes to thank Gaëlle Béquet, Director of the ISSN International Centre, for her thorough review and suggestions.

## ORCID

Clément Oury ⓘ http://orcid.org/0000-0002-0313-9919

## Notes

1. Note, however, that for blogs, websites and databases, the scope of ISSN assignment has been restricted to scholarly resources, or at least resources presenting a strong editorial content – as judged by the assigning institution. This restriction of scope has been decided because comprehensive registration of all online continuing resources was not an achievable goal. For inclusion and exclusion criteria, see *ISSN Manual*, January 2015, section 0.3.2: http://www.issn.org/wp-content/uploads/2013/09/ISSNManual_ENG2015_23-01-2015.pdf (all the URLs referenced in this paper have been checked on March 23, 2017).

2. The ISSN International Centre, or CIEPS, was established in 1975 by a treaty between UNESCO and the French government. On the objectives and history of the ISSN International Centre, see Gaëlle Béquet, "Serials Diplomacy at the ISSN International Centre: A Unique and Sustainable Experience (1975–2015)", *Ciência da Informação*, 44, no. 1 (2015): 31–46, http://revista.ibict.br/ciinf/article/view/1430.

3. See the list of member countries in the *ISSN Website*, http://www.issn.org/the-centre-and-the-network/members-countries/the-issn-network-today/.

4. This cataloging application is based on the Virtua Library System (see https://www.iii.com/products/virtua-ils/).

5. Clément Oury, "ISSN: Transitioning to Linked Data", *Proceedings of IFLA WLIC 2016 Satellite Meeting Data in libraries: the big picture*, Chicago, August 2016, https://halshs.archives-ouvertes.fr/halshs-01358415/document.

6. The Semantic Web Stack, or Semantic Web Layer Cake, has been designed by Tim Berners-Lee to illustrate the architecture of the Semantic Web. See an illustration here: https://www.w3.org/2000/Talks/1206-xml2k-tbl/slide10-0.html.

7. There are notably ISO 9000:2015, Quality management systems – Fundamentals and vocabulary, https://www.iso.org/standard/45481.html; ISO 9001:2015, Quality management systems – Requirements, https://www.iso.org/standard/62085.html and ISO 9004:2009, Managing for the sustained success of an organization – A quality management approach, https://www.iso.org/standard/41014.html.

8. See for example ISO/TS 8000-1:2011 Data quality — Part 1: Overview, https://www.iso.org/standard/50798.html; ISO 8000-2:2012 Data quality — Part 2: Vocabulary, https://www.iso.org/standard/57436.html; ISO 8000-8:2015 Data quality – Part 8: Information and data quality: Concepts and measuring, https://www.iso.org/standard/60805.html.

9. ISO 2789:2013 Information and documentation — International library statistics, https://www.iso.org/standard/60680.html.

10. ISO 11620:2014 Information and documentation — Library performance indicators, https://www.iso.org/standard/56755.html.

11. It is intended "to assess the library's success in matching the user's subject search in the catalogue and in informing the user where and how to find information on a subject" (Ibid.). Note, however, that issues related to cataloging are mentioned in other indicators, notably when the cataloging cost is used to calculate the total cost of a service.

12. Barbara Schultz-Jones, Karen Snow, Shawne Miksa, and Richard L. Hasenyager, Jr., "Historical and Current Implications of Cataloguing Quality for Next-Generation Catalogues", *Library Trends*, 61, no. 1 (2012): 49–82, https://www.ideals.illinois.edu/bitstream/handle/2142/34596/61.1.schultz-jones.pdf.

13. Peter S. Graham, "Quality of Cataloguing: Making Distinctions", *The Journal of Academic Librarianship*, 16, no. 4 (1990): 213–218, http://www.columbia.edu/cu/libraries/inside/units/bibcontrol/osmc/graham.pdf.

14. Thomas R. Bruce and Diane I. Hillmann, "The Continuum of Metadata Quality: Defining, Expressing, Exploiting", in *Metadata in Practice*, ALA Editions, 2004, https://ecommons.cornell.edu/handle/1813/7895. This list has itself been suggested by the Quality Assurance Framework for statistical data developed by Statistics Canada in 2002.

15. Diane I. Hillmann, "Metadata Quality: From Evaluation to Augmentation", *Cataloging and Classification Quarterly*, 46, no. 1 (2008): 65–80, http://www.tandfonline.com/doi/abs/10.1080/01639370802183008.

16. Ibid., p. 69 and 70.

17. David Bade, "The Perfect Bibliographic Record: Platonic Ideal, Rhetorical Strategy or Nonsense?", *Cataloging and Classification Quarterly*, 46, no. 1 (2008): 109–133, http://www.tandfonline.com/doi/abs/10.1080/01639370802183081. This article concludes that the term "perfect bibliographic record" is merely used "as a rhetorical strategy for reducing the complex and context-dependent issue of quality to an absurdity".

18. Stina Degerstedt and Joakim Philipson, "Lessons Learned from the First Year of E-Legal Deposit in Sweden: Ensuring Metadata Quality in an Ever-Changing Environment", *Cataloging & Classification Quarterly*, 54, no. 7 (2016): 468–482, http://www.tandfonline.com/doi/abs/10.1080/01639374.2016.1197170.

19. David Van Kleeck, Gerald Langford, Jimmie Lundgren, Hikaru Nakano, Allison Jai O'Dell and Trey Shelton, "Managing Bibliographic Data Quality in a Consortial Academic Library: A Case Study", *Cataloging & Classification Quarterly*, 54, no. 7 (2016): 452–467, http://www.tandfonline.com/doi/abs/10.1080/01639374.2016.1210709.

20. *Functional Requirements for Bibliographic Records. Final report*, published in 1998 and revised in 2009, http://www.ifla.org/files/assets/cataloguing/frbr/frbr_2008.pdf.

21. The Library Reference Model, or LRM, is a consolidation of the FRBR, FRAD, and FRSAD models, endorsed by IFLA Professional Committee on August 2017. The August 2017 version is available on https://www.ifla.org/files/assets/cataloguing/frbr-lrm/ifla-lrm-august-2017.pdf.

22. *Functional Requirements for Bibliographic Records...*, op. cit, p. 5.

23. *IFLA-Library Reference Model...*, op. cit., p. 95.

24. Ibid.

25. PRESS$_{OO}$ is "a conceptual model for bibliographic information pertaining to serials and other continuing resources". It was originally drafted by experts of the ISSN International Centre, the National Library of France and the ISSN Review Group; it is now an official IFLA standard maintained by a dedicated review group reporting to the IFLA cataloguing section. See https://www.ifla.org/files/assets/cataloguing/PRESSoo/pressoo_v1-3.pdf.

26. The ISSN-L linking system itself may have some shortcomings. For example, the ISSN Manual do not require assigning ISSN to reproductions in microform—they may keep the ISSN of the original version. So there is no way to distinguish between the original and the reproduction. *ISSN Manual*, op. cit., section 2.2.6, "reproductions and reprints".

27. Clément Oury, "Revising the ISSN: Involving Stakeholders to Adapt a Bibliographic Standard to its Ever-changing Environment", *Proceedings of the 2016 IFLA WLIC, Columbus*, August 2016, http://library.ifla.org/1602/1/114-oury-en.pdf.

28. The Sub-Committee 9 of the Technical Committee 46 is in charge of all standards pertaining to "Identification and Description".

29. ISO 3297:2007 Information and documentation — International standard serial number (ISSN), https://www.iso.org/standard/39601.html.

30. T. R. Bruce and D. I. Hillmann, art. cit.

31. Ibid.
32. *ISSN Manual*, op. cit., section 0.2, "scope of ISSN".
33. This definition is from ISO 11620:2014, section 2, "Terms and definitions".
34. See the press release: "ISSN International Centre and ProQuest Work Together to Improve Electronic Loading of Serial Titles Worldwide", 2016, http://www.proquest.com/about/news/2016/ISSN-and-ProQuest-Work-to-Improve-Electronic-Loading-of-Serial-Titles.html.
35. See the website: https://www.openarchives.org/pmh/.
36. Note also that, conversely, the ISSN International Centre has also set up its own OAI-PMH repository: it may be used by customers wishing to automatically retrieve information from the ISSN Register.
37. It was decided to choose South African publications for several reasons. First, South Africa is a country without a National Centre; publications from that country are therefore under the responsibility of the ISSN International Centre. Second, South African records describe a wide range of publications: not only scholarly publications, but also newspapers, magazines, trade journal, etc. Finally, as South African scholarly publications have often an international audience, they were more likely to be catalogued in other databases worldwide: so the "issuing bodies" (e.g., main universities, government bodies or research centres) were more likely to already have an ISNI.
38. GeoNames is a geographical database which covers all countries and contains over eleven million place names. See http://www.geonames.org/.
39. Nathalie Cornic, "ROAD: the Directory of Open Access Scholarly Resources to Promote Open Access Worldwide", *Positioning and Power in Academic Publishing: Players, Agents and Agendas: Proceedings of the 20th International Conference on Electronic Publishing*, 2016, pp. 37–41, https://books.google.fr/books?id=Lgy3DAAAQBAJ.
40. The Directory of Open Access Journals, launched in 2003, is a community-curated list of open access journals. It currently contains ca. 9,000 open access journals covering all areas of science, technology, medicine, social science, and humanities. See https://doaj.org/.
41. Latindex is an information system on scholarly journals published in Latin America, the Caribbean, Spain, and Portugal. It is based on a network of institutions that cooperate to provide a set of services for the gathering and dissemination of relevant bibliographic information and editorial-quality criteria. See http://www.latindex.org.
42. The Keepers Registry references electronic journals which are preserved by the "Keepers", i.e., the participating archiving agencies acting as stewards of digital content. See the website (https://thekeepers.org/) and Peter Burnhill, Gaëlle Béquet, Theron "Ted" Westervelt and Alan Darnell, "Transnational Strategies for Stewardship of Our Shared Scholarly Record (and of Each Nation's Published Heritage): Both Open and Subscribed Content", *Project Briefings of the 2016 Coalition for Networked Information (CNI) Conference*, https://www.cni.org/topics/digital-preservation/transnational-strategies-for-stewardship-of-our-shared-scholarly-record-and-of-each-nations-published-heritage-both-open-and-subscribed-content.

# Many Languages, Many Workflows: Mapping and Analyzing Technical Services Processes for East Asian and International Studies Materials

Leigh Billings (iD), Nerea A. Llamas (iD), Beth E. Snyder (iD), and Yunah Sung (iD)

**ABSTRACT**

This case study addresses a workflow analysis project undertaken in the International Studies and Asia Library technical services areas of the University of Michigan Library. The analysis was an opportunity to document existing technical services practices in three primary workflow areas: acquisitions/receiving, cataloging, and cataloging maintenance. International Studies began the project independently, and subsequently consultants were hired to work with both International Studies and Asia Library to find efficiencies and barriers, identify solutions, and propose future changes in non-Roman-language cataloging workflows. This article provides an account outlining the project background, implementation, outcomes, challenges, and lessons learned.

## Introduction

In 2013, the University of Michigan (U-M) Library reorganized, created the Research Division (Research), and hired a new Associate University Librarian (AUL) to provide services for the library across the research lifecycle. With the arrival of the new AUL for Research, the Division began the lengthy process of examining itself through a series of projects within and across its five departments, aimed at building a deeper understanding of its current work and purpose and its capacity to incorporate new and evolving responsibilities.

Within this context, the idea of a technical services workflow analysis emerged in the Asia Library and International Studies (ALIS) departments as a way to examine the tension inherent in being a library dedicated to building strong foreign language collections while facing various hurdles associated with cataloging and processing these materials. It is increasingly difficult to keep up with the work of non-Roman-language cataloging, either because budget constraints restrict the hiring of additional staff or because of a lack of qualified candidates. The U-M

Library is not alone in facing funding and staffing challenges. Many other libraries find themselves in this same situation.

Through this case study, the authors will provide insight into our process of self-reflection, shed light on our methods, and detail steps taken throughout. We discuss how we came to engage consultants and why we believe that this was beneficial to our project. Finally, we reflect on the results of our analyses and the next steps taken to implement recommendations.

## Planning and background

### Asia Library and International Studies (ALIS)

Asia Library and International Studies are administratively separate departments that have similar missions within the Research Division. Out of a total of 70 Research staff members, almost half (12 subject and functional specialists and 21 technical services professionals) are situated within the Asia Library and International Studies departments.

The Asia Library focuses on the selection, acquisition and processing of research materials in Chinese, Japanese, and Korean. International Studies has responsibility for materials selection from Sub-Saharan Africa and Latin America, and for both selection and processing of materials from North Africa, Central Asia, Eastern Europe, Latin America, the Middle East, South Asia, and Southeast Asia. Each department is home to a group of subject specialists as well as a technical services unit.

Asia Library and International Studies technical services specialists are collectively responsible for receiving and processing approximately 43,000 items annually from around the globe. These materials come in numerous formats and in more than 100 languages that can be represented in more than fifteen different scripts. Asia Library and International Studies are also organizationally independent from the library's central Technical Services department, which handles Roman script materials for the languages outside the purview of ALIS processing. As individual departments, each of the three develops their own workflows and policies.

In response to the 2013 U-M Library reorganization, which placed the Asia Library and International Studies together under the AUL for the Research Division and central Technical Services within the Collections Division, Asia Library and International Studies began to examine their relationship. The following year, these two departments launched into a strategic planning process that served to highlight their similarities and create a strong bond between the units. Since then, Asia Library and International Studies have collaborated extensively and worked toward creating a shared understanding of non-Roman-language cataloging. That said, many differences still exist in their processes, hence the desire to capture and document them.

The ALIS Workflow Analysis was realized in two distinct phases, the first of which was launched by the International Studies department to examine the workflows of its technical services professionals. This International Studies Workflow Analysis project consisted of an initial survey that was sent to staff to capture basic information, in-depth interviews with individual staff members, and the creation of maps of each of their workflows. It took two years to complete. As International Studies neared the analysis stage of their project, the Library was presented with a unique opportunity to engage Bridgeport Consulting, a firm with expertise in organizational assessment.

For the second phase of the ALIS Workflow Analysis, Asia Library, International Studies, and Bridgeport joined together and applied Lean management tools to create a unified understanding of current technical services practices within and across ALIS and to identify possible or desirable areas for change. The project timeline is outlined in Figure 1.

Overarching goals for the ALIS Technical Services Workflow Analysis Project were to:

- build a cohesive team approach to technical services functions;
- facilitate succession planning;
- articulate the resources needed to provide and improve upon access and discovery of materials;
- identify space in workflows for new functions;
- tell a compelling story of the value and impact of ALIS technical services functions;
- gain an accurate understanding of cataloging capacity; and
- understand the ordering process and standardize where possible;

Two guiding principles were articulated in launching this project: (1) changes would not be made simply for change's sake; and (2) ALIS units were not in danger of downsizing or layoffs. This was a process primarily of documentation that would allow for more informed and agile future decisions.

## Literature review

As reported in the literature, libraries have often turned to technical services workflow analysis when faced with organizational redesign,[1] changes in departmental

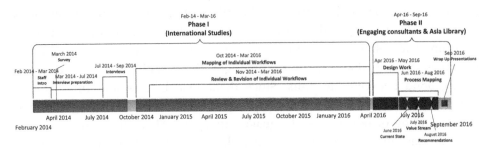

**Figure 1.** ALIS TS workflow analysis project timeline.

staffing due to retirements or employee turnover,[2] introduction of new management and reporting structures,[3] and changes in physical work spaces.[4] Shifts in format from print to electronic and practical considerations related to managing electronic resources,[5] the prospect of reduced financial resources,[6] and a desire to accelerate the "time-to-shelf" for materials have also motivated analyses.[7] Beyond these goals, many workflow analyses also aimed to gain a more accurate understanding of cataloging capacity,[8] while others were performed to solve known problems in the workflow.[9]

Reported approaches to workflow analysis include time-and-path or time-and-cost studies to quantitatively analyze workflows using time or cost measurements. These commonly took the form of slips of paper tucked into physical materials,[10] group interviews,[11] direct observation,[12] or worksheets filled out by staff.[13]

Nearly all reported workflow case studies described difficulty on the part of staff with terminology used at various stages of the process.[14] Additional challenges were discovered when workflow analyses raised anxiety [15] among the affected staff,[16] with some suggesting that negative reactions may be due to staff not being involved in the decision-making process,[17] and others reporting that "engaging staff" helped overcome initial mistrust.[18] Further, the process mapping effort was extremely time consuming for all involved.[19]

Largely absent from these analyses is a consideration of if and how variations in languages, particularly the complexities involving non-Roman-script languages, affect the flow of items through the technical services unit; in some cases reports clearly noted that the analyses were done only for Western-language materials.[20] Much of the literature treating the processing or cataloging of materials in non-Western languages has instead discussed character encoding and guidelines for including the vernacular script in records,[21] as well as language-specific cataloging challenges such as form of name/authority control, Romanization, and multilingual subject analysis.[22]

In terms of cataloging production management for non-Western language material, considerations have largely turned to outsourcing,[23] costs, and production quality, with some reporting that language expertise should be considered as a category in which libraries might cooperate and outsource to one another.[24] A backlog reduction project from an academic library that resulted in the establishment of production standards did not attempt a detailed workflow analysis but analyzed the results of established production goals.[25]

## Phase I: International Studies workflow analysis

### *Impetus for the project*

In 2014, when the first phase of the workflow analysis project was introduced in International Studies as part of a broader strategic planning and visioning exercise, there were 21 staff members and seven student assistants in the department engaged in various combinations of technical services work as well as public-facing work, such as outreach to faculty and students and support for research, teaching and learning. In keeping with the Research Division's self-reflection, International Studies set out to analyze the work performed by both subject and technical services specialists. Ultimately, that was too ambitious and the unit chose to focus its initial efforts on technical services functions: the point at which materials enter the library, are made accessible in the catalog, and become a part of the research lifecycle.

Highly individualized, language-dependent workflows have long been a hallmark within International Studies. Anecdotally, this has been attributed to the specialized expertise necessary to handle the wide variety of languages and formats passing through the unit. Although staff work in close proximity to one another, they do not necessarily know the process or steps involved in each other's work, or understand what is essential as opposed to personal preference. With the reorganization in Research, the reporting structure changed for many of the technical services staff in International Studies. Getting to know and be able to communicate workflow particulars up and down the reporting lines became a necessity. In turn, an opportunity was created to question long-standing assumptions about why and how International Studies technical processing workflows had evolved to their current state and discover if ways could be found to capitalize on existing staffing capacity to maintain or improve access to foreign-language collections.

### Objectives and structure

A Workflow Analysis Team was convened by the Head of International Studies to design a workflow analysis project to foster a common understanding of and deeper appreciation within International Studies for its own technical services work, find ways to accommodate processing needs amid fluctuating capacity and staff turnover, and be able to articulate the relevance and value of technical services functions within International Studies and to the library administration.

This International Studies (IS) Workflow Analysis Team planned to document existing workflow processes through a series of staff interviews which would be visually mapped. The data from the interviews and maps would then be available for reflection and analysis.

### The survey

The IS Workflow Analysis Team designed a brief Qualtrics survey that was administered to 23 individuals (including student assistants). The intent of the survey was twofold. First, the team wanted to broadly identify essential technical services work functions. Second, they needed to determine which individuals performed the types of work that would qualify as technical services. (This was not clear at the outset as individuals' duties and reporting lines have changed over time). The survey sought information about the source of materials received in the unit (i.e., purchase or gift), the formats worked on, and whether the language of the material in any way affected its routing or processing.

The responses influenced the team's categorization of where specific processes fell within the three broadly defined areas of Acquisitions/Receiving (how materials arrive in the unit), Cataloging (how materials are processed into the catalog), and Catalog Maintenance (how routine error-fixing and holdings updates are executed separately from the cataloging process) and helped with the formulation of interview questions and the direction of the subsequent mapping project. The survey clarified which staff members should be interviewed, demonstrating that student assistants did not always have enough control over their own workflow to serve as knowledgeable interview subjects. As a result, questions about student workflows were incorporated into the supervisor interviews. The survey answers also brought specific issues to the forefront, such as possible inconsistencies among respondents' definition of terms. This was addressed by creating a glossary so all participants could work from a common understanding.

## Interviews

Using the survey responses as a guide, the IS Workflow Analysis Team shaped and defined the interview scripts and mapping project components. The technical services life cycle became defined as the period of time from the receipt of material in the unit until it departs the unit.

Individual interviews for each workflow (Acquisitions/Receiving, Cataloging, and Catalog Maintenance) were conducted following a standardized script written by the IS Workflow Analysis Team. Care was taken to identify and record where, when, why, and how work is done; who is involved in each workflow; dependencies, redundancies, delays, and handoffs; and tools, software or systems used.

The IS Workflow Analysis Team first tested the interview technique on themselves. This allowed them to refine the content and order of the questions and determine the most effective format for each interview. Two 90-min interview sessions were planned for each cataloger, during which they were interviewed by two IS Workflow Analysis Team members, one asking the questions and the other transcribing the responses. The interviews took place in the cataloger's office so their work could be discussed or demonstrated in the context and familiarity of their own space. Seventeen people were interviewed between July and September of 2014. Depending on the job roles of those being interviewed, the sessions took more or less than the originally allotted time. Because of the tremendous time commitment, the three IS Workflow Analysis Team members rotated and divided interviewing and transcription duties across all of the interview sessions.

## Process mapping

After the interviews were complete, the IS Workflow Analysis Team formulated consistent mapping guidelines and learned how to use Microsoft Visio. As mapping commenced, refinements to the scope were made regarding what information from the interviews would be included in the visual representation of the workflows; not all information captured in the interviews was included in the maps. Figure 2 is the workflow diagram key.

The person who transcribed an interview mapped it and worked with the cataloger to review and revise it as many times as necessary until the cataloger was satisfied that it accurately depicted his or her workflow. When first introducing the workflow maps, the transcriber met with the cataloger in person to review the workflow mapping guidelines. Catalogers received copies of their own maps when they were completed, but maps were not shared widely due to privacy concerns. Before moving to the next project phase, two members of the IS Workflow Analysis Team standardized minor differences in color schemes and terminology across all of the maps and replaced all personal names with working titles to produce a unified final product.

In some cases, staff members did not have duties pertaining to one or more of the workflow areas, so no map was created for that area. On the other hand, more than one map may have been created for a cataloger if significant variation in a process occurred within the same workflow, which often happened when encountering differences in format; language (scripts and language skill of staff or students); acquisition source (book-buying trips overseas vs. ordering/approval plan vs. gifts); level of cataloging required; and staff schedules, skill levels, or job responsibilities. For example, one cataloger may have had three distinct maps produced for the cataloging workflow: one map for cataloging DVDs, one map for cataloging monographs, and a third for cataloging monographs in a second language for which a student was available to assist.

Although 17 people were interviewed during Phase I of the project, not all of those interviewed had their workflows mapped by the time Phase II began. Two people's workflows were not mapped because their activities did not constitute entire workflows (instead their duties were confined to a few actions or steps appearing within a colleague's workflow), a fact which was only discovered during the interviews. Two other people's workflows were not mapped due to time

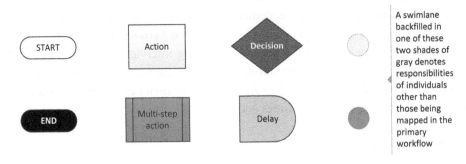

**Figure 2.** IS workflow analysis key to diagram shapes and shading. A key similar to this was created to assist in the standardization and reading of the maps.

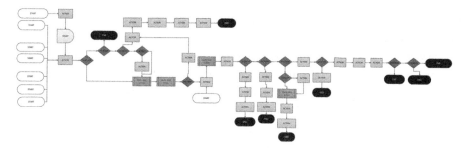

**Figure 3.** IS individual cataloging workflow sample. This image represents the number and types of steps recorded within the workflow of one individual beginning with receiving or selecting material at the point of cataloging and ending with cataloging completion. Although the specific data have been removed, the detail and complexity of the workflow are evident.

constraints, and one set of workflows was revamped completely when staff turn-over caused significant changes. By the end of Phase I, 13 IS technical services staff had had their individual workflows mapped, with a range of 4–15 maps per individual staff member, resulting in a total of 90 distinct maps. Although not all individuals' workflows had been mapped, there was representation of workflows addressing all regions of the world managed by IS. See Figure 3 for an example of one of the cataloging workflows; see Figure 4 for an example of an acquisitions workflow involving more than one individual. In both of the examples provided, the maps have been anonymized so as to show the complexity of the charts rather than the details, as staff were assured that their individual maps would not be shared outside of IS.

The time it took to map each workflow was generally lengthy, although it varied based on the complexity of the workflow and the level of detail transcribed therein. Mapping was done in addition to regular duties, so finding time to map was

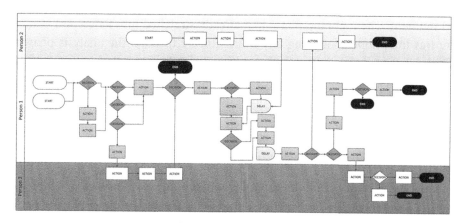

**Figure 4.** IS individual receiving workflow sample. This workflow utilizes a swimlane to represent the work of three people processing material beginning with its receipt in the unit and ending when it is ready for cataloging. The work of the individual being mapped is in the center row and is flanked above and below by the others who contribute to this workflow.

difficult, with the result that some mapping took place more than a year after the interviews were originally held.

A few of the frustrations encountered while reviewing and revising the maps were no surprise as they had also arisen during the interview process. Catalogers referring to similar procedures, systems, or tools might describe them in varying levels of detail or by using different vocabulary from one another. As a result, unifying terminology and keeping the maps to a standard scope was a struggle, even with the glossary created after the survey. It was also clear that the categorization of workflows into the three separate areas of Acquisitions, Cataloging, and Cataloging Maintenance was an artificial distinction for many. All of the work was often considered to be one fluid process by the cataloger, and trying to determine a clear beginning, middle, and end of a distinct area was difficult.

The experience gained from this first phase of the workflow analysis was invaluable for highlighting potential trouble spots and preparing everyone for the transition to the second phase of the project. Phase I was long, but in retrospect, provided foundational skills needed for the next stage. By the start of Phase II, International Studies staff members were already well versed in process mapping and had learned to contextualize their work within a larger process. Without this experience, Phase II would certainly have been more challenging and less efficient.

## Phase II: Asia Library and International Studies (ALIS) technical services workflow analysis

### Engaging a consultant

As Phase I of the IS workflow analysis project was nearing completion, the U-M Library was approached by Bridgeport Consulting. The team at Bridgeport had previously worked with other departments on campus to implement administrative changes and was now offering their services to the Library. They arrived at an ideal moment. The mapping phase had already stretched into its second year and there was little hope of moving any more quickly through the analysis phase. In addition, no one on the Workflow Analysis Team had practical experience conducting such an analysis. Therefore, a partnership with Bridgeport was explored in hopes that it would ensure completion of the project in a timely manner.

### Asia Library participation

Although Asia Library had not participated in Phase I, it was determined that a combined Asia Library and International Studies effort was warranted. It was clear that Asia Library staff could benefit as much as International Studies from understanding their own workflows. Like International Studies, Asia Library is composed of both subject and technical services specialists with technical services workflows segregated on the basis of language. Having already collaborated successfully on other projects, the two units were certain that combining forces would lead to a richer result. To this end, a combined proposal was drafted and presented to Bridgeport.

In many ways, the initial step of drafting a proposal was a test of Asia Library's and International Studies' partnership with Bridgeport. Since Bridgeport had no specific expertise in library workflows, there were multiple meetings just to understand their approach to reviewing workflows and ensure it would add value to an ALIS analysis. Success of the project would depend on two factors: (1) how well the Bridgeport team understood ALIS's needs and goals and (2) how well ALIS understood Bridgeport's approach to analyzing the data. It took multiple meetings and drafts to reach the final proposal.

### Planning Phase II

Critical issues discussed at initial meetings with Bridgeport were the need to clearly define the project scope, to develop a communication plan among project stakeholders to convey the project benefits and objectives, and to work quickly to bring Asia Library and International Studies staff to the same stage in the process.

### Project structure and scope

A Design Team–made up of the AUL for Research, the heads of both Asia Library and International Studies, the heads of ALIS Technical Services units, one IS Slavic Cataloger, and three Bridgeport team members—was charged with overseeing the project scope and design, the schedule, and the staff communication plan. This group met regularly throughout the project to discuss progress made and work through any questions or challenges that arose.

Goals set out by the Design Team were to create a shared understanding of the work of Technical Services staff by documenting the work in the areas defined in Phase I through a Lean management approach that would create three specific products: current state maps, value stream maps, and future state maps. Even though ALIS staff work with various formats, due to time constraints this workflow analysis was limited to the acquisition and cataloging of print materials, the predominant format processed in both units. Staff members were directly engaged in producing these outcomes through participation in working groups and were responsible for the ultimate recommendations of the project. The process and outcomes were guided, rather than dictated, by Bridgeport.

### Lean management

Lean management, as applied by Bridgeport, came to form the backbone of the ALIS Technical Services Workflow Analysis. This philosophy has origins in the Toyota Production System and utilizes tools such as current state, value stream, and future state maps in an iterative manner to identify and achieve process improvements.[26]

Current state maps represent end-to-end processes, and record decision points, work roles, or handoffs within a workflow. Value stream mapping takes the current state process and evaluates it for improvement opportunities through the charting of major process steps and the analysis of various metrics, roles, systems, and barriers to flow (things that impede the efficiency or completion of a process step). Future State delivers an enhanced process, which is ideally more efficient and effective, by mapping the improvement opportunities identified in the value stream analysis to the original current state maps. Throughout each of these stages, Bridgeport applies what it calls the 80/20 rule, in which steps for a process are considered or recorded if they occur roughly 80% of the time and excluded if they occur 20% of the time or less.[27]

The value stream relies on a number of specialized metrics and concepts. Process Time (PT) is the active time it takes to perform work or complete a step. Lead Time (LT) is the amount of time from when work becomes available until it is complete and passed to the next step. It includes process time and any inactive or down time before, during, or after a process until the step is complete, such as time while waiting for a system to run or to receive a handoff or occupied doing other work. The activity ratio is determined by dividing the Lead Time by the Process Time (in minutes) then multiplying by 100 to arrive at a percentage which quantifies the variation between active and inactive time and the potential for narrowing any significant differences.

Figure 5 illustrates the visual components of the Bridgeport value stream mapping system. Each process step is represented in a box, which is named and numbered. Listed within each data box are the roles and numbers of those involved in carrying out the steps. Below are listed barriers to flow, the process time (PT), and the lead time (LT) for the step. At the top of the process step is a call-out for the systems utilized within that step. Improvement opportunities, which have been

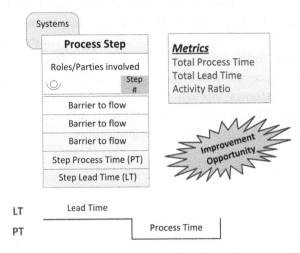

**Figure 5.** ALIS TS value stream map key. (This image is based on an image developed by Bridgeport Consulting).

determined through brainstorming, are contained within the "kaizen burst" shape. Collective metrics for the entire value stream map are noted in a separate "Metrics" textbox. Lead Time (LT) and Process Time (PT) are represented as a timeline graph which runs continuously underneath the process steps and visually links them together.

### Stakeholder engagement and rollout to staff

Throughout the workflow analysis, the Design Team took care to remain sensitive to our professional staff's needs. The team knew from experience that there would be concern about our motives for conducting the analysis. In addition, IS staff had already given significant amounts of their time to complete workflow maps. Now, the Design Team was asking for even more participation. In anticipation, the Design Team planned a layered rollout to both Asia Library and International Studies staff. Separate, hour-long kick-off meetings were held for both Asia Library and International Studies staff at which Bridgeport team members introduced themselves and made personal connections with the staff. They summarized their process and showed examples of their past projects. Design Team members invited staff to volunteer for working groups and assured them that their input would weigh heavily in the outcomes of the project. This personal attention was greatly valued by everyone involved and made a significant difference in staff's willingness to participate.

### Working groups

Bridgeport's assessment methods called for the formation and active participation of two working groups to oversee and provide the substance and metrics for the analysis. The Acquisitions Working Group focused on processes surrounding ordering and acquisitions workflows while the Cataloging Working Group focused on processes of cataloging and catalog maintenance. Each working group comprised six staff members, three from International Studies and three from Asia Library, who represented all technical services and processes from their units. Three members from the Design Team also served as group leads, with one of them participating in both groups.

The working groups met once a month to develop current state and value stream maps and provide feedback to the consultants as they created and refined the maps. These meetings encompassed brainstorming and guided discussions as team members considered tasks that they themselves performed as well as those of colleagues not present in the meetings. All of these ideas were gathered onto self-stick easel pads displayed around the room. In addition to meetings, working group members provided feedback and discussed questions and concerns through email; they also were asked to track time and provide statistics for a short period of time in order to guide discussions about metrics.

### *Adapting and transitioning Phase I work to Phase II work — Current state mapping*

The working group co-leaders representing both Asia Library and International Studies met initially with the Bridgeport lead to introduce the work done in IS during Phase I to see what data or techniques could be adapted to the combined project. This was also an opportunity to give Bridgeport its initial exposure to technical services terminology and the type of work done by the staff whose workflows would be mapped/analyzed. The devil really was in the details, and Bridgeport recognized a need to bring in an outside expert to find ways to pull back from the minutiae to illuminate the commonalities that would enable joint discussion at a higher level.

To efficiently produce high-level current state maps that would reflect processes across both Asia Library and International Studies, the working group co-leads from IS drew from data gathered in the Phase I mapping process. Due to the thoroughness of the Phase I mapping, it was relatively easy for them to create high-level maps with fewer overall steps that reflected the work done in IS. Less certain was how these mapped to Asia Library processes, since they had not previously undergone any interviews or workflow mapping. An example of the cataloging current state map is in Figure 6.

In order to address this imbalance, Asia Library Cataloging and Acquisitions Working Group members met without the IS members of the groups to discuss each of their current state processes. Using the IS high-level maps as a starting point, they worked to produce versions that matched their processes. While the cataloging maps were found to match workflows rather well, it soon became apparent that some AL acquisitions processes did not have equivalent workflows in IS. These AL acquisitions processes took more time to identify and record; the result was a current state ordering map that was unique to Asia Library. Once Asia Library and International Studies working group members had achieved a similar level of understanding of workflows and mapping, working group meetings were held jointly.

Ultimately, the working groups created five final current state maps (AL ordering and ALIS combined cataloging, cataloging maintenance, non-gift receiving, and gift receiving). These current state maps served as the framework for conversations leading to the development of the value stream maps and improvement opportunities.

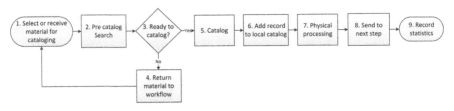

**Figure 6.** ALIS TS combined cataloging current state map.

### Value stream mapping

Next, Bridgeport provided instruction in value stream mapping and helped the working groups transform the current state maps into the more consolidated value stream format. For example, the cataloging maintenance current state map contains six steps from beginning to end (see Figure 7). For the cataloging maintenance value stream map, those six were collapsed into three measurable process steps: address error or update, record statistics, and send to next step.

The working group members were then asked to gather their own process times, lead times, and barriers to flow for each process step in each workflow and submit them to Bridgeport in advance of the value stream meeting. This ensured that working group members understood what was being asked of them and that Bridgeport had information available to guide the discussion.

At the value stream meetings, the working groups discussed all the components of the value stream, including: PT, LT, Activity Ratio (figured later by Bridgeport), systems, staff roles and numbers, barriers to flow, and process opportunities/improvements. Figure 8 shows the final catalog maintenance value stream map.

The working group completed and finalized four value stream maps: Asia Library Ordering, ALIS Receiving, ALIS Cataloging, and ALIS Cataloging Maintenance.

### Lean management learning curve

One of the difficulties during this stage was remembering that not all issues encountered by staff were required to be solved. According to Bridgeport, the current state map is meant to visualize what happens the majority (or 80%) of the time, rather than every possible iteration or variation of a process. As catalogers are often detail-oriented individuals, it was hard to keep in mind that examples of irritations or problems were often infrequent outliers, and that a problem that occurs once every two years may not be a systemic problem that requires resolution.

Another difficulty arose during the value stream mapping stage, as the Lean management terminology used by the consultants was difficult for many staff to fully grasp without examples; this was particularly noticeable during discussions of metrics, where the terms regarding process time and lead time often needed clarification. Lead time and process time are difficult for catalogers to estimate. Since this exercise relied entirely upon self-reporting by catalogers for the amounts of

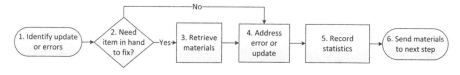

Figure 7. ALIS TS combined cataloging maintenance current state map.

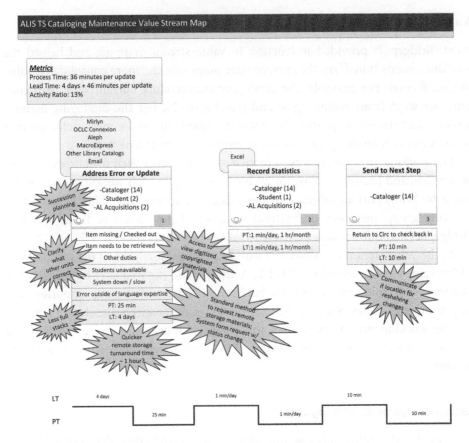

**Figure 8.** ALIS TS cataloging maintenance value stream map. (This image is based on an image developed by Bridgeport Consulting).

time each step took, one of the working group co-leads designed a spreadsheet file as an example of her own work, which was then used as a template for others to follow (see Figure 9). In addition, metrics varied significantly between individuals, which made it a challenge to come up with an average that everyone agreed upon—this is not surprising given that "catalog" stood alone as one step, which could encompass all levels of cataloging from copy to original.

### Improvement idea prioritization

While the original plan was to create a final state map illustrating new workflows, once the value stream mapping was complete it was clear that changes would not result in a new overall workflow. Instead, the teams brainstormed about how to solve the various problems listed as "barriers to flow" in the value stream maps. These recommendations were ultimately documented in a list, and conversations arose as to how best to present the ideas to the Design Team. Ultimately, each team member was asked to carefully rank each recommendation based on how difficult or easy they were to implement and the relative benefit or impact of the change to their own workflow. The team at Bridgeport compiled those rankings

| Cataloging Maintenance | | | | |
|---|---|---|---|---|
| Process step | Step includes | Process Time | Lead Time | Barriers to flow |
| Retrieve material | Picking up item from shelf, or requesting from remote storage | 1 to 15 minutes | 2 days-2 weeks | Other duties are more important; will usually wait to do these on Friday or day when I "feel like it" (may set aside and go retrieve 2-3 books at a time); if item is in remote storage I will have to wait at least a day/overnight to get from there & then have to pick up from circ |
| Address error/update | fixing call no., updating bib manually, reoverlaying bib, writing HathiTrust re: OCLC no change | 5 to 30 minutes* | | |
| Record Statistics | filling out a form once a month | less than a minute* | | Only fill out form 1 x month (1st of the month); at time of error, will record tick mark or note in record |
| Send to next step | | 1-10 minutes* | | Usually have to take to Circ to check back in if item needs relabeling |

*per title (some processes may be done as a group)

**Figure 9.** ALIS TS cataloging maintenance sample metrics.

and presented the results in a spreadsheet separated into quadrants of "Relatively High Benefit, Relatively Easy to Implement;" "Relatively High Benefit, Relatively Difficult to Implement;" "Relatively Low Benefit, Relatively Easy to Implement;" and "Relatively Low Benefit, Relatively Difficult to Implement" (see Figures 10 and 11).

Ultimately, two spreadsheets were presented to the Design Team: one for the Acquisitions Working Group, which included 13 improvement ideas in the ordering and receiving categories, and one for the Cataloging Working Group, which included 18 improvement ideas across the categories of cataloging and maintenance. Some of the major results are listed below.

### Acquisitions working group recommendations

- Human Resources and Training: train student assistants to improve search accuracy, recruit on-call trained student assistants for peak processing times, and communicate clearly and consistently with the mailroom for delivery notification and correct placement of shipments
- Space: Find or create space for an unpacking station, new arrivals, and backlog materials
- Vendor-Related: Ask vendors to normalize the size and timing of shipments, alphabetize titles on invoices/packing lists, and separate standing orders and

monographs. In terms of order lists, ask vendors to provide titles in vernacular or with correct Romanization, supply existing OCLC number, and search OPAC in order not to offer duplicates of existing library holdings.

- Other: Address the size of existing backlogs such that less time is required to manage them

| PROCESS STEP | BARRIER TO FLOW | IDEA/SOLUTION | AVG BENEFIT | AVG EASE OF IMPLEMENTATION |
|---|---|---|---|---|
| Relatively High Benefit, Relatively Easy to Implement | | | | |
| Cataloging Maintenance - Address Error or Update | Error outside of language expertise | Clarify what other units correct; clarify what corrections should be made by whom | 3.57 | 2.14 |
| Cataloging Maintenance - Address Error or Update | Insufficient staffing, fewer staff in the summer. Insufficient language expertise. Unfamiliar format. Hand-off due to language skill. Unfamiliar subject. | Succession planning | 3.14 | 1.86 |
| Relatively High Benefit, Relatively Difficult to Implement | | | | |
| Cataloging Maintenance - Address Error or Update | Item needs to be retrieved before error is fixed | Create standard method for requesting materials from remote storage (recommend a form request in the system with status change included) | 3.57 | 1.29 |
| Cataloging Maintenance - Address Error or Update | Item missing/checked out. Item needs to be retrieved before error is fixed. | Provide access for all catalogers to view digitized materials that are still in-copyright (access to scanned copy means item doesn't need to be in hand to fix) | 3.38 | 0.63 |
| Relatively Low Benefit, Relatively Easy to Implement | | | | |
| N/A | | | | |
| Relatively Low Benefit, Relatively Difficult to Implement | | | | |
| Cataloging Maintenance - Address Error or Update | Item needs to be retrieved | Quicker turnaround from remote storage (one hour?) | 2.25 | 0.63 |

**Figure 10.** ALIS cataloging maintenance improvement ideas grid.

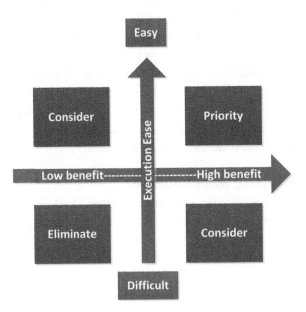

**Figure 11.** ALIS TS process improvement benefit graphic. (This image is based on an image developed by Bridgeport Consulting).

## Cataloging working group recommendations

- Human Resources and Training: Prepare for succession planning, provide standardized training for student assistants to reduce common errors, hire more permanent staff catalogers and student assistants, and provide language training for some languages
- Policy: Create or clarify cataloging policies and create central policy documentation system
- Roles and Responsibilities: Clarify who makes corrections and what types, clarify who maintains supply inventory and what the inventory entails, and clarify who performs physical processing and how
- Interactions with Other Units/Organizations: Improve notifications when the system is down or slow, standardize the method for requesting materials from other libraries and the book storage facility on campus, grant catalogers access to view digitized copyrighted materials for cataloging maintenance, and clarify responsibility for performing physical processing, such as attaching pockets for discs and tipping in loose pages.

## Reporting results

As recommendations were nearing completion, the Design Team created a roll-out plan to introduce the project and its final recommendations. This plan included several meetings and presentations with the individual working groups, the entire Research Division, and colleagues from the Library's Technical Services unit. Each meeting was led by members of the Design Team and carefully tailored to the interests of the specific audience. In the team wrap-up, we emphasized our gratitude to staff for their participation, the value of the recommendations and plans for following through with changes. In the Research all-staff meeting, the focus shifted to the larger goals of the project and how the project outcomes would guide future planning in Asia Library and International Studies. The final wrap-up with Technical Services colleagues (outside of the Research Division) was an overview of the whole process with an opportunity to discuss details of our findings. Overall, in hosting these three separate meetings we intentionally erred on the side of openness and communication so that our project was transparent to everyone either directly or indirectly affected by it.

## Communications (internal & external)

When the project was introduced, it was recognized that looking so closely at workflows might feel intrusive and be seen as a threat to staff autonomy. Thus, throughout the process those involved set out to alleviate, as much as possible, any fears about the workflow analyses. Communication lines were kept open with all staff throughout the various stages of the project through group meetings and email updates as well as individual meetings. It was stressed that the primary focus of the project was on information and documentation of processes rather than on assessment of an individual's work performance. Any reporting of results would be respectful of an individual's privacy and would be shared initially only within International Studies, Asia Library, or the Research Division. Staff needed to feel comfortable with the process and be able to trust that the information would not be used in a punitive manner.

It was also made clear to all staff that they were an integral part of this project. Staff members were considered the experts of their own work, which is complex and necessary for the success of the unit and the library. The quality of the work done by staff was not evaluated, nor were there ever discussions about improving efficiencies through reduced staffing. The final results would rely heavily on the whole team effort to discuss and illuminate their own work patterns.

## Results and outcomes

At the end of the process we had 90 individual workflow maps for International Studies staff, five current state and two value stream maps concerning Asia Library and International Studies' combined workflows, and a list of 32 working group recommendations for improvements in areas such as policy, training, documentation, space, and interactions with other units. All of the maps produced during Phase II, as well as supplementary material from Phase I, can be accessed in the University of Michigan's repository Deep Blue.[28]

The Heads of Asia Library and International Studies accepted the recommendations at face value without any question about their efficacy or validity. Upon receiving the list of recommendations, the Heads took on the task of reviewing the recommendations through an administrative lens, prioritizing them based on the availability of resources and planning for implementation. As described earlier, the recommendations were weighed and presented by the working groups based on a matrix of difficulty and benefit. In reviewing the recommendations, it is easy to see that some, such as clarifying roles and responsibilities, can and should be implemented very quickly, while others, such as documenting policy, will require additional planning and effort. Still others, such as recruiting on-call student catalogers, may be beyond our ability to implement. As the implementation phase continues, it is likely that the weights and benefits will be reevaluated as circumstances and resources change, and thus the process will no doubt continue to engage staff and require the expertise of technical services specialists.

## Lessons learned

The most important tangible outcome was in the documentation that ALIS is able to share with management, new staff, and colleagues regarding what steps are necessary when acquiring and cataloging items in non-Roman languages. No less valuable, but less concrete is the experience that staff had in sharing and evaluating their workflows. It can improve morale to see that a certain irritation is not one person's problem alone, but is an overarching theme among units, and this can provide managers a place to start when evaluating the recommendations for improvement.

A more abstract benefit of the analysis was the discovery that more communication was necessary between managers and staff, particularly as it related to the final recommendations. Staff felt that some recommendations would be almost impossible to implement, while managers thought that the same tasks had a simple solution. We hope that seeing this divide will help empower staff to bring forward future concerns with the understanding that managers may see things in a different light and be able to effect positive change on staff workflows.

In addition to the necessary communication between staff and managers, the analysis highlighted the need for more communication between staff who have similar job responsibilities. During Phase I of the project, individuals often commented "but we all do the same thing" or "you already know what I do," signifying that they were unaware of the variations among IS workflows. During Phase II, as ALIS staff tried to create a single unified high-level workflow, it became clear that while the beginning (item acquired) and end (item available for patron) might be the same for everyone, the path noticeably varied between units and individuals. Phase II enabled staff to discover for themselves the reasons behind those variances, whether they were due to differences in how individuals were trained, job responsibilities, the availability of student workers, space constraints, or changes in processes that have occurred over time. This analysis provided the forum for staff to learn that there were differences as well as similarities in how they thought and spoke about their work, creating an environment of understanding that will encourage further relationships between ALIS technical services staff.

It is impossible to overemphasize the value in having Bridgeport Consulting lead Phase II of our project. They asked thoughtful, detailed questions in order to fully understand the why and how of technical services processes; showed great respect for the knowledge and expertise of staff while keeping the working groups on track and on schedule (it is quite easy to have conversations derail as catalogers delve into the details); and ultimately created usable tools in the form of current state and value stream maps. While the working groups provided the bulk of the details, it was very helpful to have a third party ask probing questions. The objectivity of the consultants meant that their questions were taken at face value; their motives for asking questions were clear, so staff could freely talk without worry about repercussions. While International Studies staff were more familiar with the process mapping part of Phase I, it was very beneficial to have the experts explain the jargon and purpose of the Lean management tools used in Phase II. It was difficult for staff to fit their metrics into the models provided, but the consultants were able to translate very business-centric tools into something technical services staff could understand.

Overall, we learned that workflow analysis requires time, effort, and honesty. During every stage of the project, staff members continued to perform their regular job duties as well as participate in the time-consuming workflow analysis. This meant that Phase I of the project took almost two years to conclude, and there were still some individual maps left incomplete. Even though Phase II was complete in six months, it was an intense, exhaustive process of self-reflection for all parties involved. If staff had not been encouraged to participate and provide candid and detailed feedback, the process most certainly would have failed.

While we may not have achieved all of the goals originally set out during the project, we believe that this project was successful because we ultimately obtained information that can be used to attain those goals at a later date. For instance, none of the recommendations addressed the ambitious original goal of "Identify [ing] space in workflows for new functions," but now that we have a more accurate understanding of our current cataloging capacity due to the metrics recovered during the value-stream-mapping part of Phase II, we can begin to plan for future needs. Having workflow maps will be useful during succession planning, and the complexity of some of the individual workflows and the metrics involved tell a compelling story of the value of Asia Library and International Studies technical services. In the end, this project encouraged staff to learn from one another and be less guarded when discussing their processes. For this reason alone, we call this project an unqualified success.

## Recommendations

Overall, a workflow analysis can be a useful tool for any library to document and study their processes. Workflow analyses are also inherently complicated and require significant attention to detail to complete successfully. However, such a project requires a considerable time commitment. Anyone who undertakes such a project should articulate clearly the need and value of this work in their particular context. We cannot overstate the need for a plan at the outset that specifies the goals of the project, steps to take, and expected outcomes.

First and foremost, a detailed timeline is essential. The timeline should include milestones for the project, but also provide enough flexibility to accommodate the inevitable delays. It should be assumed that complications will arise and the project will take longer than expected, so account for this in your timeline. In Phase I of the project described here, there was no set timeline to complete the interviews and workflow maps. Because the analysis team did not anticipate the time required to complete the project, it dragged on for almost two years, without any end in sight.

The process Asia Library and International Studies took was unfamiliar to staff and naturally provoked questions and doubts. Attention to communications is another vital aspect of a successful project. Transparency is the key—be very clear with staff about expected outcomes of the project and expectations regarding individual involvement. There should be a multi-pronged plan that includes regular updates throughout the project, as well as opportunities for staff to provide feedback on the process. ALIS's process involved as many staff as possible, which went a long way to ensuring transparency.

One of the possible drawbacks to doing such a high-level analysis is that in focusing on the broad strokes in order to facilitate discussion among different units, the details of the individual workflows can be lost. However, the opportunity remains for International Studies staff to revisit their own workflows and discuss possible smaller or more individualized changes at a later date.

## Conclusion

At first glance, the 90 workflows prepared during Phase I of the project seem to point to inefficiencies in our handling of material in International Studies. And while it is true that some of these workflows may need individual improvement, we learned during Phase II that these workflows were necessary. They had intentional differences due to the complex nature of technical services work, especially when considering the added complications of dealing with languages that require specific expertise to handle. Asia Library and International Studies gained the tools necessary to explain the basics of technical services work to other parties and received recommendations on how best to handle inefficiencies that affected both departments' technical services units. We built relationships between the units as the working groups strove to compare and contrast our workflows, paving the pathway for future opportunities.

## Acknowledgments

The workflow analysis undertaken by Asia Library and International Studies was a team effort. It was made possible by the dedication and engagement of many individuals within the two units. The authors particularly would like to acknowledge the contributions of the Asia Library and International Studies Technical Services staff, whose expertise was critical to the analysis. In addition, we acknowledge AUL, Research, Elaine Westbrooks for supporting and encouraging our process. We would also like to thank Bridgeport Consulting for their expertise and guidance during Phase II. Our thanks to Evyn Kropf for her expert contributions to the International Studies Workflow Analysis Team and her counsel and contributions to this article. Finally, we are grateful to Dawn Lawson and Paul Grochowski for their feedback on the writing of this article.

## Funding

We acknowledge the U-M Library administration for funding Phase II.

## ORCID

Leigh Billings  http://orcid.org/0000-0002-9260-8392
Nerea A. Llamas  http://orcid.org/0000-0002-7714-2475
Beth E. Snyder  http://orcid.org/0000-0001-7694-5068
Yunah Sung  http://orcid.org/0000-0002-5801-5489

## Notes

1. Cheryl Martin, "Workflow Analysis as a Basis for Organizational Redesign at McMaster University Library," in *Innovative Redesign and Reorganization of Library Technical Services: Paths for the Future and Case Studies*, ed. Bradford Lee Eden (Westport, Conn.: Libraries Unlimited, 2004): 199–246.

2. Patricia Dragon and Lisa Sheets Barricella, "Assessment of Technical Services Workflow in an Academic Library: A Time-and-Path Study," *Technical Services Quarterly* 23, no. 4 (2006): 1–16.

3. Kristen Blake and Erin Stahlberg, "Me and My Shadow: Observation, Documentation, and Analysis of Serials and Electronic Resources Workflow," *Serials Review* 35, no. 4 (2009): 242–252.

4. Kitti Canepi, "Work Analysis in Library Technical Services", *Technical Services Quarterly*, 25, no. 2 (2007): 19–30, DOI: 10.1300/J124v25n02_02.

5. Tonia Graves and Michael A. Arthur, "Developing a Crystal Clear Future for the Serials Unit in an Electronic Environment: Results of a Workflow Analysis," *Serials Review* 32, no. 4 (12, 2006): 238–246; Blake and Stahlberg, "Me and My Shadow"; Elsa K. Anderson, "Workflow Analysis," *Library Technology Reports* 50, no. 3 (April 2014): 23–29; Alexandra Hamlett, "Keeping Up with the Flow: Electronic Resource Workflow and Analysis," *Serials Librarian* 70, no. 1–4 (January 2016): 168–174.

6. Stuart Hunt, "Improving performance in cataloguing and technical services workflows," *Catalogue & Index*, 161 (2010): 10–15, http://wrap.warwick.ac.uk/id/eprint/3910.

7. Terry Hurlbert and Linda L. Dujmic, "Factors Affecting Cataloging Time: An In-House Survey," *Technical Services Quarterly*, 22, no. 2 (2004): 1–14; Dragon and Barricella, "Assessment of Technical Services Workflow in an Academic Library"; Sally Gibson, "Utilizing a Time-to-Shelf Study to Start a Conversation on Change," *Faculty and Staff Publications – Milner Library*, Paper 66 (2015), http://ir.library.illinoisstate.edu/fpml/66.

8. Blake and Stahlberg, "Me and My Shadow"; Gibson, "Utilizing a Time-to-Shelf Study to Start a Conversation on Change."

9. Melanie McGurr, "Improving the Flow of Materials in a Cataloging Department: Using ADDIE for a Project in the Ohio State University Libraries," *Library Resources & Technical Services*, 52, no. 2 (Apr 2008): 54–60.

10. Dragon and Barricella, "Assessment of Technical Services Workflow in an Academic Library."

11. Martin, "Workflow Analysis as a Basis for Organizational Redesign at McMaster University Library."

12. Blake and Stahlberg, "Me and My Shadow."

13. Canepi, "Work Analysis in Library Technical Services."

14. Dragon and Barricella, "Assessment of Technical Services Workflow in an Academic Library."

15. Blake and Stahlberg, "Me and My Shadow."

16. Canepi, "Work Analysis in Library Technical Services."

17. Robert B. Freeborn and Rebecca L. Mugridge "The reorganization of monographic cataloging processes at Penn State University Libraries," *Library Collections, Acquisitions, & Technical Services*, 26, no. 1 (2002): 35–45.

18. Martin, "Workflow Analysis as a Basis for Organizational Redesign at McMaster University Library."

19. *Ibid.*; Hurlbert and Dujmic, "Factors Affecting Cataloging Time"; Blake and Stahlberg, "Me and My Shadow"; McGurr, "Improving the Flow of Materials in a Cataloging Department," 2008, 56.

20. Peter Haddad, "Cataloging and Classification of Pacific and Asian Language Materials at the National Library of Australia," *Cataloging & Classification Quarterly* 35, no. 3/4 (April 2003): 483–489.
21. Jacqueline Byrd, "Library catalogs and non-Roman scripts." *College & Research Libraries News* 65, no. 8 (September 2004): 424–425; Michele Seikel, "No More Romanizing: The Attempt to Be Less Anglocentric in RDA." *Cataloging & Classification Quarterly* 47, no. 8 (November 2009): 741–748; Zahiruddin Khurshid, "Arabic Script Materials: Cataloging Issues and Problems." *Cataloging & Classification Quarterly* 34, no. 4 (October 2002): 67–77.
22. Atoma Batoma, "Cataloguing Africana: The Case for the Integration of Onomastics into Training Programs." *African Research and Documentation* no. 111 (2009): 31–44; Mohd Ikhwan Ismail and Nurul Azurah Md. Roni, "Issues and challenges in cataloguing Arabic books in Malaysia academic libraries," *Education For Information* 28, no. 2–4 (June 2010): 151–163; Magda El-Sherbini and Sherab Chen. "An Assessment of the Need to Provide Non-Roman Subject Access to the Library Online Catalog." *Cataloging & Classification Quarterly* 49, no. 6 (August 2011): 457–483; Hikaru Nakano, "Non-Roman Language Cataloging in Bulk: A Case Study of Japanese Language Materials." Cataloging & Classification Quarterly 55, no. 2 (February 2017): 75–88.
23. Magda El-Sherbini, "Outsourcing of Slavic cataloguing at the Ohio State University libraries: evaluation and cost analysis," *Library Management* 23, no. 6/7 (September 2002): 325–329.
24. Magda El-Sherbini, "Sharing Cataloging Expertise: Options for Libraries to Share Their Skilled Catalogers with Other Libraries," in *Cataloging and Classification Quarterly: 21st Century Metadata Operations: Challenges, Opportunities, Directions: Special Issue*, ed. Bradford Lee Eden 48, no. 6–7 (2010): 525–540.
25. Jacqueline Byrd, "Cataloging production standards for non-western languages: from a project to permanent standards." *Indiana Slavic Studies* 16 (2006): 31–46.
26. Rob Ptacek. *Today's Lean! The Wiki (or Quick) Kaizen Approach to Continuous Improvement* (Chelsea, MI: MCS Media, 2012).
27. Bridgeport Consulting, "Process Mapping Overview." Unpublished slideshow, last modified May 25, 2016. PowerPoint file.
28. Research Unit: ALIS Technical Services Workflow Analysis (2016), University of Michigan Deep Blue Depository: http://hdl.handle.net/2027.42/136195

# Cataloging from the Center: Improving e-Book Cataloging on a Consortial Level

Emily Alinder Flynn (iD) and Erin Kilkenny (iD)

**ABSTRACT**

In 2014, the Ohio Library and Information Network (OhioLINK) overhauled its consortial cataloging workflows by switching to what has been termed a model of "cataloging from the center." For more than 20 years, the Ohio academic library consortium relied on volunteers from its member institutions to catalog consortially purchased materials. Consolidating the consortial cataloging into the OhioLINK office allowed for revising the various workflows. Since 2014, the cataloging workflows for these shared electronic resources have improved efficiencies, allowing records to be provided to members in a more timely manner.

## Background

OhioLINK is a statewide academic library consortium in Ohio, consisting of 121 member libraries from 91 institutions. Member institutions serve users from public universities, four-year and two-year institutions, and Ohio residents via the State Library of Ohio. While probably best known for print resource sharing, also called patron-initiated circulation (PCIRC), consortially purchased electronic resources (e-resources) are a large part of OhioLINK services.[1] Over the years, OhioLINK increased its consortial purchasing of electronic material which it loaded into shared platforms. This began first with electronic journal (e-journal) content in the 1990s and then adding electronic books (e-books) in the 2000s. Because OhioLINK's e-journal collection is relatively stable with few new journal subscriptions, this article focuses on e-book cataloging. The majority of cataloging performed in the Ohio-LINK office is for consortially purchased e-books, cataloged at the title level. The number of OhioLINK e-books has more than doubled from 72,022 in fiscal year (FY) 2011 to 149,341 in FY2016. OhioLINK purchased nearly 20,000 e-books in FY2016 alone. Beyond cataloging new e-books, OhioLINK also updates and improves older catalog records and now handles 15,000–30,000 MARC records per year, on average.

As OhioLINK began purchasing e-books, volunteer catalogers from member institutions cataloged the records on behalf of the consortium. Since new vendors and collections were added slowly over time, this process worked well. However, as vendor record batches increased in size with more publications each year and with OhioLINK continuing to purchase more e-books, there were sometimes significant delays between when records were received for cataloging and when they were provided to members to load into their catalogs. Volunteer catalogers had to fit consortial cataloging into their regular work as demand continued to grow for e-books and their catalog records. As there was no rotation in volunteer cataloging to share the burden, it made sense to consider other options including a dedicated consortial cataloger.

There were many contributing factors to OhioLINK's switch to centralized cataloging. Increased demand for e-books among OhioLINK institutions prompted an increase in purchases, which in turn drove the need to catalog them. At the same time, changes in staffing created open positions in the OhioLINK office, and in 2014 OhioLINK was able to hire for areas of growing need, such as e-book and e-journal cataloging without increasing OhioLINK member dues. Since the initial hire of a full-time cataloger in 2014, the consortial cataloging staff has expanded to include a part-time cataloging assistant and a part-time cataloging consultant as OhioLINK continues to purchase new collections in addition to its yearly renewals and receives more e-books to catalog.

This article will cover the reason why OhioLINK moved from using volunteer catalogers to a consortial staff cataloger, the associated challenges, efficiencies gained, and possible transferrable lessons for other libraries and consortia.

## Literature review

This literature review will cover three main areas: consortial cataloging, vendor record quality, and tools that make batch cataloging more efficient.

Academic consortia have largely been at the forefront of cooperative cataloging. Cary and Ogburn explain The Virtual Library of Virginia's (VIVA) efforts to avoid duplicating cataloging work and share cataloging knowledge and training.[2] Shieh, Summer, and Day detail VIVA's cooperative cataloging project to provide MARC records to its member libraries.[3] In 2003, OhioLINK began its cooperative cataloging endeavors with volunteers from member libraries, although Preston notes that many other similar efforts were attempted but did not succeed.[4] In addition to cataloging efforts, many institutions and consortia collaborate on best practices. Maurer, Gammon, and Pollock describe how OhioLINK member libraries created consortial best practices for cross-institutional technical services cataloging collaboration and cite many related projects from other libraries.[5]

Another trend across the literature is the concern for and difficulty managing vendor record quality. Mugridge and Edmunds surveyed large research libraries about batchloading and found the biggest challenges included inconsistent record quality, staffing, ongoing maintenance, vendor technical support, local technical support, and funding the purchase of records.[6] Batchloading catalog records since 2006, Martin and Mundle enumerate the varying quality of vendor records and suggest that libraries not only give feedback to vendors regarding metadata quality, but also use it as a factor in vendor negotiations.[7] David and Thomas underscore this point, having calculated the local cost of record correction for negotiation purposes.[8] It is not just vendors who bear responsibility for record quality. In relation to their collaborative batch cataloging, Young, Culbertson, and McGrath discuss difficulties in the quality of crowdsourcing in the OCLC WorldCat, which cannot improve if libraries never share their corrected records back.[9] Van Kleeck et al. at the University of Florida detail their process of quality management for batches of MARC records, emphasizing that the "intent is to catch and correct errors so that they do not permanently reside in the OCLC WorldCat database and in the shared catalog."[10]

Many tools and resources are available to make batch cataloging more efficient. Sanchez et al. note the various tools useful for cooperative cataloging, including MarcEdit, macros, and Excel, as well as helpful standards and practices, such as file naming conventions and workflow documentation.[11] Mugridge and Poehlmann conducted a survey on benchmarking of cataloging as an assessment tool to improve efficiencies. Although respondents indicated interest in the topic, few libraries reported using benchmarking in this way.[12] Naun and Braxton emphasize that records need to be flexible enough to satisfy local standards and concerns.[13] Turner argues for more flexible cataloging standards so that more records are available sooner, as well as relying on OCLC WorldCat members and automation to improve upon them, thus improving cataloging efficiency.[14] This assumes everyone will do their part for the benefit of all, and catalogers are willing and able to share their improved records with WorldCat.

Quality control is an important aspect of cataloging and a reoccurring theme in the literature. Vendor provided MARC records can vary in quality which affects the amount of time needed for cataloging. To combat low-quality records that consume lots of staff time, some institutions such as Duke University have created policies that streamline cataloging down to core needs in order to increase staff productivity and reduce turnaround time for the increasing number of vendor provided records.[18]

One thing not addressed in other articles is the potential for the quality of the vendor provided records to change. It seems some operate under the assumption that vendor provided records are stable in their quality. However, it is possible for record quality to decrease, requiring more cataloging time. While it is unclear how often record quality changes occur, such changes can be difficult to adjust to, depending on the severity of the degradation. OhioLINK has encountered this unfortunate phenomenon and is currently working with a vendor to try to remedy the reduction in quality. In the meantime, the time spent cataloging the affected collection has doubled, slowing down access to members because the records are not distributed as quickly as before.

Whenever possible, OhioLINK shares back record corrections and improvements with OCLC WorldCat via the Connexion Client thus benefitting thousands of libraries that use OCLC records. While other catalogers have mentioned this in many articles, it bears repeating, that everyone should share back improved records to OCLC and correct master records whenever possible. Turner says it best, "Catalogers already involved with updating WorldCat records should do all they can to encourage peers in their own and other institutions to join the effort. Local policies which mean that some edits cannot be made to the master record should be re-evaluated in light of the new reality. All cataloging is now global."[19]

## Consortial volunteer cataloging

The shared union catalog, called the OhioLINK Central Catalog (Central), connects member institutions' catalogs and allows for OhioLINK to be successful in sharing print materials throughout the state. It has also paved the way for shared access to consortially purchased e-resources. Central runs on the INN-Reach product from Innovative Interfaces, Inc. which requires at least one participating institution to contribute a record in order for it to display in the union catalog; all other records for the same title then attach their holdings with minimal local information displayed, including additional local proxy links. As more records for the same title are added to Central, the system runs through a list of priorities, including the presence of authorized headings, to select the most complete record for display. Since not all OhioLINK member libraries are able to do local authority control, this benefits all users of Central, by ensuring the best catalog record for each title is displayed.

When OhioLINK began purchasing consortial e-books, it relied on member catalogers to volunteer to create and review catalog records. Prior to 2014, OhioLINK had at least eight volunteer catalogers who each focused on a particular vendor. An OhioLINK staff member helped coordinate the volunteers, but this staff member was not a cataloger and acted more as an intermediary. Generally, the Ohio-LINK staff member sent volunteer catalogers batches of vendor records to improve and then shared the final records back to OhioLINK member libraries for local loading and contribution to Central. Since each vendor differed in its workflows for sharing records with OhioLINK, the OhioLINK office needed to keep separate tracking documents. In some instances, OhioLINK tracked when records were sent to and returned from volunteer catalogers. In at least one case, a volunteer managed the workflow entirely, including logging into the vendor system to download files and sending OhioLINK the final records. Because each vendor was managed slightly differently, it is difficult to compare and calculate volunteer time spent and financial implications for member libraries.

In her 2011 article, Preston describes the efforts of OhioLINK member libraries to coordinate volunteer cataloging for the consortium.[20] A few expert catalogers divided up the work and then provided the final MARC record batches to member libraries for local loading. As record batches tended to be large, sometimes complex, or needed to be upgraded to full-level standards, there were few in the Ohio-LINK community who were able to process the records. Volunteer catalogers found time during their everyday work to catalog consortial e-book records to benefit the whole community. This placed an undue burden on volunteer catalogers who rarely, if ever, rotated to share the consortial cataloging responsibilities and were treated almost like staff instead of volunteers.

## Moving to centrally consolidated cataloging

In 2014, for the first time, OhioLINK hired a cataloger as a staff member in the central office. This was the first step in consolidating consortial e-book cataloging and beginning the practice that the OhioLINK office calls "cataloging from the center." OhioLINK made the decision to hire a cataloger after considering the burden of consortial cataloging on the few volunteer catalogers, the increasing number of consortially purchased e-books, and the reduction of member library staffing and budgets. Open positions at the OhioLINK office also provided the opportunity to hire a consortial cataloger. The transition from volunteers to the OhioLINK office cataloger occurred over a few months, allowing volunteer catalogers to finish their current batches and share any documentation or workflows for the vendors they cataloged. Due to proximity, one volunteer cataloger was able to train the new OhioLINK office cataloger in-person, covering some of the more complex issues to watch for in a particular vendor's records. The decision to catalog from the center resulted in numerous benefits for all OhioLINK member libraries. More recently, in addition to the full-time cataloger, OhioLINK hired a part-time cataloging assistant in July 2015 and a part-time cataloging contractor in May 2016 to help with consortial e-book cataloging.

Based on current trends noticed in the OhioLINK office, the amount of e-book cataloging is ever-increasing and will be for the foreseeable future. Each year, vendor collections contain new e-book titles that each need a new catalog record. Also, collections tend to increase in the number of e-books they contain year-after-year, varying from 400–16,000 e-books during 2013–2016 for OhioLINK vendors. Since volunteer catalogers had to fit cataloging consortial resources into their other responsibilities, record delays and longer turnaround times were inevitable. By centralizing cataloging, records can be provided in a more timely manner, allowing member library users access sooner. This is crucial for e-books because without a bibliographic record in the catalog, there is no access to the content through Central, local catalogs, or discovery layers.

As a result of e-book cataloging moving to the central office, OhioLINK added paid subscriptions to OCLC Connexion, Library of Congress (LC) Classification Web, and the RDA Toolkit, as well as utilizing free MarcEdit software. OhioLINK uses a File Transfer Protocol (FTP) server to provide members with record batches and email listservs for notifications and to manage corrections and errors among members. OhioLINK staff also loaded a complete set of all previously cataloged e-book records into a locally managed integrated library system (ILS) called the Office Catalog to better manage all of the OhioLINK e-resource records in the office. This also allows OhioLINK to consider clean-up projects that would not have been possible before the records were together in a single ILS, rather than being stored in folders as separate MARC batches.

When dealing with such large batches of records, errors can slow down batch cataloging or, if not caught and corrected, affect member institutions' local catalogs and Central. For these reasons, batch e-book cataloging within OhioLINK became an important focus to ensure the best quality records were provided to members so that library users could find and use the consortially purchased materials. To help facilitate better findability, OhioLINK does full-level cataloging, ensuring that call numbers and subject headings are included and that descriptive metadata is accurate, especially the title field and author(s)/editor(s).

## Benefits of centrally consolidated cataloging

Both the OhioLINK office and OhioLINK member libraries benefited in multiple ways by bringing e-book cataloging into the central consortial office. First, the volunteer catalogers could return to devoting their time to their regular work. While OhioLINK could not have cataloged e-books without the hard work and dedication of these volunteer catalogers, the strain such work placed on those member libraries must also be acknowledged. By cataloging from the center, volunteer catalogers are able to focus on local work, which can have a meaningful impact as many libraries are looking to increase local efficiencies due to staffing and budget constraints.

Another benefit is that local and national standards were applied consistently to all record sets. As OhioLINK policies and standards changed over the years, more recently acquired vendor collections applied updated standards, but older collections did not always incorporate the updates. Variability between volunteer record sets was easier to notice after cataloging consolidation, and subsequent cataloging projects in the OhioLINK office were able to revise all records, bringing them up to current local standards.[21]

Dedicated central office staff spends the necessary time to provide member libraries high-quality, full-level records, which means that member library staff are able to spend less time duplicating that work. When the scale of the 120 libraries is considered, the OhioLINK office staff time spent cataloging consortial e-books has magnifying implications for all members. It is difficult to provide data regarding member library time and money saved by OhioLINK office staff cataloging. However, it can be estimated that five minutes spent cataloging in the OhioLINK office saves each member library those five minutes locally, which in total is 605 minutes (or 10+ hours) of collective member time, assuming every library would have made the same record updates. Volunteers previously saved the member libraries this time. When deciding whether to spend time fixing an issue, this thought-experiment offers a worthwhile perspective. Beyond the consortial members, sharing records back to OCLC for global library users only further expands the impact of centrally taking time to make improvements. However, it should be noted that some changes can be shared back to a PCC record, while other changes cannot and so not all significantly improved records updated by OhioLINK can be updated in OCLC.

Cataloging from the center has also allowed OhioLINK staff to create a schedule for providing records to members. As volunteer catalogers finished record batches, they were released in an ad hoc manner. With a schedule in place, members are able to expect new e-book record batches and enjoy the consistency of the release schedule. Sometimes only one vendor record batch is provided while other scheduled releases have multiple vendor record batches. A standardized naming convention was also implemented to provide consistency between the vendor record files to facilitate better file organization.

In addition to a regular, consistent schedule of record batch releases, record files are being provided more frequently. As volunteer catalogers had to make time for consortial cataloging, there were time lags for record files. Now, with a dedicated central staff, vendor records are provided more quickly to members. For example, volunteer records for one vendor were provided on average every six weeks, whereas that timeframe is now down to three weeks. Another vendor took an average of four months, currently down to one month. While OhioLINK significantly improved turnaround time for some vendor records, other vender record workflows were already as efficient as possible. One vendor record turnaround averaged one month, which OhioLINK catalogers only improved to three weeks. Between the dedicated cataloging staff and refined workflows, OhioLINK overall is providing more records batches in less time than before.

One of the most useful benefits of centralized cataloging is the ability of Ohio-LINK catalogers to be nimble in cataloging practices. When there are problems with vendor records, OhioLINK catalogers can quickly identify these changes and respond with vendor communication or minor workflow changes. For example, one vendor was found to be including records in their batches for collections to which OhioLINK did not subscribe. The office catalogers were able to spot the issue, discuss a workaround, and remove the records when the record provider was unable to remove these records. In other cases, staff were able to contact vendors about issues and remedy them, usually within two to four weeks. This was the case when one vendor supplied foreign languages records instead of English language records. Being nimble also means that changes to local or national standards can be more easily incorporated consistently to all vendor records. Looking forward, OhioLINK can more easily adapt to a national change in record format such as BIBFRAME.

With a dedicated focus on consortial e-book cataloging, the OhioLINK cataloging staff are able to more easily notice changes in record batches from a vendor. Recently, OhioLINK cataloging staff noticed a significant change in the quality of a particular vendor's records. The problems are documented and example records are set aside, both in their original state and after applying cataloging improvements, to show the difference in quality. At this point, the OhioLINK cataloger is compiling a brief report with the information and example records that will be used to discuss the problem with the vendor and record provider. Building and maintaining good relationships with vendors is important even when dealing with very specific issues such as cataloging records, as both the vendor and the library want the best experience for users and the librarians managing library resources. Since this issue was identified at the consortial level, OhioLINK will be able to use its existing vendor relationships to discuss record quality with this vendor, improving user experiences to the benefit of all parties involved. Depending on the duration and severity of issues with cataloging records, there is always the option for these issues to become a factor in future negotiations for other libraries or consortia.

Central cataloging has done more, though, than allow for analysis of the records received. OhioLINK cataloging staff have been able to begin new projects, such as tracking each e-book collection to ensure records have been received for all e-books purchased by the consortium. Before centrally consolidated cataloging, records cataloged by volunteers were provided to members without any tracking or comparison to entitlements lists of purchased items. OhioLINK is now able to view a larger portion of the lifecycle of e-books, which makes it easier to implement a tracking process. OhioLINK began this process in 2016 and has already compared Springer and Wiley e-book collection entitlements with OhioLINK catalog records. Such a project requires working with vendors, organization of entitlements lists, and the time to clean-up and compare multiple data sources. While this project is still in process, preliminary results suggest that this is a worthwhile exercise as consortial e-book purchases can now be reconciled to guarantee records and access for members.

The OhioLINK catalogers have also been able to complete record maintenance projects. Over the years, while volunteer catalogers provided records to member libraries, record maintenance was minimal. The focus had always been on providing high-quality records with authority control at the time provided. Once these records were locally loaded in member catalogs and then contributed to Central, they remained static unless a user found and reported an error. Usually misspellings or broken links are reported by members and corrected but even with the best records, some errors were able to get through. Now with a dedicated consortial cataloging staff, it is possible to review older records and do record maintenance.

Record maintenance projects prioritize user access as well as record standardization and consistency to ensure all e-book records meet current consortial cataloging standards. The first project included updating 43,000 records that lacked OCLC record numbers. For purchased e-resources, it is a consortial standard for records to contain an OCLC number in order for Central to match records correctly for display purposes. A total of 78,882 inconsistent or incomplete fixed fields (006 and 007) in records were also updated to comply with OhioLINK and national standards. The focus then turned to e-resource access. Staff updated 94,336 links and standardized the associated subfields. Corrections to 120 database records reflected correct LC standards and current holdings. During these projects, staff discovered and deleted 2,070 duplicate and inaccessible e-resource records in Central. Altogether, the staff updated a total of 218,408 records between July 2015 and May 2017.

Beyond record maintenance, OhioLINK is now able to manage consortial cataloging-related projects among the members. The most recent consortial project was the mapping of material types from local catalogs to Central, which resulted in nearly 52 million local records being recontributed to Central. The material type project mapped local bibliographic material types to Central material types. Although a list of Central material types was available years ago, mapping had never taken place, which caused several problems in Central. Some records were displayed without material types because local codes were not recognized. Other records did not display the correct label and icon (such as e-book or thesis/dissertation) for the item due to a mismatch of local-to-Central codes. Occasionally, local codes did not match in Central for the same item, which created duplicate records that would have otherwise been consolidated into one record. The mapping resulted in a more user-friendly catalog by eliminating incorrect duplicate records and ensuring correctly categorized labels and icons. In addition, members voted to expand the list of material types to include more specific categories for electronic materials, which are now searchable in Central's advanced search.[22]

Another consortial project removed about three million non-sharable e-resource records from Central. Some member libraries individually buy or subscribe to online content, making the content inaccessible to users from other member libraries. By removing these non-sharable e-resources, the search results in Central now only contain content available to all members and prevents any confusion and frustration that users experienced when trying to access content not available to them. This completed project also improved the user experience of Central by refining the content to only consortially available e-resources in the shared catalog.

The OhioLINK cataloger also serves as a contact for member libraries who experience problems with or have questions about certain records. Corrections to records in Central are more easily fixed as there is now a consortial cataloger as a point of contact. This setup allows OhioLINK to reach out to the member libraries that need to make record updates, giving authority for the requested change.

Although there is a roster of contacts that members can use to communicate about record errors, in practice, most requests are sent to OhioLINK. Beyond issue reporting, having a central cataloger has also facilitated discussions about the e-book cataloging records and related concerns. As one example, this led to a discussion during an OhioLINK committee meeting with member catalogers about adding a local-use-only field for the record batch name to all record files starting in 2016, since many member libraries inserted one anyway. These discussions are now possible with a central contact managing the entire cataloging process and utilizing member knowledge to better understand issues and concerns, as well as to find solutions that work best for everyone.

## OhioLINK cataloging workflow assessment and refinement

Once cataloging workflows for each vendor were transitioned to the OhioLINK office, each workflow was assessed. While some workflows were straightforward and did not need much improvement, others were able to be refined for efficiency. In general, if vendors provided higher quality records, fewer adjustments were required to a particular workflow. However, in some cases major changes were made to the workflows.

As an example of this, in one instance, vendor records did not contain OCLC numbers, a consortial requirement. OhioLINK cataloging staff find records manually, many of which are of low-quality. These records can be missing crucial fields for access such as call numbers or subject headings. They may also contain significant errors in author and editor fields, or even an incomplete title and subtitle. For one particular vendor, OhioLINK uses OCLC Connexion Client and their macros feature to cut cataloging time in half. The work is frontloaded since all the records must be found by title and major errors are corrected by hand. However, once records are organized, a macro can complete the rest of the necessary record changes and updates. This includes deleting all URLs, inserting customized URLs and proxies, adding consortial notes, and setting holdings. Once the batch is exported from Connexion, the records are ready to be provided to member libraries. Searching for titles is made easier with Connexion's batch search features and typically works best with titles that are coded as e-books, in electronic format, and in English. There is some labor required to move data between a spreadsheet, text files, MarcEdit and Connexion to put this macro to use, but the end result saves a considerable amount of time. The macro was written specifically for OhioLINK by a member librarian, and OhioLINK staff have since adjusted it to fit consortial e-book cataloging needs. While the OCLC macro is specific to OhioLINK, it was written using Visual Basic, which could be used to create something similar by library or information technology staff with programming skills for other libraries or consortia.

The main tool used for batch cataloging at OhioLINK is the free software called MarcEdit by Terry Reese, which is a versatile program that allows for many manipulations to MARC records beyond just batch editing.[23] Beneficial to all workflows are MarcEdit Assigned Tasks (also known as macros) that can be pre-programmed and run on any record file. Assigned Tasks can range from simple changes such as adding a new field with specific wording and indicators (creating a note field) to more complex changes such as copying a field and adding subfields with different wording to both the original and duplicate field (generating a second proxied URL with a custom public note for example) or even sorting data in a certain field (moving all non-electronic ISBNs from active to cancelled/invalid subfield based on qualifying information). OhioLINK has several assigned tasks that are run routinely on most record batches: adding consortial standard notes in fields 506 and 710, moving print ISBNs from subfield a to z, adding a proxy link and subfield z wording, and correcting 082 Dewey Classification field to update standard indicators. These tasks are some of the most common staff edits and are run on most vendor record files. It made sense to create these macros to speed up routine edits to ensure they are easy to apply consistently. Assigned Tasks is a powerful MarcEdit tool that enables both simple and complex batch editing that can be easily customized for local needs.

Organizing and creating documentation for cataloging has been an important refinement to the overall process. To better track and organize cataloging files, the OhioLINK cataloger created a comprehensive running to-do spreadsheet for all vendors. This provides a quick view of what still needs to be cataloged in addition to more detailed data, such as the dates when a record batch was cataloged, when it was proofed, and when it was provided to members. While vendor files were originally stored electronically in separate folders containing their MARC records, the cataloger added more levels of organization to each folder. The main folder now contains only the files yet to be cataloged, with everything else in a subfolder based on the type of item (documentation, title lists, etc.). Each vendor folder also contains a subfolder for records provided to members arranged by fiscal year to keep the folders from being too cluttered. All files downloaded to a vendor folder are added to the cataloging to-do list. An alternate organization for the cataloging to-do list is to use separate sheets within a workbook or tabs within a spreadsheet for each vendor, which would give an overview by vendor. The OhioLINK cataloger prefers to view all vendor files together to get a sense of the movement of all the records.

## Transferrable lessons

While the benefits for OhioLINK members are clear, there are also takeaways for other libraries and consortia.

As OhioLINK transitioned from volunteers to central office staff, prior documentation or notes from volunteers were invaluable in assessing cataloging workflows. The degree of thoroughness and age of documentation from each volunteer cataloger varied but in all cases it served as a starting point for assessment. OhioLINK reviewed the volunteers' workflows at least once with a vendor record batch and made updates or adjustments to improve timeliness or other factors that changed over time. With older documentation, some of the steps differed, for example, how to download the files or what edits need to be made. Volunteers were open to questions as they arose, which helped in forming new workflows and dealing with known issues.

Adding additional organization to the management of vendor record files further streamlined cataloging. Creating more folder levels, a filing system, a comprehensive tracking spreadsheet with record batch details, and using a naming convention across all vendor files makes it easier to manage such a large number of files. At a glance, it is possible to know what has yet to be cataloged or when a particular set of records was provided to members. File organization and documentation have been especially helpful with the addition of cataloging staff.

When reviewing workflows for all of the vendors, there were standard changes that most record batches required. Identifying these tasks meant they could be automated to save time and ensure consistency among OhioLINK cataloging staff. Using Connexion's macro feature and MarcEdit's Assigned Tasks, routine simple and complex batch edits were streamlined. While it may take time for the initial set-up, macros are a powerful feature for refining workflows by reducing editing time.

Finally, monitoring and noting changes in record quality is important. Some problematic trend or noticeable reduction in quality records leads to an increase in time spent. Taking time to track and to document problems and to follow up with vendors and record providers is more likely to produce a resolution than simply waiting for records to improve or to report problems record-by-record.

## Conclusion

Since 2014 when OhioLINK began cataloging on behalf of its member libraries, records are more consistent with local consortial and national standards, workflows are refined, and records are provided to members more quickly on a regular schedule with consistent file names across vendors. Cataloging from the center returns member volunteer cataloger time back to their institutions, employs a central cataloging representative to moderate discussions and cataloging issues, and allows for more nimble cataloging practices. It has also made possible centralized e-book record updates and maintenance, as well as consortial cataloging projects. E-book cataloging will likely remain an important need, as publishers continue to release yearly collections of new items that increase in number each year. Beyond benefiting OhioLINK members, by making the effort to share corrected and improved records with OCLC, OhioLINK cataloging efforts continue to improve records for the wider cataloging community.

## ORCID

Emily Alinder Flynn ⓘ http://orcid.org/0000-0002-0566-9796
Erin Kilkenny ⓘ http://orcid.org/0000-0002-9161-0802

## Notes

1. Gwen Evans and Theda Schwing, "OhioLINK – Recent Developments at a United States Academic Library Consortium," *Interlending & Document Supply* 44, no. 4 (2016): 172–177, doi:10.1108/ILDS-06-2016-0021.
2. Karen Cary and L. Ogburn Joyce, "Developing a Consortial Approach to Cataloging and Intellectual Access," *Library Collections, Acquisitions, & Technical Services* 24, no. 1 (2000): 45–51, https://doi.org/10.1016/S1464-9055(99)00095-0.
3. Jackie Shieh, Ed Summers, and Elaine Day, "A Consortial Approach to Cooperative Cataloging and Authority Control: The Virtual Library of Virginia (VIVA) Experience," *Resource Sharing & Information Networks* 16, no. 1 (2002): 33–52, https://doi.org/10.1300/J121v16n01_04.
4. C. A. Preston, "Cooperative E-Book Cataloging in the OhioLINK Library Consortium," *Cataloging & Classification Quarterly* 49, no. 4 (2011): 257–276, https://doi.org/10.1080/01639374.2011.571147.
5. Margaret Beecher Maurer, Julia A. Gammon, and Bonita M. Pollock, "Developing Best Practices for Technical Services Cross-Institutional Collaboration: Cataloging Collaborations and Partnerships," *Cataloging & Classification Quarterly* 51, no. 1–4 (2013): 179–193, http://doi.org/10.1080/01639374.2012.733795.
6. Rebecca L. Mugridge and Jeff Edmunds, "Batchloading MARC Bibliographic Records: Current Practices and Future Challenges in Large Research Libraries," *Library Resources & Technical Services* 56, no. 3 (2012): 155–170, https://doi.org/10.5860/lrts.56n3.155.
7. Kristin E. Martin and Kavita Mundle, "Notes on Operations Cataloging E-Books and Vendor Records: A Case Study at the University of Illinois at Chicago," *Library Resources & Technical Services* 54, no. 4 (2010): 227–237, https://doi.org/10.5860/lrts.54n4.227.
8. Ravit H. David and Dana Thomas, "Assessing Metadata and Controlling Quality in Scholarly Ebooks," *Cataloging & Classification Quarterly* 53, no. 7 (2015): 801–824, doi:10.1080/01639374.2015.1018397.
9. Philip Young, Rebecca Culbertson, and Kelley McGrath, "Collaborative Batch Creation for Open Access E-Books: A Case Study," *Cataloging & Classification Quarterly* 51, no. 1–3 (2013): 102–117, doi:10.1080/01639374.2012.719075.
10. David Van Kleeck, Gerald Langford, Jimmie Lundgren, Hikaru Nakano, Allison Jai O'Dell, and Trey Shelton, "Managing Bibliographic Data Quality in a Consortial Academic Library: A Case Study," *Cataloging & Classification Quarterly* 54, no. 7 (2016): 452–467, doi:10.1080/01639374.2016.1210709.
11. Elaine Sanchez, Leslie Fatout, Aleene Howser, and Charles Vance, "Cleanup of NetLibrary Records: A Methodical Front-End Process," *Technical Services Quarterly* 23, no.4 (2006): 51–71, doi:10.1300/J124v23n04_04.
12. Rebecca L. Mugridge and Nancy M. Poehlmann, "Benchmarking as an Assessment Tool for Cataloging," *Technical Services Quarterly* 32, no. 2 (2015): 141–159, doi:10.1080/07317131.2015.998465.
13. Chew Chiat Naun and Susan M. Braxton, "Developing Recommendations for Consortial Cataloging of Electronic Resources: Lessons Learned," *Library Collections, Acquisitions, & Technical Services* 29, no. 3 (2005): 307–325, doi:10.1080/14649055.2005.10766068.
14. Amy H. Turner, "OCLC WorldCat as a Cooperative Catalog," *Cataloging & Classification Quarterly* 48, no. 2/3 (2010): 271–278, doi:10.1080/01639370903536237.
15. David and Thomas, "Assessing Metadata and Controlling Quality in Scholarly Ebooks."
16. Martin and Mundle, "Notes on Operations Cataloging E-Books and Vendor Records."
17. Young, Culbertson, and McGrath, "Collaborative Batch Creation for Open Access E-Books."

18. Turner, "OCLC WorldCat as a Cooperative Catalog."
19. Ibid., 273.
20. Preston, "Cooperative E-Book Cataloging in the OhioLINK Library Consortium."
21. Database Management and Standards Committee. "Standards for Cataloging Electronic Monographs," *OhioLINK Database Management and Standards Committee,* June 2010. https://platinum.ohiolink.edu/dms/catstandards/electronicmonograph.pdf.
22. OhioLINK Database Management and Services Committee. "OhioLINK Values for Material Type." *OhioLINK,* September 2016. https://platinum.ohiolink.edu/dms/DMSdocs/BCODE2.htm.
23. Terry Reese, "MarcEdit Development: Features," 2013, http://marcedit.reeset.net/features.

# Achieving and Maintaining Metadata Quality: Toward a Sustainable Workflow for the IDEALS Institutional Repository

Ayla Stein 🆔, Kelly J. Applegate 🆔, and Seth Robbins

**ABSTRACT**

This article documents the steps taken to assess metadata errors within the IDEALS repository. It describes the workflows established to create accurate and consistent metadata, focusing especially on the batch ingest and retroactive metadata remediation processes. It also seeks to address theoretical issues surrounding the concept of metadata quality.

## Introduction

The Illinois Digital Environment for Access to Learning and Scholarship (IDEALS) is the institutional repository for the University of Illinois at Urbana-Champaign (UIUC). IDEALS collects the research and scholarly output of the University's staff, students, and faculty. Like many repositories, IDEALS relies on "mixed metadata",[1] i.e., metadata created by both humans and machines. Objects in IDEALS are either deposited by their creators, approved individuals, or are legacy publications digitized and uploaded by Library staff in batches. While metadata errors are introduced via both deposit methods, the types of errors and how often they occur vary between collections. IDEALS staff determined that the vast majority of the errors were introduced when batches of materials were uploaded due to a lack of comprehensive quality assurance review procedures. Determining the cause and content of the metadata errors, however, was quickly overshadowed by the imminent need to fix existing errors and mitigate them in the future.

In this article, the authors describe the workflows created in the quest to improve metadata quality prior to uploading batch ingests in order to mitigate the introduction of new metadata errors, as well as retroactively clean legacy metadata.

Both goals have been aided by incorporating extensive use of the open source software application OpenRefine, rather than reviewing and correcting metadata within the repository interface. This article also seeks to address theoretical issues regarding metadata quality.

## Literature review

The existing literature on metadata quality assurance workflows and evaluation methods in digital repositories focuses, for the most part, on metadata for digitized special collections or archival materials, although there are a handful of papers specific to institutional repository metadata on these topics. The same can be said of the literature for retroactive metadata cleaning. Regardless, there are significant gaps in the library literature in regards to metadata quality assurance workflows and retroactive metadata remediation. This article helps address these gaps by identifying common metadata issues found in institutional repository metadata and the multi-pronged strategy undertaken at the University of Illinois at Urbana-Champaign to address them in IDEALS. The literature review is divided into categories, which are as follows: Measuring Metadata Quality; Quality Assurance Methods; Institutional Repository Metadata Quality Issues; Retroactive Metadata Remediation Case Studies; Automated Tools; and Repurposed Metadata Issues.

### *Measuring metadata quality*

Measuring metadata quality is often quite difficult because, as noted throughout the literature, there is no universally accepted definition or set of best practices for what exactly is meant by the term "quality metadata".[2] Park proposes a synthesized definition of quality metadata, where "the quality of metadata reflects the degree to which the metadata in question perform the core bibliographic functions of discovery, use, provenance, currency, authenticity, and administration".[3] Park also found that the most commonly used measurements of metadata quality are completeness, accuracy, and consistency.[4]

In a separate study, Park and Tosaka surveyed cataloging and metadata professionals to evaluate metadata quality control practices in digital repositories. They found that one of the most important tools for creating high quality metadata is best practices documentation, especially if it is embedded into the repository's item submission workflow. Despite metadata standards being used for multi-institution projects, usage guidelines are often not shared between institutions. Survey results also showed that metadata element semantics were not considered very important by respondents but also that schema semantics and their definitions were often unclear, which likely leads to inconsistent application of terms across institutions.[5]

Yasser's article provided a framework for the categorization of problems found in both digital repository and catalog metadata records. According to Yasser, there are five universal metadata problems: "Incorrect Values, Incorrect Elements, Missing Information, Information Loss, and Inconsistent Value Representation".[6]

### Quality assurance methods

There are a plethora of methods and frameworks for creating quality metadata. Boock and Kunda described a professional staff review quality assurance workflow where matriculating graduate students directly deposited their electronic theses and dissertations into the Oregon State University repository. The metadata was reviewed by library staff for correctness and enhanced. The review and enhancement process was time intensive, requiring "30–60 minutes [per ETD record], depending on the difficulty of assigning subject headings".[7]

Kelly, Closier, and Hiom detailed a case study that implemented the QA Focus Methodology, a quality assurance framework, derived from the Joint Information Systems Committee (JISC) funded project, QA Focus. The Social Science Information Gateway (SOSIG) implemented the methodology by employing and training subject specialists; developed documentation that specifies policies, step-by-step instructions, and cataloging rules; employed controlled vocabularies and authorities whenever possible; used automatic checks for spelling and links; reviewed metadata regularly; and assessed metadata using the self-assessment toolkit developed by the QA Focus team.[8]

Owonibi and Koenig-Ries advocated applying data quality management (DQM) principles from industry data warehousing in research data repositories. They proposed a QA workflow that customized the described DQM principles and techniques for semi-automatic checking of biodiversity research data in spreadsheet formats when deposited into a data repository. This article is significant because it reiterated that libraries and scholarly repositories do not need to reinvent the wheel, and should instead capitalize on connections between database administration and data warehousing practices for the scholarly digital repository field.[9]

Palavitsinis, Manouselis, and Sanchez-Alonso noted that while a plethora of QA frameworks and proposals exist, there was little work on the applicability of these models to more than one repository. The authors described the metadata QA framework they developed, the Metadata Quality Assurance Certification Process (MQACP) and their attempts to apply it to the metadata creation workflows of two types of repositories. The authors found that their framework resulted in improved metadata quality and understanding of the metadata schemas in both cases.[10]

### Institutional repository metadata quality issues

Although there is a significant amount of work on metadata quality in digital repositories, literature focusing on quality of metadata in institutional repositories (IRs) has been fairly lacking. In the beginning stages of the development of DSpace, the prevailing notion was that it would be primarily used for the capture of born digital text-based materials. However, as early repositories grew, ingest of digitized items and the reuse of legacy metadata, typically MARC records, also rose.[11] While this change is good for populating institutional repositories, it has also added an increasing number of entry points through which metadata errors can be introduced, particularly through batch ingests developed in response to this now common influx of legacy material. In their research, Chapman, Reynolds, and Shreeves discovered very few institutional repositories putting "extra effort into augmenting, correcting, or editing the metadata coming into the repository," even though most IRs already acknowledge that metadata quality is a problem, largely due to the influx of metadata being mapped and converted from other systems.[12]

Sandy and Dykas found that it was essential to have adequate numbers of qualified metadata professionals for the production of quality metadata. Their study surveyed fifty open access (OA) repositories registered with the Directory of Open Access Repositories (OpenDOAR). With an emphasis on how IRs suffered primarily from staffing shortages, the researchers reported on the quality of metadata in repositories, how metadata quality is perceived by repository managers, and ideas that repository managers had for how to alleviate this problem.[13] Budget restraints are also often noted as a reason that metadata is not properly quality checked. Another survey-based study, conducted by Alexandra Chassanoff, stated, "A few institutions reported that quality checking was done on an ad-hoc basis due to budgetary concerns, with certain collections receiving prioritized attention".[14] Presumably, these budget concerns encompassed staffing shortages, but may also include not investing in tools that might aid in metadata quality or remediation.

Another theme in the literature is metadata inconsistency and a lack of authority control. Chapman, Reynolds, and Shreeves also addressed this issue saying, "Authority control and management of authors in institutional repositories is notoriously difficult. Yet it is essential that an IR be able to accurately identify the researchers who deposit their materials for preservation, access, and rights reasons. Traditional library catalogs have struggled with author identity through the establishment of name authority records, but this approach may not extend well to the IR environment".[15] Salo cited this problem as well and argues that the problem with names may even have a damaging effect on IRs as a whole.[16]

### Retroactive metadata remediation case studies

There is a surprising dearth of literature on retroactive metadata analysis and remediation. Metadata remediation projects are often undertaken when migrating or implementing repository or catalog systems. When making improvements to large amounts of legacy data, reviewing and editing metadata records individually by hand are exceedingly time consuming. To save time, metadata professionals have developed batch procedures to remediate metadata records en masse. West-brook et al. audited the University of Houston Digital Library metadata by sampling records from each collection. They found three broad types of corrections that needed to be made: changes to individual records, changes at the collection level, and changes made to policies.[17] Huffman lays out a workflow where, in preparation for migrating to a new archival information system, the author uses Extensible Stylesheet Language Transformations (XSLT), OpenRefine,[18] and Excel to "analyze all these terms, dedupe them, normalize them, and update the XML before importing it into ArchivesSpace".[19]

Weidner and Wu, building on a previous "Metadata Upgrade Project"[20] developed scripts and used OpenRefine to extract, analyze, and match descriptive metadata values and names from their CONTENTdm collections to controlled vocabularies and name authorities, laying the groundwork for transforming their metadata into linked data.[21]

### Automated tools

A significant portion of the literature on metadata focuses on the use of automated tools to make metadata workflows more efficient. Several authors have focused on giving technical accounts of procedures and tools used in metadata workflows. Phillips, Tarver, and Frakes detailed their use of Open Refine, Google Fusion Tables, and a local Python-based tool called m2m to clean and crosswalk metadata as part of a workflow to digitize and make accessible a collection of photographs from the Oklahoma Publishing Company Photography Collection.[22] Kan and Tan present an overview of matching algorithms and describe how they can be used to clean metadata in digital libraries where "metadata inconsistencies are a significant barrier to locating and collating knowledge that end users and reference librarians have had to adapt to".[23] Phillips details the usage of tools available at the UNIX command-line and some custom python tools written at the University of North Texas to "focus technology development resources on tools that can easily be integrated into this command-line environment".[24]

A subset of the literature on automating metadata workflows has specifically addressed quality control and metadata reuse in the context of batch ingesting into institutional repositories. Leveraging data collected by ProQuest UMI Dissertation Publishing, Averkamp and Lee detail a workflow for ingesting graduate theses and dissertations into the bepress repository at the University of Iowa.[25] After an ingest of items from the Native Health Database to the University of New Mexico's IR, Lobovault, Nash and Wheeler "mapped the metadata to items that had been uploaded using the accession numbers... and transformed metadata fields...to a Comma Separated Values (CSV) file which was imported into LoboVault".[26]

Walsh describes two batch ingest workflows for the Knowledge Bank IR at Ohio State University. In one workflow, librarians created a mapping from "vendor-supplied, article-level metadata" which was used by developers to create "Perl scripts to transform the vendor metadata into the DSpace schema of DC [Dublin Core]." The second project used Perl scripts to "create the tables of contents" for repository items from the metadata.[27]

Although not a case study on batch uploading to IRs, Sun depicts a case study of repurposing metadata from a historical photograph collection to create descriptive metadata of the digitized images and using the built-in-house Workflow Management System (WMS) to upload both the metadata and images to a Fedora repository.[28]

### Repurposed metadata issues

The challenge of converting, cleaning, and mapping metadata from diverse sources and platforms is a major topic in almost all of the literature on metadata workflows, but certain authors focus specifically on dealing with diversity of technology platforms, formats, or descriptive practices within these workflows. The reasons for this focus are mapped out by Hillman, who, looking back on early digital library metadata efforts, identified the need to develop metadata quality improvement workflows that can be deployed throughout the lifetime of a project or collection, rather than focusing all metadata effort at the initial description step. Such workflows "must be designed to operate in an environment of considerable (and probably increasing) diversity [of metadata]" and should rely less heavily on traditional cataloging standards since "libraries attempting to use Dublin Core or metadata standards other than MARC have been hampered by a view of their task much too tied to the MARC world".[29]

A number of authors have provided case studies illuminating the challenges in dealing with this diversity of metadata, especially when migrating metadata from one platform to another. In an early example, McClelland et al. reported on a metadata import project, using Open Archives Initiative Protocol for Metadata Harvesting (OAI-PMH), at the University of North Carolina at Wilmington. The authors enumerated several challenges that stemmed from the variety of descriptive practices and noted "that not all the problems will be solved merely by adopting a common metadata element schema".[30]

Deng's approach to the analysis of metadata workflows is centered on metadata repurposing, defined as "using [meta]data in a new context that was not originally intended".[31] The repurposing methods used for several projects are discussed including the repurposing of metadata collected for an archival collection of papers and other materials relating to the poet Albert Goldbarth to add each of his "individual poems as a separate entry to [the Online Computer Library Center (OCLC)] and Voyager," and reuse of metadata collected for a number of Wichita State University's digital library collections that had been selected for deposit into the Institutional Repository.[32] Deng highlights the "[c]ollaboration and coordination within the library and beyond" as being key to success in metadata projects.[33]

Metadata workflows are not born fully-formed, and often have to be developed iteratively. This is especially true when the workflow requires mapping between complex and unrelated models. Faced with the task of "batch loading records from MARC into Variations," a music digital library system with a Functional Requirements for Bibliographic Records (FRBR)-like metadata model, Riley, Mullin, and Hunter performed a series of experiments in "a series of four iterations, each time applying a defined mapping routine to a set of approximately 10,000 MARC bibliographic records representing sound recordings," refining their mapping algorithm with each successive iteration.[34]

While diversity of technological platforms and formats present challenges addressed by the authors above, Khoo and Hall focused on diversity of practices and behaviors exhibited by different project members involved in a metadata overhaul at the Internet Public Library (ipl2). The project involved "crosswalking ipl2 metadata from the original custom format to Dublin Core and ... moving that metadata from a MySQL database to a new Fedora database." The authors found that the information technology staff and librarians working on the project belonged to different networks of practice and were "aligned with different technological frames," such that "Each group tended to take their frames for granted, and ... these frames were not articulated explicitly".[35]

## Background

Like many institutional repository initiatives, the IDEALS team has developed methods to create, verify, and correct metadata, to varying degrees. As touched on in the literature review, there is no universally accepted practice or standard defining quality metadata; similarly, there is no set of rules for describing institutional repository materials like *Resource Description and Access* (RDA)[36] for bibliographic cataloging or *Describing Archives: A Content Standard* (DACS)[37] for archival description. Criteria for creating high-quality metadata must be determined by the individual institutional repository. This is not to say that local institutions should utterly disregard recommended metadata practices by external organizations when setting internal measurements of quality; rather, institutional repositories can and should take into consideration external metadata recommendations, especially if an IR contributes metadata to an aggregation initiative such as SHARE.[38] Ultimately, however, metadata best practices and quality standards are implemented locally.

In IDEALS, high quality metadata meets the following criteria:

1) Includes all of the required elements, as defined in the IDEALS Metadata Policy.[39] (See Table 1)
2) Values for specified metadata elements are drawn from controlled vocabularies indicated by the "Controlled Vocabularies and Standards in Use" portion of the Metadata Policy.[40]

3) Element values adhere to the IDEALS data entry and formatting rules, which are specified in the Metadata Best Practices.[41]

**Table 1.** Required metadata elements in IDEALS.

| Metadata Element | Depositor or Software Supplied | Free Text/Controlled | Display Label |
|---|---|---|---|
| dc.title | Depositor supplied | Free text | Title |
| dc.date.issued | Depositor supplied | Controlled | Issue Date |
| dc.date.accessioned | Software supplied | Controlled | Not Displayed |
| dc.date.available | Software supplied | Controlled | Date Available in IDEALS |
| dc.subject | Depositor supplied | Free text, although controlled vocabularies are encouraged. | Subject(s) |
| dc.identifier.uri | Software supplied (Depositor may supply additional URIs) | Controlled | URI |
| dc.description.provenance | Software supplied | System generated text that may be altered if needed. | Not Displayed |
| dc.type | Depositor supplied | Controlled | Type |

Repository system functionality impacts how metadata is created and entered. The IDEALS Metadata Best Practices were developed to facilitate discovery of materials through the DSpace software search utility. For example, the IDEALS Metadata Best Practices recommend formatting personal names in the "LastName, FirstName, Middle Initial" format. IDEALS does not maintain an author or contributor registry or local name authority file, so all name queries are string searches. Structuring creator and contributor names in this format aids in the discovery and visual presentation of author and contributor names in the DSpace search results.

Despite the existence of the Metadata Policy and Best Practices documentation, a variety of errors have been introduced into the IDEALS repository metadata via the user-submission workflow and batch ingests of materials. In a 2013 article, Chapman, Reynolds, and Shreeves gave an account of IDEALS metadata procedures and provided some of the reasons that they historically did not engage in retroactive metadata remediation: "Chronic staffing shortages," and the difficulty of "editing metadata on an item-by-item basis" in the interface.[42] Since this article was written, the University of Illinois at Urbana-Champaign University Library has hired additional staff for Metadata Services, including a second full time Metadata Librarian. The increase in staff, coupled with the migration to DSpace version 5 from 3.2, were the impetus for starting a retroactive metadata cleaning project.

## Repository metadata review workflow

### *CSV generation for repository metadata review*

The metadata review and cleaning of existing metadata in IDEALS should take place at regular intervals throughout the year. Instead of focusing on a single batch ingest, metadata from across the entire IDEALS repository is reviewed for adherence to best practices. During the regular metadata cleaning process, CSV files containing all of the values for a particular metadata field are exported from the IDEALS database itself, inspected, revised if necessary, and then re-imported into IDEALS using a custom metadata import script. This process should occur once a semester.

To facilitate the cleaning of existing metadata, the IDEALS Repository developer wrote a program to allow import of CSVs that contain new metadata values for fields across the repository, called "MetadataValueUpdate." DSpace has a similar function built in called "Batch Metadata Edit,".[43] However, the native functionality only allows for exporting metadata for all items in a single collection and lacks the ability to export only certain fields. While this might work well on a smaller scale, IDEALS has a complex structure with heavily populated collections and many items cross-mapped to multiple collections.

"MetadataValueUpdate" was designed to work with a long-established process of generating CSV reports containing all the values of a specified metadata element directly from the database. Metadata value information is stored in a table called metadatavalue, which is standard in DSpace. In this table each row is one metadatavalue and includes two foreign keys: one which relates to the IDEALS item and one which relates to the metadata field. The IDEALS team decided that it would be useful to edit the reports generated from this table directly. The "MetadataValueUpdate" program was created to allow the edited CSVs to be reuploaded in the repository.

"MetadataValueUpdate" takes advantage of DSpace's launcher, a configurable framework for running server side processes at the command line. DSpace comes with a number of predefined launcher tasks that perform an assortment of backend processes, including batch imports, indexing, and fixity checks. Scripts that are run by the launcher have full access to the DSpace API, which provides a more convenient platform for interacting with the database and search indices than dealing with them directly. The source code for DSpace is written in the Java programming language, so the launcher-run scripts take the form of Java classes that have a "Main" method, which provides the entry point for the launcher-run code. These classes are then recorded in DSpace's "launcher.xml" configuration file and assigned a name by which they will be called at the command line.[44]

The "MetadataValueUpdate" script takes a CSV file of metadatavalue rows as input, compares them to the existing values based on the row ID and writes any changes to the repository. CSV files are used because they can be read and edited by any spreadsheet software and can also be easily processed by most programming languages. A CSV is structurally similar to a single spreadsheet, in that it represents a table with rows and columns of textual data, but it cannot be used to store formulas or any of the other special formatting supported by spreadsheet software.

To be used as input by the "MetadataValueUpdate" script, the CSV should have a header row for column names. The following rows contain the metadata values and should only contain a single value. The CSV must have a "metadata_value_id" column containing the database row identifier of the metadatavalue and a "text_value" column for the new values themselves. An empty "text_value" cell will result in the deletion of the metadatavalue upon re-import of the CVS into the database. These two columns are all that is needed for the basic case of changing the text of an existing metadatavalue, but the developer also extended the "MetadataValueUpdate" functionality to create new metadatavalue entries and to change the associated metadata field of a metadatavalue entry.

Creating a new metadatavalue record requires the presence of two additional columns. First, metadata in DSpace applies to items, so the CSV must also have an "item_id" column to associate the new metadatavalue with an item in the repository. Second, each metadatavalue has an associated metadata field that specifies the function of the metadatavalue (e.g., title, creator) and is specified in a "metadata_field_id" column. If these two columns are present then a row with an empty "metadata_value_id" cell will result in a new record for the item referenced in the "item_id" column. These two columns also need to be present to support changing the metadata field.

The procedure for using this script, diagrammed in Figure 1, involves first querying the database for the desired metadata fields and values, then exporting the results of that query to a CSV file. The CSV is then delivered to the metadata team, who reviews and cleans the field values. The revised CSV is uploaded to the IDEALS server and is used as input for the launcher script.

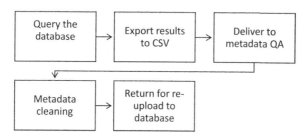

**Figure 1.** Repository metadata QA review workflow.

Compared to the native DSpace Batch Metadata Editing process, this workflow better supports our typical use case, wherein the Metadata Team examines and remediates the values of a particular metadata field across multiple collections and communities when they do not match specified IDEALS best practices. The downside is that this process requires a team member with the appropriate knowledge and access to query the database and run server-side processes.

## *OpenRefine process for repository metadata review*

OpenRefine is a tool specifically designed for cleaning messy data. It was chosen as the tool to clean IDEALS metadata primarily because of its capacity for wrangling metadata records in batches. The CSV generated for reviewing a specific metadata element across IDEALS usually has between 12,000 and 90,000 rows. OpenRefine allows for easy navigation between changing thousands of records simultaneously to editing individual cell values.

The cleaning procedures dictate using only CSV files to facilitate portability across multiple spreadsheet editing platforms, as well as OpenRefine. Whenever possible, utilization of Microsoft Excel is avoided in order to reduce the introduction of encoding errors into the database when the cleaned data is re-imported back into the IDEALS, as Excel is known to add proprietary encoding to files edited with it.[45]

In April 2015, as preparation for migrating to DSpace 5, we began the process of reviewing and cleaning the most visible fields in the user interface: Author (dc.creator), Contributor (dc.contributor), and Title (dc.title). The Graduate Assistant recommended that this review and remediation work be completed biannually, after completion of the fall and sprng semester electronic theses and dissertations (ETDs) batch uploads.

Once a CSV has been imported into OpenRefine for cleanup, there are several steps that apply to both author and contributor names. OpenRefine's "Cluster and Edit" feature has two clustering methods, key collision and nearest neighbor. In these workflows, only the key collision method is used. The nearest neighbor method is too slow for results that are not any more useful than what the key collision method finds. The key collision method in Open-Refine has four keying functions, the first three of which are applied in these workflows: fingerprint, ngram-fingerprint, metaphone3. Cologne-phonetic, the fourth keying function, is specific to the German language. They all group different values together based on the likelihood that they are semantically identical. For example, the values "Avis Steinberg" and "A.S. Steinberg" might refer to the same person, and "Champaign-Urbana" and "champaign-urbana" are the same name but differ in capitalization.[46]

After using the cluster-and-edit feature on the name metadata, several regular expressions are used for additional corrections. Regular expressions (regexps) are a way to search for specific patterns. OpenRefine can use regexps to identify metadata values matching the particular criteria specified by the expression, all instances of which can then be changed using a single replace command. Common search parameters that lead to error discovery are:

  1) data entries with one or more set(s) of parentheses. This returns values containing parenthetical expressions, such as those found in a Name Authority Entry label, e.g., "Lancaster, F. Wilfrid (joint author)," or "Ricketts, G. E. (Gary Eugene)";

2) fields that contain three or more characters followed by a period. This helps locate extraneous periods after given and middle names;

3) data values containing a comma followed by a string of four numbers, followed by a dash. This locates creator and contributor name fields that have inadvertently carried over birth-death date ranges that are likely from a main entry field in a bibliographic record, for example "Wesson, Alfred, 1929–1993"; and

4) first and middle initials with an extra space in between them. IDEALS Metadata Best Practice is to have no space between two initials, such as "Applegate, K.J." instead of "Applegate, K. J."

The final step for name remediation is standardizing organization and entity names that occur multiple times in IDEALS. For example, the name for the "University of Illinois at Urbana-Champaign" has appeared in multiple iterations (U of I, UIUC, Univ. of Illinois, etc.). All these variations can be edited in bulk using the "Cluster-and-Edit" feature to correctly read the formal standard name of the school. Abbreviations can be standardized to be more formal as well; for example, we change all instances of "Dept." to "Department" if it is listed as part of a creator or contributor name.

The Title (dc.title) value spreadsheet is a slightly different process. OpenRefine has the ability to translate string text to ALL CAPS, Title Case/Initial Capitalization, or all lowercase. Unfortunately, it does not have an option for Sentence Case, which is the preferred case according to the Metadata Best Practices. However, OpenRefine can still be used to find titles in uppercase as well as encoding and diacritic errors using regexps. Using the text filter feature the regexps, ^[^a-z]*$ and (/b[A-Z]+\b\s){2,}, are used to find titles where all the letters are in uppercase. The first regex finds any group of characters that does not include lowercase letters. The second expression finds groups of two or more words that are composed entirely of capital letters. Unfortunately, the process here is limited in its efficiency, because the only way we have found to correct the titles is to edit them individually.

In addition to OpenRefine, the metadata team also uses OpenOffice Calc, an open source spreadsheet software similar to Microsoft Excel, to clean title data. OpenOffice Calc has the capability to mass-convert all text in a given range to sentence case. However, it does not capitalize the first letter of a word after a colon nor does it account for proper nouns. Therefore, each row must be reviewed to ensure that proper nouns, scientific nomenclature, chemical compounds, and mathematical equations within title strings, are capitalized properly.

In developing and reviewing these quality assurance procedures, it has been debated whether or not the usage of sentence case for title information should be removed from the Metadata Best Practices since there seems to be little benefit other than uniform presentation. Additionally, it is easier to enforce this rule when reviewing smaller batch ingests than it is with an exported CSV of all titles in the IDEALS database.

## Batch ingest workflow

### *Batch ingest metadata review*

Review of IDEALS metadata is subject to two separate processes: one for batch ingests and another for regular repository metadata cleaning. Batch ingests occur when a collection of multiple items and the associated metadata, are imported into the repository through an automated process. Much of the material in IDEALS is ingested via a backend batch process that uses DSpace's "ItemImport" launcher task, rather than the submission user interface. To be ingested in a batch, files must be packaged together with their metadata in the form of a Simple Archive Format (SAF) package.[47] The packaging process involves collecting the metadata into a specifically formatted CSV spreadsheet, which becomes the input for SAFCreator,[48] a tool that packages the spread-sheet and content files into a SAF directory. The origin of the spreadsheet data could be another campus or library department, or generated by the IDEALS developer using catalog records. Before creating packages, the spread-sheet is reviewed by the metadata team. An overview of the Batch ingest metadata review workflow is depicted in Figure 2.

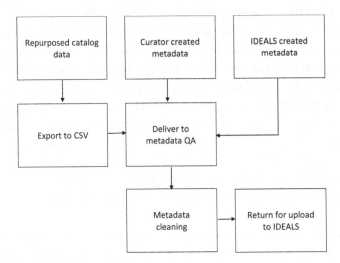

**Figure 2.** Batch ingest metadata review workflow.

The addition of metadata review to the batch ingest process began with the real-ization while examining the metadata for initial review for migration that many of the quality issues being identified were introduced via batch ingests, especially those batches whose metadata was repurposed from existing catalog records. MARCXML metadata is formatted for use in SAF packages using an XSLT style-sheet. Developers would often need to customize the stylesheet for individual batch ingests to deal with unexpected values or non-standard field usage in the catalog records. The stylesheet output was used as the metadata for the SAF formatted ingest packages, which when ingested using DSpace's batch import functionality, become individual DSpace items.

The need to upload new materials in these cases often preempted adherence to the metadata best practices. The use of an XSLT stylesheet typically ensured that the metadata was "good enough" to warrant the item would be discoverable based on title or author information, but did not verify that the field values followed stated repository best practices. Reviewing and changing the metadata once the ingest packages were generated was difficult since the metadata for each item was stored in its individual package. This set of circumstances led to the creation of a metadata review step as part of the ingest process. Our standard procedure for batch ingests now includes four steps

1. A CSV file containing the metadata is generated for the ingest.
2. The metadata is reviewed and edited by the IDEALS metadata team.
3. Packages are generated using the edited metadata CSV file.
4. The packages are uploaded to the server and ingested using the DSpace "import" script.

### CSV generation for batch ingests

Batch ingest metadata typically comes from one of three sources: repurposed catalog data for materials held by the Library; original metadata spreadsheets created by a curator (either a subject specialist or a representative from a campus department); or original metadata created by an IDEALS graduate student. In most cases, the analog materials digitized for ingest into IDEALS had existing records in the Library's catalog. The PDF files that result from the digitization are named with the catalog ID and placed in a shared directory. The CSV generation process starts with a script written in the Ruby programming language[49] that examines each of the PDF files and retrieves a MARCXML representation of the catalog record from the Get Bib Record Web Service, a locally developed tool.[50] To build a DSpace compatible representation of the metadata, the previously mentioned XSLT script was repurposed to crosswalk the MARCXML record into the much simpler XML format used for DSpace SAF packages. This format is a flat representation of Qualified Dublin Core records and can be directly transformed into a CSV row by the Ruby script.

Prior to the addition of the metadata review process, ingest packaging was managed by having a developer write a short one-off Ruby script that leveraged a locally developed library of Ruby code, as well as the XSLT stylesheet, for writing SAF metadata. With the addition of the metadata review process, which requires the creation of a metadata CSV, the Texas Digital Library's SAFCreator has been adopted to build packages for DSpace ingest instead. The SAFCreator application builds packages based on a specifically formatted CSV. CSVs that are generated for metadata review are pre-formatted to be used by SAFCreator to create ingest packages once the review is complete.

In the SAFCreator CSV format, each row represents a package and each package, when ingested, will become a DSpace item. The CSV also must include a header row, which consists of metadata elements as column labels. The first column lists the names of files by bundle. Bundles are a concept in the DSpace data model. Typically, in DSpace an "item" is used to represent a particular publication. However, an item may logically contain many files. For example, in addition to the main content files, there is always a text file containing the IDEALS deposit license, the main content itself may consist of several files, and there may be multiple representations of the main content. DSpace uses the concept of bundles to group files within a repository item by function, with the main content files belonging to the "ORIGINAL" bundle, the license files belonging to the "LICENSE" bundle, and so on. The header for the file column is formatted with the word "bundle" followed by a colon, followed by the bundle name. For example, the column "bundle:ORIGINAL" would list the main content files. In a typical case, only a "bundle:ORIGINAL" column is present in the CSV, although if an item had, for instance, plaintext derivative files for full-text search, those would be listed in a different column called "bundle: TEXT." The license file is automatically added by the SAFCreator, removing the need for a "bundle:LICENSE" column. If more than one file is included in a bundle, it is possible to provide multiple entries in a cell by concatenating the entries with double pipe characters "||", though this situation has been rare for batch ingests.

In addition to the file column, there is also a column for each metadata field that has at least one associated value in the batch. If an item has multiple entries for a given metadata field, those should be concatenated with the double pipe symbol. The main DSpace metadata model is a superset of Qualified Dublin Core but DSpace allows additional schemas, which consist of prefix, element, and qualifier sets outside of the base Dublin Core set.

Once the generated CSV has been reviewed, it can be used by SAFCreator to generate the ingest packages. SAFCreator has a graphical interface, where the CSV and the directory of files to be packaged can be selected. Once ingest packages are created from the cleaned metadata, they are then moved to the filesystem on the IDEALS production machine, and ingested using DSpace's "ItemImport" launcher script.

### OpenRefine workflow for batch ingests

Batch ingest metadata CSVs have a slightly more complex process for quality control than the regular metadata review workflow. The metadata for batch ingests originates from one of several possible sources: repurposed catalog record data in CSV spreadsheets, as described previously; created by the individual or campus department that owns the analog materials; or created by the IDEALS Metadata Graduate Assistant if the collection is not prohibitively large. If the materials to be digitized are held by the Library, the materials must be cataloged before digitization.

First are preliminary checks.

1) A collection ID number is included either as a column in the spreadsheet or with any corresponding information (e.g., relevant emails or meeting notes).
2) Every item has a filename.
3) Columns for each required Qualified Dublin Core (QDC) element (dc.title, dc.date.issued, dc.subject, dc.type). All other required elements are automatically generated on successful system ingest.
4) Any cells for fields that contain more than one item (subjects, authors, etc.) should be divided by "||". If instead they are divided by ";" they should be replaced en masse.

Like the dc.title CSVs discussed above, batch ingest spreadsheets also have capitalization style issues. However, since batch ingests are typically smaller than regular metadata review CSVs, titles can simply be reviewed and edited row by row in OpenOffice Calc.

Different departments and colleges will submit their own spreadsheets with their own preferences when requesting batch ingests from IDEALS, and as a result IDEALS staff reviews spreadsheets that include varying degrees of additional metadata fields. As long as the metadata fields are in the IDEALS schema they are allowed, and the QA proceeds ensuring that each field conforms to our best practices.

When working with metadata created by external campus units (outside of the Library), a common issue encountered with name data is the conflation of contributors and authors; sometimes contributors are incorrectly listed as creators. Any name in the dc.creator field containing a parenthetical title such as (editor) or (illustrator), is moved to the contributor column.


## Positive outcomes

As a result of these efforts, the number of unique creator and contributor names decreased significantly, which is a major step for name disambiguation. Nearly all of the titles that had diacritic or special symbol errors have been found and corrected. The creation and implementation of the batch ingest review workflow has led to fewer metadata errors introduced via the batch upload process. Reviewing metadata for ingest of new materials into already existing collections has enabled the identification and standardization of previously inconsistent field values in particular collections. For example, while reviewing the metadata for a batch of Illinois State Water Survey (ISWS) materials, inconsistencies were found in the Series/Report field values of the ISWS Circular and Bulletin collections. Some used the abbreviation "no." for number while others did not, some items capitalized "No." while others did not, etc. It was as a result of quality control review on one CSV file that led to the retroactive remediation of the metadata fields for two entire collections, significantly improving the quality and consistency of the metadata.

Another outcome of the batch metadata review process is greater insight into which communities and collections receive batch ingests most frequently, and the types of materials deposited in them. For example, IDEALS receives batch ingest requests from the Prairie Research Institute, the parent community of the ISWS sub-community and collections, multiple times a year. IDEALS also serves as the designated repository for several annual conference proceedings, such as the International Symposium on Molecular Spectroscopy. Greater understanding of incoming material types enabled the design of custom metadata CSV templates, which can be shared with external departments or contacts for easy communication of metadata requirements based on content types.

## Future work

A number of areas stand out as potential foci for future improvement of these workflows. It is essential to review, clean, and standardize values for many of the metadata fields not already mentioned in this paper. In particular, the dc.type.genre (Genre) field, whose values should only include terms from the IDEALS Genre controlled vocabulary list,[51] and the dc.subject (Subject Keywords) field, have been identified as being in need of significant future attention. The Genre field is controlled by a checkbox in the submission user interface, but many other terms have crept in through direct addition to the database via batch ingests. Subject Keyword field input is free text in the submission user interface and the IDEALS metadata best practices, so while any term is technically allowable, remediating dc.subject field values would improve discoverability of topically similar materials through spelling consolidation, as well as enforcement of sentence case capitalization, since keyword browsing in DSpace functions as a capitalization-sensitive string search. A long-term goal is to examine the cost and benefits of implementing a controlled vocabulary for the Subject Keyword field. However, there is likely no single controlled vocabulary that will meet the needs of all the disciplines represented in IDEALS, so multiple controlled vocabularies would need to be recommended. Implementation of controlled vocabularies could theoretically limit the number of subject keyword terms in the database, thus making it easier to locate thematically related materials. However, repository staff would need to monitor the vocabularies for substantial changes. Linked data vocabularies could help ameliorate the onerous task of keeping terms up to date, and are an area of future exploration.

Another possibility is the creation of a local folksonomy of previously entered subject keyword terms that could make suggestions to users in order to help mitigate wide variations of keyword term data. Folksonomy terms generated from existing IDEALS keyword data could also be published as a linked data vocabulary.

A third, and more immediately feasible, option is to pilot reconciling batch ingest metadata against existing linked data vocabularies as a way to begin testing the utility of various vocabularies.

Validation of metadata field input is also a future implementation priority since all field values, including dates, are stored in the database as free text. Additionally, any and all of the metadata elements for an item can be edited via the administrative interface, which does not include any form of validation or element definitions. This may be addressed in part by built-in DSpace authority control features that have not been enabled in IDEALS at this time.

## Discussion: Practical challenges to metadata quality

Metadata "quality" is a relative term, defined largely by the needs of whatever organization or institution is using said metadata and to what end, be it for their own easy retrieval of data, or increased discoverability for external users. When initially developing the new batch ingest and remediation of existing repository metadata workflows, the team's goals and methods were pragmatic but perhaps naïve to the magnitude of the project and metadata quality's broad multi-faceted scope.

Although implementation of any standard or best practice varies to some degree at the local level, to the best of the authors' knowledge, there is a lack of community-developed guidance for description of academic and scholarly materials that serves a similar role as Describing Archives: A Content Standard (DACS) does for archival materials. Shreeves, Riley, and Milewicz provide high level guidance for making digital repository metadata more "shareable" but it is not specific to scholarly communication needs.[52] The OpenAIRE Guidelines perhaps come closest to filling this gap, but are still designed to suit the needs of a specific aggregation system.[53] A community-developed best practice for content description of institutional repository materials could improve metadata interoperability and utility.

Furthermore, current default implementations of metadata schemas in institutional repositories do not accurately represent recent trends in scholarly communication metadata. For example, if a DSpace repository does not have metadata authority control functionality enabled, there is no standard metadata element that could be used to record an author identifier number such as ORCID or ResearcherID. As it currently stands, the only default identifier element is for identifying objects, not authors or contributors. Of course, DSpace does allow additional metadata schemas through the Metadata Registry, but this impacts interoperability. The current generation of turnkey institutional repository systems are not keeping up with trends in scholarly communication at an efficient enough pace.

The necessity to develop workflows such as the ones described in this article underscore a problem that seems to be inherent across digital repository systems: the lack of truly useful built-in tools for metadata management and manipulation beyond basic editing of item-level records. While DSpace attempts to fill this gap with the Export Metadata and Batch Import tools, significant limitations in their functionality preclude implementation into daily workflows of a large institutional repository. Vendors and repository developers should pay more attention to the use cases, functional requests, and workflows of non-developer administrative users to design systems with more powerful metadata management tools, natively.

Finally, current evaluations of metadata quality rely almost entirely on technical criteria. In this era of growing awareness of how implicit bias and power systems work their way into search engine algorithms, controlled vocabularies, and classification schemas, metadata professionals need to move beyond purely technical or domain specific considerations of metadata quality. This evaluative expansion could likely fit under the concept "currency of metadata," which does not seem to have a communally accepted definition. How to incorporate a critical theory lens into quality evaluations of institutional repository metadata is a research question that becomes ever more vital as information systems and data become increasingly linked, personalized, and actionable.

## Conclusion and next steps

The team had a revelation that when implementing the new metadata workflow a comprehensive metadata audit should have been conducted prior to starting a metadata remediation project. However, as mentioned previously, due to time constraints for a software upgrade, metadata remediation of the most publicly visible metadata elements needed to be expediently completed. Now with the workflows in place, the team intends to take a more systematic approach to improve the rest of the repository metadata by undertaking an extensive metadata audit. This will allow the metadata team to quantitatively evaluate and prioritize elements for remediation moving forward. It will also help identify gaps in data entry requirements and documented best practices, both for metadata elements available in the user-submission interface and those elements visible only to community or repository administrators. A single data dictionary and content standard unifying the IDEALS metadata documentation, need to be created. This information is presently in three different places, with varying levels of completeness: the Best Practices documentation, the DSpace metadata registry, and the IDEALS metadata policy text.

Once initial remediation of prioritized metadata values is completed, a regular metadata review and cleaning schedule needs to be devised and implemented, as well as enshrined in official IDEALS policies and procedures. The IDEALS team is also interested in ways to further automate the metadata review, remediate, and update process. Beyond the planned metadata audit and additional retroactive metadata cleaning, the IDEALS team will work on improving the end-user submission workflow through a combination of stakeholder engagement and implementation of enhanced system heuristics. The IDEALS team intends to engage with stakeholders in several ways: survey IDEALS stakeholders, including faculty, administrators, and students, for ways to improve the submission process; reach out to departments that utilize IDEALS heavily for their insight regarding which metadata fields should be prioritized for periodic review or metadata that need to be revised for improved consistency across their collections; and advise campus units with frequent batch ingests on the requirements and best practices for IDEALS material description. Enhancements to submission workflow heuristics are being explored such as integration of IDEALS' best practices documentation into the submission form itself, as well as implementing improved metadata entry validation. Since the vast majority of metadata errors are introduced via batch ingests, investigating data validation for IDEALS spreadsheet templates by non-metadata experts is also a priority.

This article arose out of a desire to share our two-pronged metadata quality assurance strategy, and our challenges in creating it, with the community. As described above, we developed practices to clean metadata values both retroactively and pre-emptively. To facilitate this cleaning we adopted a set of open source software tools, some of which were developed in-house, to partially automate our procedures. We encountered challenges in the cleaning process stemming from the mixed metadata model of the institutional repository and the variety of metadata sources. The lack of controlled vocabularies and enforcement of best practices necessitated cleaning the most publicly visible metadata fields, which has in turn underscored the need for a larger metadata audit. In the future, we intend to develop and implement more automation workflows for "technical" metadata review and remediation, and investigate evaluation methods for currency and inclusion.

## ORCID

Ayla Stein ⓘ http://orcid.org/0000-0002-6829-221X
Kelly J. Applegate ⓘ http://orcid.org/0000-0002-1316-793X

## Notes

1. John W. Chapman, David Reynolds, and Sarah A. Shreeves, "Repository Metadata: Approaches and Challenges," *Cataloging & Classification Quarterly* 47, no. 3–4 (April 2009): 310–311, https://doi.org/10.1080/01639370902735020.
2. Jung-Ran Park, "Metadata Quality in Digital Repositories: A Survey of the Current State of the Art," *Cataloging & Classification Quarterly* 47, no. 3–4 (April 2009): 213–28, https://doi.org/10.1080/01639370902737240; Jung-Ran Park and Yuji Tosaka, "Metadata Quality Control in Digital Repositories and Collections: Criteria, Semantics, and Mechanisms," *Cataloging & Classification Quarterly*, 48, no. 8 (September 2010): 696–715, https://doi.org/10.1080/01639374.2010.508711; Ravit H. David and Dana Thomas, "Assessing Metadata and Controlling Quality in Scholarly Ebooks," *Cataloging & Classification Quarterly* 53, no. 7 (October 2015): 801–24, https://doi.org/10.1080/01639374.2015.1018397; Marieke Guy, Andy Powell, and Michael Day, "Improving the Quality of Metadata in Eprint Archives," *Ariadne*, no. 38 (2004), http://www.ariadne.ac.uk/issue38/guy; Amanda Harlan, "Metadata Quality Assurance | TDL Metadata," December 2010, http://sites.tdl.org/metadata/2010/12/13/metadata-quality-assurance/.
3. Park, "Metadata Quality," 213.
4. Ibid., 218–219.
5. Park and Tosaka, "Metadata Quality Control," 696–715.

6. Chuttur M. Yasser, "An Analysis of Problems in Metadata Records," *Journal of Library Metadata* 11, no. 2 (April 2011): 51, https://doi.org/10.1080/19386389.2011.570654.

7. Michael Boock and Sue Kunda, Electronic thesis and dissertation metadata workflow at Oregon State Libraries, *Cataloging & Classification Quarterly*, 47, no. 3–4 (April 2009): 302, https://doi.org/10.1080/01639370902737323.

8. Brian Kelly, Amanda Closier, and Debra Hiom, "Gateway Standardization: A Quality Assurance Framework for Metadata," *Library Trends* 53, no. 4 (Spring 2005): 637–650.

9. Michael Owonibi and Birgitta Koenig-Ries, "A Quality Management Workflow Proposal for a Biodiversity Data Repository," In *Advances in Conceptual Modeling*, Lecture Notes in Computer Science 8823, ed. by Marta Indulska and Sandeep Purao, (Cham, Switzerland: Springer International, 2014), 157–167.

10. Nikos Palavitsinis, Nikos Manouselis, and Salvador Sanchez-Alonso, "Metadata Quality in Digital Repositories: Empirical Results from the Cross-Domain Transfer of a Quality Assurance Process," *Journal of the Association for Information Science & Technology* 65, no. 6 (June 2014): 1202–1216, https://doi.org/10.1002/asi.23045.

11. Margret Branschofsky, Rebecca Lubas, MacKenzie Smith, and Sarah Williams, "Evolving Metadata Needs for an Institutional Repository: MIT's DSpace," *International Conference on Dublin Core and Metadata Applications*, September 28, 2003, 237–238.

12. Chapman, Reynolds, and Shreeves, "Repository Metadata," 310.

13. Heather Moulaison Sandy and Felicity Dykas, "High-Quality Metadata and Repository Staffing: Perceptions of United States–Based OpenDOAR Participants," *Cataloging & Classification Quarterly* 54, no. 2 (January 2016): 101–116, https://doi.org//10.1080/01639374.2015.1116480.

14. Alexandra M. Chassanoff, "Metadata Quality Evaluation in Institutional Repositories: A Survey of Current Practices," (Master's thesis, University of North Carolina at Chapel Hill, December 2009): 29. https://cdr.lib.unc.edu/record/uuid:1e82a108-6404-4382-b775-d66c0a9711e3

15. Chapman, Reynolds, and Shreeves, "Repository Metadata," 324.

16. Dorothea Salo, "Name Authority Control in Institutional Repositories," *Cataloging & Classification Quarterly* 47, no. 3–4 (April 2009): 249–261, https://doi.org/10.1080/01639370902737232.

17. R. Niccole Westbrook, Dan Johnson, Karen Carter, and Angela Lockwood, "Metadata Clean Sweep: A Digital Library Audit Project," *D-Lib Magazine*, June 2012, http://www.dlib.org/dlib/may12/westbrook/05westbrook.html.

18. "OpenRefine," accessed March 10, 2017, https://openrefine.org/.

19. Noah Huffman, "Adventures in Metadata Hygiene: Using Open Refine, XSLT, and Excel to Dedup and Reconcile Name and Subject Headings in EAD | Library Workflow Exchange," August 5, 2015, http://www.libraryworkflowexchange.org/2015/08/05/adventures-in-metadata-hygiene-using-open-refine-xslt-and-excel-to-dedup-and-reconcile-name-and-subject-headings-in-ead/.

20. Andrew Weidner and Annie Wu, "Metadata Quality Control for Content Migration: The Metadata Migration Project at the University of Houston," *International Conference on Dublin Core and Metadata Applications*, September 5, 2015, 112–118.

21. Santi Thompson and Annie Wu, "Metadata Overhaul: Upgrading Metadata in the University of Houston Digital Library," *Journal of Digital Media Management* 2, no. 2 (November 1, 2013): 137–147.

22. Mark Phillips, Hannah Tarver, and Stacy Frakes, "Implementing a Collaborative Workflow for Metadata Analysis, Quality Improvement, and Mapping," *The Code4Lib Journal*, no. 23 (January 17, 2014), http://journal.code4lib.org/articles/9199.

23. Min-Yen Kan, and Yee Fan Tan, "Record Matching in Digital Library Metadata," *Communications of the ACM* 51, no. 2 (February 2008): 94, https://doi.org/10.1145/1314215.1314231.

24. Mark Phillips, "Metadata Analysis at the Command-Line," *The Code4Lib Journal*, no. 19 (January 15, 2013), http://journal.code4lib.org/articles/7818.

25. Shawn Averkamp and Joanna Lee, "Repurposing ProQuest Metadata for Batch Ingesting ETDs into an Institutional Repository," *The Code4Lib Journal*, no. 7 (June 26, 2009), http://journal.code4lib.org/articles/1647.

26. Jacob L. Nash and Jonathan Wheeler, "Desktop Batch Import Workflow for Ingesting Heterogeneous Collections: A Case Study with DSpace 5," *D-Lib Magazine* 22, no. 1/2 (2016), https://doi.org/10.1045/january2016-nash.

27. Maureen P. Walsh, "Batch Loading Collections into DSpace: Using Perl Scripts for Automation and Quality Control," *Information Technology & Libraries* 29, no. 3 (September 2010): 120.

28. Li Sun, "Batch Loading in Metadata Creation: A Case Study," *Electronic Library* 29, no. 4 (2011): 538–549, https://doi.org/10.1108/02640471111156786.

29. Diane Hillmann, "Metadata Quality: From Evaluation to Augmentation," *Cataloging & Classification Quarterly* 46, no. 1 (March 1, 2008): 67, https://doi.org/10.1080/01639370802183008.

30. Marilyn McClelland, David McArthur, Sarah Giersch, and Gary Geisler, "Challenges for Service Providers When Importing Metadata in Digital Libraries," *D-Lib Magazine* 8, no. 4 (2002), https://doi.org/10.1045/april2002-mcclelland.

31. Sai Deng, "Optimizing Workflow through Metadata Repurposing and Batch Processing," *Journal of Library Metadata* 10, no. 4 (2010): 220, https://doi.org/10.1080/19386389.2010.524862.

32. Sai Deng, "Optimizing Workflow," 225.

33. Sai Deng, "Optimizing Workflow," 227.

34. Jenn Riley, Casey Mullin, and Caitlin Hunter, "Automatically Batch Loading Metadata from MARC into a Work-Based Metadata Model for Music," *Cataloging & Classification Quarterly* 47, no. 6 (2009): 525, https://doi.org/10.1080/01639370902936446.

35. Michael Khoo and Catherine Hall, "Managing Metadata: Networks of Practice, Technological Frames, and Metadata Work in a Digital Library," *Information and Organization* 23, no. 2 (April 2013): 81–106. https://doi.org/10.1016/j.infoandorg.2013.01.003.

36. RDA Steering Committee, "About RDA | Www.rda-Rsc.org," accessed March 5, 2017, http://www.rda-rsc.org/content/about-rda.

37. Society of American Archivists, "Describing Archives: A Content Standard, Second Edition (DACS) | Society of American Archivists," http://www2.archivists.org/standards/DACS.

38. SHARE initiative, "SHARE," accessed February 14, http://www.share-research.org/.

39. "Metadata Policy - IDEALS - Illinois Wiki", last modified October 6, 2016, https://wiki.illinois.edu/wiki/display/IDEALS/Metadata+Policy.

40. "Controlled Vocabularies and Standards in Use - IDEALS - Illinois Wiki," last modified October 4, 2016, https://wiki.illinois.edu/wiki/display/IDEALS/Controlled+Vocabularies+and+Standards+in+Use.

41. "Metadata Best Practices - IDEALS - Illinois Wiki", last modified March 7, 2017, https://wiki.illinois.edu/wiki/display/IDEALS/Metadata+Best+Practices.

42. Chapman, Reynolds, and Shreeves, "Repository Metadata," 320.

43. "Batch Metadata Editing," DSpace 5.x Documentation, last modified September 14, 2016, https://wiki.duraspace.org/display/DSDOC5x/Batch+Metadata+Editing.

44. "Application Layer - DSpace 5.x Documentation - DuraSpace Wiki," DSpace 5.x Documentation, last modified July 30, 2014, https://wiki.duraspace.org/display/DSDOC5x/Application+Layer#ApplicationLayer-CommandLauncherStructure.

45. Mark Ziemann, Yotam Eren, and Assam El-Osta, "Gene Name Errors Are Widespread in the Scientific Literature," *Genome Biology* 17 (2016): 177, https://doi.org/10.1186/s13059-016-1044-7.

46. "Clustering In Depth · OpenRefine/OpenRefine Wiki," OpenRefine/OpenRefine Github Repository, last modified December 9, 2016, https://github.com/OpenRefine/OpenRefine/wiki/Clustering-In-Depth.

47. "Importing and Exporting Items via Simple Archive Format - DSpace 5.x Documentation - DuraSpace Wiki," DSpace 5.x Documentation, last modified January 10, 2017, https://wiki.duraspace.org/display/DSDOC5x/Importing+and+Exporting+Items+via+Simple+Archive+Format.

48. James Creel, "Batch Importing into DSpace with the SAFCreator," May 24, 2016, http://hdl.handle.net/2249.1/76289.

49. Ruby Programming Language https://www.ruby-lang.org/en/

50. Get Bib Record Web Service. http://quest.library.illinois.edu/GetMARC

51. "Controlled Vocabularies and Standards in Use - IDEALS - Illinois Wiki."

52. Sarah L. Shreeves, Jenn Riley, and Liz Milewicz, "Moving towards shareable metadata," *First Monday*, 11, no. 8 (2006), https://doi.org/10.5210/fm.v11i8.1386

53. "OpenAIRE Guidelines — OpenAIRE Guidelines 3.0 Documentation," accessed May 16, 2017, https://guidelines.readthedocs.io/en/latest/index.html.

## Appendix

**Table A1.** Regular expressions used to clean IDEALS metadata CSVs in OpenRefine.

| Cell transform functions | |
|---|---|
| value.replace(";","\|\|") | Replaces semicolons with double pipes in cells containing more than one value |
| value.replace(/\.\s*$/, "") | Removes extraneous periods that don't belong (i.e., at the end of a first name) |
| text.replace(/, [0-9]{4}\-/,"") | Removes birth-death ranges after an author name |
| value.replace("\. ", "\.") | Replaces double space with single space between two initials in a name |
| **Regular expression filter functions** | |
| [()]+ | finds all the text_value cells that contain one or more parentheses. Useful for finding birth-death dates, more than one version of a name (i.e., Lancaster, F. Wilfrid (Frederick Wilfrid), and finding creators that should be contributors (i.e., Appleby, Kate (editor)) |
| [A-Za-z]{3}\. | Find any string of three characters followed by a period. This string helps locate extraneous periods after first and middle names where there shouldn't be any. |
| | It also finds instances where someone has entered 'joint author' after a co-authors name, which is unnecessary as IDEALS lists all authors separately and all authors are indexed in the author list. |
| , [0–9]{4}\- | Finds any comma followed by a string of four numbers followed by a dash. This string finds birth-death ranges that are part of the author name. These should not be a part of this metadata field, it is intended for names only. |
| [A-Z]{1}\. [A-Z]{1}\. | Finds all double sets of initials with extra space in between. IDEALs metadata best practice is no space, as in Applegate, K.J. *not* Applegate, K. J. |
| ^[a-z]*$ | Finds all cells containing ALL CAPS |
| " | Finds quotation marks and/or diacritics that were corrupted during metadata CSV batch upload |
| ^[a-z]*$ | Finds any group of characters that does not include lowercase letters |
| (\b[A-Z]+\b\s){2,} | Finds groups of two or more words that are composed entirely of capital letters |

# Index

**Note**: *Boldface page numbers refer to tables; italic page numbers refer to figures; page numbers followed by "n" denote endnotes.*

# INDEX

For Product Safety Concerns and Information please contact our EU
representative GPSR@taylorandfrancis.com Taylor & Francis Verlag GmbH,
Kaufingerstraße 24, 80331 München, Germany

Printed and bound by CPI Group (UK) Ltd, Croydon, CR0 4YY
08/06/2025
01896999-0014